Memorial Space
The triumph of memory in Eugenio Montale

A mia Helen, al nostro cucciolo

Memorial Space, Poetic Time

The triumph of memory in Eugenio Montale

Gregory M. Pell

t

Copyright © 2005 Gregory M Pell and Troubador Publishing Ltd

Apart from any fair dealing for the purposes of research or private study, or criticism or review, as permitted under the Copyright, Designs and Patents Act 1988, this publication may only be reproduced, stored or transmitted, in any form or by any means, with the prior permission in writing of the publishers, or in the case of reprographic reproduction in accordance with the terms of licences issued by the Copyright Licensing Agency. Enquiries concerning reproduction outside those terms should be sent to the publishers.

Published by
Troubador Publishing Ltd
9 De Montfort Mews
Leicester LE1 7FW, UK
Tel: (+44) 116 255 9311
Email: books@troubador.co.uk
Web: www.troubador.co.uk

Series Editor
Professor George Ferzoco
University of Leicester, UK

ISBN 1 904744 86 9

Typesetting: Troubador Publishing Ltd, Leicester, UK

CONTENTS

Introduction		vii
Chronology		xvii
1	Memory, Death and the Void	1
2	'Il Balcone' as overture: Montale and nothingness	25
3	The Occasioni and the 'Mottetti': Late motifs and latent images	41
4	'La casa dei doganieri': "Memoria che giova" and "memoria peccato"	95
5	La bufera: Guarding the Ark of Memory from the Storm	119
6	Flashes: Meta-poetic montage	145
7	Dreams born in the void	169
8	'Ezekiel saw the Wheel': Reconciling the Past	187
9	Perhaps one morning a hologram	203

INTRODUCTION

*Lo stupore
quando s'incarna è lampo che ti abbaglia
e si spegne. Durare potrebbe essere
l'effetto di una droga nel creato,
in un medium di cui non si ebbe mai
alcuna prova.*[1]

This book was first meant to be an investigation of the thematics of memory in Eugenio Montale's poetry. In the process of the work, I became aware that Montale's opus is replete with aporia and contradictions in both the way he perceives the world in which he lived and the way he portrayed it in his writing. His allusive, obscure poetry remains in the balance between the world of appearances and the world of reality. At times, Montale's pronouncements – in the vein of Zeno of Elea, Parmenides, Plato and Kant – seem to be a *reductio* (literally) *ad absurdum*: because poetry is a rhetorical contrivance, Montale was able to construct a world which defies the objective world that most of us have come to know through common experience and science, empirically or otherwise. Only in such a virtual world could Montale present a reality which is 'more real' than empirical reality; only there could a void be something more than nothing; only there could a man isolate privileged moments out of the overall flux of time. The poem which most effectively demonstrates these concepts, and which took my study in a new direction, is 'Forse un mattino andando' from his first collection, *Ossi di seppia* (1925):

> Forse un mattino andando in un'aria di vetro, / arida, rivolgendomi, vedrò compirsi il miracolo: / il nulla alle mie spalle, il vuoto dietro / di me, con un terrore di ubriaco. // Poi come s'uno schermo, s'accamperanno di gitto / alberi case colli per l'inganno consueto. /

Ma sarà troppo tardi; ed io me n'andrò zitto / tra gli uomini che non
si voltano, col mio segreto.

This one work stands as a pivotal point in understanding the chapters to follow in this book. Key is the idea that there is a phenomenal reality that the poet experiences as illusion or appearance, while a 'real' reality exists behind it as the source of this illusory projection. Before long, I could not help but see how Montale's conception of the cosmos paralleled aspects of cinematic experience, as well as those of physics where the world can be explained in terms of being a hologram.

'Forse un mattino andando' addresses the interstitial, void spaces between each image on his visual field. Montale is indirectly speaking of the notion of cinematic after-images, for which the after-image theory ascribes the apparent movement that a viewer of a motion picture perceives. The after-image is the persistence on the visual receptors (i.e., the retina) of one image as the subsequent image enters the same field, creating the illusion of movement. The after-image 'fuses' the images, thereby avoiding the 'flicker-effect' that *should* occur as the result of separate, still, frames passing over a screen, which *do* have spaces in between them. (This is why older films often present a continuity that is not synchronized with the movement portrayed in them; hence, the flicker.) The difference, in the poetry at hand, would be that the void in between the cinematic frames becomes the void among the myriad instants that exist as a holographic cosmos for Montale: all is there simultaneously as projection behind which there is a noumenos (or 'real' reality[2]), if only the poet can obtain a reprieve from the illusion of reality just long enough. The world as hologram presupposes a world as the Buddhist 'Maya;' an illusory perception. But in the single image are all images, as each image contains the whole; hence, the holistic aspect of the term 'hologram.' Separate but simultaneous are the images of a holographic world, which assumes that each moment is but a syneddoche of a whole. This takes Zeno's paradox of the arrow to a new level. Zeno's paradox imagines the movement of the arrow in flight. If it moves, he maintained, then it must be standing still, for it simply is where it is at any given instant, occupying a space equal to itself. Therefore, if it only occupies that one instant, it is at rest – this resembles the primitive frame-by-frame 'movement' of a flip book, which is, of course, the basis for the move from still photography to motion pictures. For Zeno, the seemingly continuous order is made up of discrete, infinitely divisible elements. There is no movement (or time) but the illusion of it as the resultant fusions of after-images which occur on the retina between each discrete instant.[3]

In a cinematic, holographic projection that is the cosmos, measurable, concrete, geologic time (to which I will refer as 'calendric' time) does not truly exist. Time is merely the movement of the system as it is being perceived by the viewer – in this case, Montale. To this insoluble logic, Montale is able, in his literary creations, to offer something that does not have to answer to science or rigorous philosophy. His poetry, his art, is, in that sense, an analogy of the very paradoxes that he tries to uncover through it. Though Montale has no empirical proof for his intuitions, he considers himself unique in his suspicion that there is an alternative, real universe behind the screen of images in the everyday world.

Montale's view of his world as being divided into the realm of appearances and the realm of reality (the phenomenal and the noumenal, respectively) begins in the *Ossi di seppia*, which reflect the conditions of the poet's childhood surroundings. Born in 1896 in Genova, he frequently summered in Monterosso (one of the Cinque Terre), where the rugged, seaside landscape offered him images of harsh coasts, sun-baked earth, and a rough sea, which seemed indifferent to his presence. This was the locus of "divina Indifferenza" ('Spesso il male di vivere'). Here, the stone wall surrounding the family's summer property would form a symbolic barrier, preventing him from arriving at the secret truth. This barrier is represented as the objective correlative of 'Meriggiare pallido e assorto' in the "rovente muro." In this poem – the earliest of Montale's works, from 1916 – the final image is foreboding as he highlights that this wall has, "in cima cocci agguzzi di bottiglia." The wall was meant to deter those from getting in, as much as it keeps the poet inside, enclosed in an existential prison. But, Montale felt, in the silence and hallucinogenic sun, there lurked a possibility that the existential miracle would occur, allowing him to move beyond the wall to see into the 'void' behind the world of appearances. Montale provides his theory most explicitly in the third stanza of the most programmatic work of the *Ossi*: 'I limoni:'

> Vedi, in questi silenzi in cui le cose / s'abbandonano e sembrano vicine / a tradire il loro ultimo segreto, / talora ci si aspetta / di scoprire uno sbaglio di Natura, / il punto morto del mondo, l'anello che non tiene [...]

So, he waits, patiently for this miracle, consoling himself with a virtual solution in his poetry. This miracle, the break in the chain ("una maglia rotta nella rete" from 'Godi se il vento'), does not occur, so he looks to those whom he feels pertain to the noumenal world, and who have accessed, if only briefly, a view of the truth.

The character with whom Montale maintains dialogue during his search is the institutional *tu*. Inevitably, this *tu* becomes the female addressee in whom he finds existential salvation. From the *tu* of 'Casa sul mare' and 'Godi se il vento' (*Ossi*), the poet's interlocutor evolves into the feminine character, seen first as Esterina in 'Falsetto' (also from *Ossi*). Esterina is divine in her actions, while her physical bearing is that of the lizard that resists, even embraces, the sun. Her friend is the sea, a "divino amico," and something separates her existence from Montale's mere living: "Ti guardiamo noi, della razza / di chi rimane a terra." Esterina's ability to resist the sun explains a variation of this motif to be found in "Portami il girasole," in which the sunflower is the ultimate correlative of illumination. Not accidentally, then, did Montale choose the *senhal* (code-name) for his female savior of *Le occasioni* (1939). Her name, Clizia, comes from the mythical female figure, whom we know in English as Clytie, the water-nymph from Ovid's *Metamorphoses*, who was turned into a sunflower ("girasole") as an indirect result of her love for Helios (Apollo).

In the *Occasioni*, Clizia will become Montale's equivalent of Petrarch's Laura or Dante's Beatrice. Montale had met the American Irma Brandeis, the inspiration for Clizia, in Florence in 1933, while he was working as the director of the library called the Gabinetto Vieusseux, which was a cultural and literary attraction among Anglophile ex-patriots. The fact that she was a medieval scholar,[4] not only ensured common interests, but solidified her purpose to Montale, whose poetry would see in her an embodiment of the abstract notions he had begun to expound in the *Ossi*, and make of her the focus of his poetry in the style of the troubadours. In this sense, the poem, 'Il balcone,' which serves as a program poem for the 'Mottetti,' eponymously refers to the locus of the lady whom the troubadour would admire from below.

Brandeis is the dedicatee of the 'Mottetti' (as well as the entire collection of the *Occasioni*), which remain among Montale's most allusive, hermetic works. Though these poems would make up a pseudo-*canzoniere*, in the tradition of a Petrarch, the backdrop – for them, and for the rest of the poems in the *Occassioni* – is the fascist Italy of the 1930s. That Brandeis was Jewish made things more difficult, if not inspirational. Montale saw her as being cast in a different metal from him, but in the face of the racial laws against Jews, which would cause Brandeis' return to America, he imagined her as a force, or essence, of salvation. This intuition about Clizia's fortitude was played out in 'Nuove stanze' (*Occasioni*). During her exile from Florence, Montale pondered the nature of absence and death, and consequentially that of time and space. The key term that encompasses these dimensions is memory.

After the singular lyric, 'Forse un mattino andando,' the 'Mottetti' are perhaps the most important poems for the purposes of my study. Though they comprise a sort of *canzoniere* dedicated to a woman, Clizia, the thematic of love is nearly absent. Instead, she is as much Virgil as Beatrice: she guides him as much as she offers him the prospect of salvation from the world of appearances. This world of appearances is delineated from the real world behind it, by the "schermo d'immagini," introduced in the sixth motet, 'La speranza di pure rivederti.' Montale leaves this screen motif vague enough as to suggest many interpretations, among which are the cinematic and holographic scenarios, along with the photographic images of memory as they insert themselves into the montage within the poet's visual field. This screen even recalls the infinite receptivity of Sigmund Freud's 'Wunderblock,'[5] which, itself, stood as a precursor for the notion of hypertext technology.

In 'La casa dei doganieri' (*Occasioni*), Montale's obsession with memory causes him to reassess the continuum of space and time. To his Clizia character, Montale adds an addressee who remains anonymous. She is the same woman from 'Incontro' and 'Godi se il vento' (both from the *Ossi*) and to whom Montale will refer in various sources as Arletta.[6] In 'La casa dei doganieri,' Montale presents Arletta as negligent for not remembering – however, that which she should have remembered was a time that preceded Montale's and her meeting. In this poem, Montale insists that there is a unified presence, a world-as-Being, in which all moments are contained in one permanent, continuous present, which he knows empirically as memory, and can be found in the noumenal void. By now, the barrier wall of 'Meriggiare pallido e assorto' has become the "varco" ("channel," passage, or opening), beyond which the world continues its role of becoming while he rests within the memorial confines of the shore.

Arletta, Esterina and Clizia, are, at times, rather interchangeable. As they evolve into the Gertrude and Dora Markus characters (both from *Le occasioni*), into the more mundane "Volpe" (Montale's anti-Beatrice, from the *Bufera* collection), and even into his wife (Mosca) from *Xenia*, they are less women than markers for abstract concepts in Montale's discourse on the world that surrounds him, however real it may be. Each, as in the Arletta character from 'La casa dei doganieri,' becomes the interlocutor-as-premise for a larger, overarching discussion on the nature of memory, space, and time. If "Volpe" is no longer a force of salvation (a visiting angel), then her terrestrial presence acts in counterpoint to Montale's inability to resign himself to the concrete world and accept it. Even in his dialogue with Mosca in the afterlife (*Xenia*), one intuits Montale's uneasiness with the world, as his wife had always been rather well adjusted to it (despite her obvious physical ailments – primarily her spondylitis). Mosca is not the Clizia with "occhi d'acciaio" from 'Nuove stanze.' She is a domestic insect ('mosca' means 'fly' in Italian) of 'Non ho mai capito se io fossi' ('Xenia 5'); she is the "insetto miope" who, despite her frail existence among the rhetoric of important politicos and men of letters, manages to orient herself amidst the falseness of the world with her "radar di pipistrello." Montale maintains that all is illusion – not just the false rhetoric – and that we are all dead without knowing it. If that is the case, then there is no separation between life and death, past and future, memory or dream.[7] In a world where past and future are indistinguishable, Arletta can be castigated for not remembering a moment in time that Montale and she could not – for reasons of time and space – have possibly shared.

During his years in Florence (1927–1948),[8] Montale composed the *Occasioni* and most of his third collection, *La bufera ed altro* (1956). These years would see Montale fight a silent battle against fascism, which culminated in his being removed from the directorship at the Gabinetto Vieusseux. (Montale would joke that he was removed for the same reason that he was initially hired: he was the only candidate without a Fascist Party membership card.) But these times of fascist censorship, highlighted by Clizia's exile, would force Montale's poetry more inwards – hermetic poetry, by default. Amid the false rhetoric of fascism leading up to the war, during the war, and in the eerie aftermath, Montale felt detached from any sense of harmony with the world. This detachment would cause many of his detractors[9] to see Montale as a-political, or disinterested in the struggles of humankind. But Montale would see himself still in the light of his poetic *alter ego* from 'Forse un mattino andando,' and the others as the "uomini che non si voltano" to see the reality behind the rhetorical and false appearances.

Montale's Florentine years were perhaps not those in which he experienced his formation as a poet – the Ligurian coast will haunt his poetry throughout his career – but in these years he would mature his ideas and poetry. Fundamental during this period was the literary café that he frequented, *Le Giubbe Rosse*.[10] For it was here that he would encounter such personalities as Ottone Rosai, Piero Bigongiari, Mario Luzi, Tommaso Landolfi, Alessandro Parronchi, Elio Vittorini and Arturo Loria. Among the regulars of the *Giubbe Rosse*, Montale would enter a literary dialogue that resulted in the establishment of such journals as *Solaria*, *Frontespizio*, and *Campo di Marte*. His collaboration in such journals meant that he came into contact with the avant-garde of Florence, as well as that of Europe and the

Americas. (Through the literary journal *Solaria*, Montale would discover the works of T. S. Eliot, in whom he would find a literary kindred spirit.) This center of activity and literary personalities was also a second home to the hermetic poets and their trademark anti-fascism. Among them, Montale's own inherent introspection would develop a confident poetic voice. Perhaps this voice would remain too introspective, as Montale's anti-fascism was never recognized at the level of a Vittorini, and few could appreciate, at the time, the wit of his sardonic commentary.

With the peace after World World II and the submission of fascism, Montale would slightly alter his style, however. He no longer sees the urgency of salvation found in his Clizia, and his Clizia-like characters; rather, Montale attends to the banality of the post-war. Though Montale's *Bufera* was published in 1956, it is important to remember that the substantial portion of its works were penned in the 1940s. Therefore, much of the satiric nature of his post-war cynicism would not be seen until his later publications: *Satura* (1962), *Xenia* (1966) and his *Diario del '71 e del '72* (published together in 1973 by Mondadori). Conversely, his prose work, the *Farfalla di Dinard* (1956), performs the task of amalgamating his poetic, metaphysical philosophy on memory and the space-time continuum with self-depreciation and a facetious look at his society. Each *farfalla*, or short story, in the collection adds to Montale's discourse and, moreover, is essential as an exegetical tool for the reading of his poetry.

Having studied the *Farfalla di Dinard*, ultimately, I cannot but help confirming my suspicion that in his first three poetic collections – and, to an extent, in his later poetry, which was often recycled material and themes – Montale was writing about a hologram projected from the 'void,' or noumenos, of the cosmos, which could be viewed as a film. This 'film' was taken for memories, and past, present, and future, by those who could not read it correctly outside the flux of time; by those who did not realize that there was one unified present with myriad discrete, simultaneous images. This is especially seen in such *farfalle* as 'La casa delle due palme,' 'Sul limite,' 'Reliquie,' 'Il regista,' and 'Sulla spiaggia.'

Though the short stories from *Farfalla di Dinard* are esoteric and full of philosophical and phenomenological paradox, without them, Montale's poetry has less impact. In *Farfalla*, one begins to sense that Montale shared affinities – even unbeknownst to him – with Marcel Proust, Jorge Luis Borges, Henri Bergson, the cinematic theories of Gilles Deleuze and Sergei Eisenstein, and contemporary hologram theories, such as those of Michael Talbot. Through the *Farfalla*, Montale's lyrics take on new meaning, as in the photo-cinematic "derelitte lastre" of 'Quasi una fantasia' (*Ossi*), or the virtual "punto dilatato" of 'Voce giunta con le folaghe' (*Bufera*). Without them, his poetry seems like a series of sporadic, impressionistic canvasses; with them, one can trace a parabola of consistency throughout his entire opus. This parabola covers the duration of Montale's poetic career, but for the purposes of discussion, I will limit it to the period between *Ossi* and *Bufera*.

Because this book primarily focuses on the first three collections of Montale's poetry, I will, when an English rendering becomes necessary, refer to the Galassi translations, which are the most insightful and accurate versions that currently exist for the English-speaking public.[11] All English translations will be taken from Galassi, unless otherwise specified.

Notes

1. Excerpt of 'Annetta' taken from Eugenio Montale. *Diari del '71 e del '72*. Milano: Mondadori, 1973.
2. The idea is that the phenomenal is that which is experienced relatively, as appearance. The noumenal is the absolute, the source of the appearance. In this paradigm, the idea of reality precedes reality itself. This means that an order exists in the world before even entering into the receptive soul.
3. Though Zeno's paradox is a rhetorical trick – a *reductio* – of convenient fiction, it is still the object of much discussion in philosophy and physics. Perhaps he was fully aware of his own bad philosophy, as this notion may have been a satyrical criticism of the fallacious philosophical arguments aimed at his teacher, Parmenides, by those in disagreement with his logic.
4. Irma Brandeis later went on to teach medieval literature at Bard College in the United States. Her most notable work of scholarship was: *The Ladder of Vision: A Study of Dante's Comedy*. Garden City (NY): Doubleday and Company, 1961.
5. This magical writing pad was the subject of a short 'note' by Freud. It is the waxen tablet covered by a clear sheet of celluloid used by many children as a drawing surface. If one runs a stylus over the clear sheet while it is laid over the waxen tablet, a series of darkened images will result from the impressions. When the sheet is lifted, the darken traces 'magically' disappear. In Freud's analogy for the psyche's mnemonic ability, theoretically the original incision still exists somewhere in the infinite layers of impressions. These latent images are not unlike the undeveloped, albeit present, images on the photographic paper prior to its being developed. Each layer is a palimpsest of a unique experience. See Sigmund Freud. 'A Note upon the 'Mystic Writing-Pad'. *Sigmund Freud: Collected Papers*, vol. 5. Ed. James Strachey. (New York: Basic Books, Inc., 1959): 175–181
6. Many years later, she will appear as Annetta in the eponymously entitled poem from *Diario del '72*.
7. See the fourth poem of the first *Xenia* collection, 'Avevamo studiato per l'aldilà:' "Mi provo a modularlo nella speranza / che tutti siamo già morti senza saperlo."
8. In 1948, Montale will relocate to Milano, where he will begin a twenty-five year career as a journalist for the cultural pages of *Il corriere della sera*, in particular writing music reviews for *Il corriere d'informazione*.

9. The most famous of these is Pier Paolo Pasolini. Many years later – during the rise of the culture of contestation, the Communist Party, and social movements – Pasolini would finally take Montale to task for his lack of overt political commitment in his review of *Satura*, in *Nuovi Argumenti*, 21, 1971: 17–20. Montale would respond in kind by penning "Lettera a Malvolio" (Diario del '71) in which the title refers to Pasolini himself.
10. For an anecdotal account of the literary activity of the famous café see Arnaldo Pini's *Incontri alle Giubbe Rosse*. Firenze: Edizioni Polistampa, 2000. In Montale's words: 'Sotto il profilo della maturazione culturale i venti anni che ho passato a Firenze sono stati i piú importanti della mia vita e lì ho scoperto che non c'era solamente il mare, ma anche la terraferma: la terra ferma della cultura, delle idee, della tradizione, dell'umanesimo' (90–91).
11. Eugenio Montale. *Collected Poems: 1920–1954*. Ed. and trans. Jonathan Galassi. New York: Farrar, Straus and Giroux,

CHRONOLOGY

The names, dates and events listed in this chronology are based on a whole host of sources. Of particular importance in compiling this list, two works stand out: Marco Forti's *Per conoscere Montale: antologia corredata di testi critici* (Mondadori, terza ristampa, 1995) and Giorgio Zampa's edition of Montale's collected poetry, *Tutte le poesie* (Mondadori, 1990).

1896 Eugenio Montale is born in Genoa on October 12 (Columbus Day). He is the youngest of six children born to Domenico Montale and Giuseppina Ricci Montale.

1900 Domenico and his cousins begin construction of family villa at Fegina (Monterosso) in the Cinque Terre along the Ligurian coast.

1905 Villa at Fegina is finished. This will remain Montale's summer holiday destination until he is almost 30 years of age. The rugged seaside and coastal landscape form the basis of his first poetic compositions.

1907 Carducci (Nobel Prize for Literature in 1906) dies. Carducci, Pascoli and D'Annunzio together make up the three most important Italian poets to influence the early 1900s.

1912 Pascoli dies.

1915 Undertakes opera training with the baritone Ernesto Sivori. Obtains his diploma as an accountant, working briefly for his father's business. Italy enters World War I; his three brothers are conscripted – he bides his time by reading assiduously at the Biblioteca Comunale.

1916 Pens first version of 'Meriggiare pallido e assorto.'

1917 Maintains a diary which will be published in 1983 as *Quaderno genovese*. This work provides background on his intellectual formation, often times under the tutelage of his sister, Marianna, who introduces Montale to philosophy (particulary that of Boutroux and contingentism). Called into military service; begins officer training at Parma, where he meets Sergio Solmi.

1918 Assigned to the 'Liguria Bridage' (the 158th infantry regiment). Volunteers for assignment on the front in Trentino, where he commands a post in Valmorbia, which he will later immortalize in *Ossi di seppia*.

1919 D'Annunzio leads the expedition of Fiume to occupy the territory with a militia of young, rebellious fascists.

1920 Officially discharged from the service. Meets writer Angelo Barile and painter-poet Filippo de Pisis. In Fegina meets the degli Uberti family, among whom is the sixteen-year old Anna, who will later become "Arletta." Writes his first published review: that of *Trucioli* by fellow Ligurian Camillo Sbarbaro, with whom he will share a friendship.

1921 Recommences operatic training with Sivori.

1922 Publishes 'Accordi;' writes 'I limoni.' Collaborates on *Primo tempo*, the literary review of Giacomo Debenedetti and Sergio Solmi.

1923 Death of Ernesto Sivori; Montale ends his opera career (before it began). Writes a number of important poems, including: 'Portami il girasole,' 'Forse un mattino andando,' 'Non chiederci la parola' and 'Vasca.' Meets Roberto 'Bobi' Bazlen, a Triestine who will remain his confidant and who introduces him to the works of Svevo.

1925 His essay, 'Stile e tradizione,' appears in *Il Baretti*, whose anti-fascist editor, Piero Gobetti, publishes Montale's *Ossi di seppia* in the same year. Publishes his article 'Omaggio a Svevo,' which will contribute to bringing notoriety to the Triestine novelist. Montale signs the anti-fascist manifesto (*Manifesto degli Intellettuali Antifascisti*) by Giovanni Amendola and Benedetto Croce

1926 Gobetti dies in exile in Paris as a result of trauma suffered at the hands of the fascists. Offered a position at the publishing house of Bemporad & Figli in Florence. Writes 'Incontro' (formerly known as 'Arletta') and 'Due nel crepuscolo.' Publishes 'I morti' and 'Vecchi versi.' Meets Umberto Saba in Trieste. Collaborates on the journals, *Il convegno* and *La fiera letteraria*.

1927 Moves to Florence to begin work with Bemporad. Solidified friendships with such writers as Arturo Loria, Elio Vittorini, C. E. Gadda, and Alessandro Bonsanti, which will lead to the founding of *Solaria*, the literary journal. The center for intellectual and social activity is the famous café in Piazza Vittoria (now, Repubblica), *Le Giubbe Rosse*. His 'Arsenio' is published in *Solaria*.

1928 Mario Praz translates 'Arsenio' into English; T. S. Eliot publishes it in his journal, The Criterion.

1929 Offered directorship of the Gabinetto Scientifico Letterario Vieusseux, the library and reading room located in the Palazzo di Parte Guelfa. Becomes a border in the home of Matteo and Drusilla Tanzi Marangoni. Drusilla, known as 'Mosca,' will become a life-long friend of Montale, and eventually his wife. Becket translates 'Delta' into English.

1930 Publishes 'La casa dei doganieri.'

1931 Death of Montale's father, Domenico. Wins the Premio Antico Fattore.

1932 Having won the Antico Fattore the previous year, his 'La casa dei doganieri' and four other verses are published in a 'plaquette' (chapbook). Writes 'Omaggio a T. S. Eliot.'

1933 Irma Brandeis, a young American scholar who has read his *Ossi di seppia*, visits Montale at the Gabinetto Vieusseux.

1934 Publishes three of his 'Mottetti.'

1937 Writes 'Non recidere, forbice, quel volto.' Publishes four more of the 'Mottetti.'

1938 His sister, Marianna, dies, age 44. Montale loses directorship of the

Vieusseux because he is not a member of the Fascist Party – the Vieusseux is taken over by the fascist Ministero di Cultura Popolare for purposes of propaganda. Irma Brandeis suggests Montale return to the United States with her, in order to pursue a teaching career; he declines. Montale finishes writing the poems that will comprise the 'Mottetti.' D'Annunzio dies.

1939 Unemployed, Montale begins work as a translator of American and English fiction. His collaborator, Lucia Rodocanachi, is considered to be his ghost writer in many cases. Takes up residence with Drusilla Tanzi Marangoni. *Le occasioni* are published by Einaudi. This work is immediately a success with the younger generations.

1940 Publishes the second edition of *Le occasioni*, in which four new poems, including 'Ti libero la fronte dai ghiaccioli,' appear. Translations of Steinbeck.

1941 Publishes the poem 'La bufera.' Translations of Cervantes, Bécquer, Marlowe and Dorothy Parker.

1942 Mother, Giuseppina Ricca, dies. Translations of Hawthorne, Melville, Twain and Faulkner.

1943 Montale's 'plaquette,' *Finisterre*, is smuggled into Switzerland by friend and critic, Gianfranco Contini. Winter of 1943-1944, Montale offers aid and comfort to Umberto Saba and Carlo Levi who are in hiding, as Jews living in Italy; he keeps them clandestinely in his home.

1944 Battle of Florence. Mosca hospitalized for several weeks with an acute attack of ankylosing spondylitis, a debilitating bone disease.

1945 Named as member of Committee for Culture and Art within the Committee for National Liberation (CLN in Italian). Joins the Partito d'Azione. Writes theater reviews for *La Nazione del Popolo* of Florence. Begins painting in Vittoria Apuana, where Mosca is recovering from her illness. Writes 'Ballata scritta in una clinica' based on Mosca's convalescence.

1946 Publishes 'Ezekiel saw the Wheel…' and 'Intenzioni: Intervista immaginaria.' Begins writing for *Il Corriere della Sera* and *Il Corriere d'Informazione.*

1947 Publishes 'Voce giunta con le folaghe.'

1948 Hired permanently by *Il Corriere della Sera*; moves to Milan. On British tour, meets T. S. Eliot at Faber & Faber. Publishes 'L'anguilla.'

1949 Meets Maria Luisa Spaziani ("la Volpe") at the Università di Torino. Translation of Shakespeare's *Hamlet*.

1950 Trip to New York City for the inaugural flight of Alitalia's Rome-New York route. Wins the Premio San Marino for poetry.

1952 Delivers address at the International Congress of Cultural Freedom in Paris; title: 'La solitudine dell'artista.' Inaugurates a column called 'Letture' in *Il Corriere della Sera*.

1954 Begins writing regular music review column for *Il Corriere d'Informazione*.

1956 Publishes *La bufera e altro* with Neri Pozza (Venice). Awarded the Premio Marzotto for his poetry. Publishes his short stories in *Farfalla di Dinard*, also with Neri Pozza.

1957 *La bufera e altro* published by Mondadori.

1959 Made a member of the French Legion d'Honneur. Quasimodo wins the Nobel Prize for Literature. Though they correspond, Montale is frustrated by this choice by the Nobel committee.

1960 *Farfalla di Dinard* published by Mondadori.

1961 Receives a degree in Letters (*laurea honoris causa*) from the Università di Milano.

1962 Publishes *Satura*. Religious marriage to Mosca. Wins the Premio Lincei.

1963 Civil marriage to Mosca in Florence on April 30; she will die months later in Milan on October 20. She entrusts Montale to Gina Tossi – their housekeeper – who will remain Montale's companion until his death.

1965 Delivers lecture, 'Dante ieri e oggi,' in Florence at the Congresso Internazionale di Studi Danteschi, which marks the 500th anniversary of Alighieri's birth. Long-time confidente, Bobi Bazlen, dies. *Selected Poems* is published in the United States under the direction of Glauco Cambon, with translations by Mario Praz, Robert Lowell, and Irma Brandeis, among others.

1966 Publishes *Xenia*, poems dedicated to the memory of Mosca, and *Auto da fé: Cronache in due tempi*, cultural criticism. Gallimard (Paris) publishes a French translation (by Patrice Angelini) of *Ossi di seppia*, *Le occasioni*, and *La bufera e altro*.

1967 Honorary degree, doctor of letters, conferred by the University of Cambridge. Named 'senatore a vita' by Italian Presidente Giuseppe Saragat.

1969 Publishes his travel writings (his correspondences to *Il Corriere della Sera*) as *Fuori di casa*.

1971 Publishes *Satura (1962–1970)*, an expanded edition. Publishes prose work entitled La poesia non esiste. Private edition of *Diario del '71*, a collection of poems.

1973 Publishes *Diari del '71 e del '72*. Among these poems is 'Lettera a Malvolio,' in which he defends his political choices throughout his life. Chief in his defense against the accusation of 'qualunquismo' (non-commitment) by Pasolini, who is the target of the poem. Retires from *Il Corriere della Sera*.

1974 Receives the *laurea honoris causa* from the Università di Roma.

1975 Awarded Nobel Prize for Literature; his acceptance speech is entitled: 'È ancora possibile la poesia?'

1976 For Montale's eightieth birthday, Mondadori publishes a collection of his musings on poetry in a work entitled *Sulla poesia*. The first edition of Marco Forti's *Per conoscere Montale* is published.

1977 Named 'cittadino onorario' by the city of Florence. Mondadori publishes *Tutte le poesie*.

1980 Einaudi publishes the Bettarini-Contini edition of Montale's poetry as *L'opera in versi*.

1981 Montale dies in the Clinica San Pio X in Milan on September 12; a State funeral follows on the 14th in the Duomo of Milan. On the 15th, Montale is buried next to his wife in the cemetary of San Felice a Ema (Florence). Mondadori publishes a collection of Montale's music criticism in the volume *Prime alla Scala*.

1983 Mondadori publishes *Quaderno genovese*, edited by Laura Barile.

1984 Mondadori publishes *Tutte le poesia*, edited by Giorgio Zampa.

1991 Mondadori publishes *Diario postumo: Prima parte: 30 poesie*, edited by Annalisa Cima. Cima claims that Montale had, beginning in 1969, given her a packet of inedited poems each year until his death. He entrusted them to her under the condition that she not publish them until after his death. Much controversy has been generated, as critics believe Cima – not Montale – composed these works from snippets of conversations with the poet; others believe that she forged them outright. Though such names as Maria Corti, curator of the library at the Università di Pavia, corroborate the authenticity of them, there is still debate. Needless to say, this is the sort of polemic that Montale would have enjoyed, and many feel that this was his own version of a practical joke from the grave.

1996 Mondadori publishes *Diario postumo: 66 poesie e altre*, edited by Annalisa Cima, in honor of the centenary of the poet's birth. Mondadori also publishes a two-volume edition of all of Montale's published writings in *Il secondo mestiere: Arte, musica, società* and *Il secondo mestiere: Prose 1920–1979*, edited by Giorgio Zampa.

CHAPTER 1

Memory, Death and the Void[1]

The poetry of Montale is thematically concerned with absence and presence as visual manifestations occurring on the 'screen of images' between the worlds of the phenomenal and the noumenal. This initially transpires in the world of "remote spectral landscapes"[2] of the *Ossi,* where Montale senses his own disharmony with the world and yet perceives a truer, more real empirical reality behind it, as expressed in his poem 'Forse un mattino andando.' His poems are concerned with fighting that absence and creating a connection to real presence in the void. He fills the void through his constant harking back to his memory in order to compare his current environment with some quality, or facet, of a person from his past so that he can designate a locus in the present as the point in the present that has the perfect visual juxtaposition to stand as a sort of linguistic expression of that past. Initially this is a voluntary, existential struggle; inevitably and involuntary resignation into a world of "predestined memory."[3] To further fill the void, Montale also creates dialogues with the dead, the absence of whom would be the equivalent of conversing with a living person who is absent; far off. He looks into empty space – where the figures of his past are no longer – to see if he has evoked them or found a way of materializing their absence in his surroundings. He creates an essential alphabet by searching for a sign of *something* in his environment to which he can attribute Clizia's presence as in 'Bassa marea', where "il vagheggiamento supremo di una realtà assente, saturata di lancinante nostalgia," which has its "formula piú elementare" here, where "la sensazione presente, il 'segno,' libera un secondo piano di ricordo, squarciando di colpo il velo sopra un vivente sottosuolo sentimentale, di cui la realtà attuale finisce col configurarsi come una specie di colorita e allucinata materializzazione."[4] A 'sensation', or stimulus, affects the photoreceptors of his retinal nerves and the result produces a perfect facsimile of a vision which had originally implanted itself in his mind. He wonders how a glimmer, or a blowing leaf, could not be a sign of her presence. She is there if he believes it, the way a god exists (truly) for believers and is an abstract construct for non-believers. For Arrowsmith the void – the emptiness containing her absence – is:

the inexpressible X that precedes images or words, the X from which we come and into which we vanish. We remember it darkly only when we cease remembering, then if at all, we sense it growing inside us, a fate that depends on us (as God depends on his believers, like Clizia) to confront and freely define.[5]

Montale's desire to have her with him is projected into the void that is the "arduo nulla" of 'Il balcone' and the poems of the *Occasioni* – especially of the 'Mottetti' – literally become his every latest motif ("ogni mio tardo motivo") that he conjoins to the emptiness: his fight against entropy becomes, "la possiblità...di trovare nella creazione artistica l'unica via di salvezza dalla distruzione."[6] His poems are not an image but a list of the perfect juxtaposition of signs in his visual field which will produce the same retinal stimuli. In this regard, his metaphor for memory as creation approaches the process of cinema. He will add his latest motif like a projection on the void; the poem itself will become the object:

Le occasioni, nell'ordinamento voluto dall'Autore, si reggono per intero sulla memoria, come è dimostrato dalla prima introduttiva poesia Il balcone: "Ora a quel vuoto ho congiunto / ogni mio tardo motivo, [...] La vita che dà barlumi / è quella che sola tu scorgi." È di qualità memoriale ciò che rende unitaria la centrale serie dei Mottetti.[7]

Thus, the culmination of his hopes, his memory, his search for Clizia (and, indirectly, faith and truth) is represented in the poems which become the ultimate presence in the void.[8] Clearly, the point of intersection of past and present and also the point where dead and absent become equal states for the recalling party, as in 'Voce giunta con le folaghe.' All of these notions can be reinterpreted, however, with the cinematic, even holographic, metaphors of memory which become clearer in his later works, particularly in *Farfalla di Dinard*.

Montale's experience of memory is not likely to fall into the category of an 'ubi sunt' motif. "Egli non afferma, come il Leopardi e il Baudelaire, che il presente è una decadenza rispetto ad un passato storico o individuale, oggetto di rimpianto. Non è ossessionato dalla nostalgia di altre epoche o luoghi contrari."[9] Rather, he perceives the present and the past as "atomi equivalenti."[10] Nor does it open up passageways into itself as an analysis of the past for the past's sake. Rather the nature of memory is, like a photo, a mental presence which indicates further absence from the present moment. In fact, in 'Mottetto 18' he envisions a memory "che si sfolla," easily brought to a state of fog or mist ("nebbia"):

Non recidere, forbice, quel volto, / solo nella memoria che si sfolla, / non far del grande suo viso in ascolto / la mia nebbia di sempre. / Un freddo cala ... duro il colpo svetta. / E l'acacia ferita da sé scrolla il guscio di cicala / nella prima belletta di novembre.

Montale had already created some linguistic precursors for the discussion of memory and its cinematic appearance in his earlier *Ossi di seppia*, for example, in 'Flussi' ("lampi") and 'Sarcofaghi' ("derelitte lastre"). In the *Ossi* the expressions are more objective descriptions about memory, which is a simple function of living and being human. Though they are not quite the preoccupied, concerned syntagma of *Le Occasioni*, and they have a secondary role in the poetry, one can see their linguistic relation to the syntagm of *Le Occasioni*, where they take on a primary role: "memoria stancata" ('Fine dell'infanzia'); "scialba memoria" ('Valmorbia'); "memoria grigia" ('Ripenso il tuo sorriso').

In fact, very much in the way that cinema cuts simultaneous actions together in a parallel montage, the second strophe of 'Non recidere' occurs as an exterior parallel of his inner state, as well as an example of the process of forgetting; so easy to forget; so cold like the November mud. Of course, the image is compounded by the use of the "guscio" ("shell"), the molted exoskeleton of the cicada, which speaks of an ephemeral, passing stage. The shell is a remnant of the past, and may even suffice as an amulet of remembrance for the poet if it were not so fragile; if it did not, itself, mimic undoing over time which dissipates memory: "Memory itself can be understood metaphorically as a great 'husk,' the flimsy remains of living, tangible experience."[11] Though Montale does not literally say it in 'Mottetto 18,' one can infer that he was thinking this for later, in 'L'ombra della magnolia,' the image returns: "...la vuota scorza / di chi cantava sarà presto polvere / di vetro sotto i piedi."

In the void of space, unoccupied now by Clizia, there is at least his own consolation that she is with him still. That is, she is either part of a sempiternal holographic cinema that can be projected on his visual photoreceptors or she is there in the juxtaposition on the 'screen of images'. Metaphorically what is left of her is the husk of a shell, but metaphysically Montale feels literally connected to her even in this reduced shell-of-a-state. When the cicada occupied its shell, it was alive, but in a different form. So, already the fact that it has molted means it has transmuted; gone from one living form to another. The fact that a shell is left behind means that it is remembered, like the latent images we leave behind in a photograph; a photograph which is implied as the object of the scissor cutting action of verse one. Perhaps in this sense, the fan of 'Il ventaglio' (*Bufera*), albeit a physical, tangible object, is a sort of 'husk' of experience, like many souvenirs. The shell is a memory, but when it is shaken from the acacia to the ground (perhaps to be reduced to dust) it is a memory of a memory; a memory twice removed as we will clearly see in 'La casa dei doganieri.' Therefore, if memory is being forever reduced to mist and overshadowed by hard, physical aspects of the world (as seen here in nature with an acacia, an axe chop, cold mud) perhaps he will have to look to the exterior world, perhaps the "schermo d'immagini" ('Mottetto 6') with which he will create by virtue of objective, physical presence of things, a presence where there would only be absence, outward appearances to which to tie the memory of Clizia. To truly perceive motion, time is necessary; but in an open, eternal system, where each individual frame – to an infinite division – can be perceived without impeding one's overall understanding. Objects will stimulate a point in his memory to dilate – the "punto dilatato" of 'Voce giunta con le folaghe' – and throw him into the infinitely expandable continuum of space (without time) within memory: a holographic world of perfect connectivity.

Even the structure of 'Mottetto 18' seems to represent his struggle to associate the abstract and the ephemeral with the concrete and the lasting. It alternates from line to line: verse 1 includes cutting scissors; verse 2, emptying memory; verse 3, the face on the photograph; verse 4, fog; verse 5, a cold which seems to represent the physical cold outside and the correlative of the coldness of the moment in the cold steel of the axe (a double correlative, as it were); then ellipses and a hard chop lops the top of the acacia; verse 6, again, the acacia; verse 7, the shell, a presence which indicates an absence, and which soon will be absent, turned to dust; and verse 8, the final image of all that rests here, now, in the present. All that remains is a cold November, wet and muddy.

Montale portrays memory as having enough resources in itself to replace the absence, as in 'Debole sistro al vento' where there is a "lament for the inability of life (or poetry) to defeat the void."[12] Montale elucidates his conception of this via Clizia, who comes to him like a voice. Voices of the dead and voices of the absent amount to the same thing, for to talk with either one must rely on memory. As in 'Delta,' there is a "presenza soffocata" ("a character who is presented as dead, or at least permanently absent, 'suffocated,' only able to 'surface' in the poet's memory.")[13] Like the "guscio di cicala," memory has a duration: it is here, perhaps even mutates, but eventually dies, in all its forms, even its vestiges (in this case, the shell which will turn to dust). But in this duration it is not negative, for it is alive and brings joy to whomever is recollecting. The expression "fin che giova" ('Voce giunta con le folaghe') calls our attention to the joy of remembrance:

Io rammento quelle / mie prode e pur son giunta con le folaghe / a distaccarti dalle tue. Memoria / non è peccato fin che giova. Dopo / è letargo di talpe, abiezione / che funghisce su sé...

But it becomes the lethargy of moles, abjection which builds mold upon itself. Also in 'Sul Llogebrat' the reader experiences a woman who "assumes the superego role that is proper to the father, condemning a useless and too-private memory":[14]

Dal verde immarcescibile della canfora / due note, un intervallo di terza maggiore. / Il cucco, non la civetta, ti dissi; ma intanto, di scatto, / tu avevi spinto l'acceleratore.

It is a fragmentary cul-de-sac that, assuming it is lasting, will only bring Montale to the memory locus; not a beginning of another creative link, or process, though we recall that in 'Sul limite' (FD), memory is no longer private, as the author's confident has 'viewed' the film of the former's life.

Even the negative aspects of memory, and the fear of being lost in memory, present in 'Voce giunta,' find their precursors in 'I morti.' Galassi speaks of the 'morti' as "[t]ormented by their continued life in the minds of those who survive them rather than released into the salvation posited throughout *Ossi* but unavailable for most."[15] The dead are not conforted by knowing that the living are quick to forget, for any possibility of their individual mortality is what is remembered in the living.

In this same poem ('Voce giunta'), Montale refers to memory as an "obscure reminiscing sense." It is a sense which is perceivable to him before it can be attached to any exterior images or words, as "il vuoto inabitato / che occupammo" (the uninhabited void that we occupied)[16] "e che attende fin ch'è tempo / di colmarsi di noi, di ritrovarci..." (and which awaits to fill itself with us, when we will find each other again). This concept is perhaps introduced to Montale's reader as early as 'Forse un mattino andando,' where

il protagonista della poesia di Montale riesce, per una combinazione di fattori oggettivi (aria di vetro, arida) e soggettivi (ricettività a un miracolo gnoseologico) a voltarsi tanto in fretta da arrivare, diciamo, a gettare lo sguardo là dove il suo campo visuale non ha ancora occupato lo spazio: e vede il nulla, il vuoto.[17]

So, if it is perceivable to the poet, but not clearly attached to exterior images or words, he turns to the void around him, which is only void because it contains an absence, yet it is filled with all the possible occasions that the outside world offers to him. A disembodied voice or the spirit of a dead loved-one is perceivable to Montale here, though its perceivable presence, like the abstract of memory, is its apparent absence. Memory's presence implies an absence of the seminal event. Montale himself clearly speaks of this: "Le vide inhabité qui se fait en nous juste avant que nous soyons ou que nous disions oui à la vie: le vide qui se fait dans la pendule une seconde avant que ne sonne l'heure."[18] This brings us back to further consider Arrowsmith's commentary when he speaks of the:

> *inexpressable X that precedes images or words, the X from which we come and into which we shall vanish. We remember it darkly only when we cease remembering; then, if at all, we sense it growing inside us, a fate that depends on us (as God depends on his believers, like Clizia) to confront and freely define. The ancient Greeks would have called that void Chaos..., not so much anarchic disorder as the matrix of the possible – the undifferentiated 'ditch' of things.*[19]

Montale ties together the progression of memory to the concept of the conversation with the dead and with the absent. These factors have the commonality of being presences which are never materialized. If the world is a phenomenal hologram, in *Farfalla di Dinard* we see the hologram for what it is: non-reality. In the afterlife, Montale's alter ego is in the void: in this 'real' reality, he sees that the holographic projection of a phenomenal reality was just as illusory as the reality projected in a cinema. The photo grams of cinema are present as absence, as in the instance where Clizia and Montale's father exchange words which the poet cannot hear:

> *L'ombra fidata e il muto che risorge, / quella che scorporò l'interno fuoco / e colui che lunghi anni d'oltretempo / (anni per me pesante) disincarnano, / si scambiano parole che interito / sul margine io non odo.*

The uninhabited void reveals itself before being tied to images or words in 'Voce giunta.' "Cosí" ("Thus"), he tells us, the void reveals itself, as if to say that these disembodied souls and memories, not being linked to ontological images, require the experience of a present situation to which to tie them. His trip to the cemetery, wondering where his father could be spiritually, having passed on to the other life, becomes the treatise on Montale's preoccupation with death and the death, or fleeing, of memory, and the spiritual faith needed to get over his fear of the void. Montale, associated with the image of his dead father, cannot accept the abstract without material links or external correlatives. Clizia seems comfortable with being detached from the terrestrial ties to life. It seems that Clizia is in a privileged position – she is far off. Let us call this an irrational fear on Montale's part. By the female companion being so far away, or spiritually remote, Montale feels excluded, as if her being far away somehow means she is (*a priori*) closer to the miracle or epiphany, and he farther from it.

The uninhabited void that we occupy could be the real reality behind the illusion of the phenomenal world. It remains uninhabited because it is a projection – a world as sensation and stimuli. Memories and ghosts are there, but do not occupy a physical space. They reside within that infinitesimally small point, which upon being recalled, expands. It does not even truly exist in its immaterial form until it is recalled on the screen of images that is the brain or the brain-as-hologram where memorial images are projected. We see through our eyes, but not with them, so the screen of images could be on the retina, or in a virtual space of the brain as hologram which, in turn, is a division of the world as hologram. In this regard, whether internal or external, the visual field becomes the reality of the seer, even when it does not reflect the phenomenal reality. In the *Ossi*, the world was cinematically 'overexposed' by the "canicola." The bounds of phenomenal reality are explored in 'Voce giunta', where multiple images are edited together as if by a trick of the holographic projection:

> *Il vento del giorno / confonde l'ombra viva e l'altra ancora riluttante in un mezzo che respinge / le mie mani, e il respiro mi si rompe / nel punto dilatato, nella fossa / che circonda lo scatto del ricordo.*

A "punto dilatato," which Galassi translates as "swelling point,"[20] leaves just as great a margin of interpretation as Montale's original Italian wording. This is not novel to the poetry of Montale. After all, in 'Quasi una fantasia' he speaks of a time when the entire realm of the past will have appeared in front of him in one focused point: "Lieto leggerò i neri / segni dei rami sul bianco / come un essenziale alfabeto. / Tutto il passato in un punto dinanzi mi sarà comparso." Perhaps this point can be overlooked or misinterpreted, despite the universe within it. In 'Gli uomini che si voltano,' Montale mentions a point that seems like an ordinary sign, and yet, like a hieroglyphic character, not only can it be interpreted, it can be interpreted and expanded into volumes out of just one character: "metterli controluce è ingigantire quel segno, formare / un geroglifico piú grande del diadema che ti abbagliava." The mention of "controluce" implies a process of holography whereby all images are simultaneously present, but only visible when illuminated at the proper angle. So perhaps then the "vuoto inabitato" is the holographic void which is omnipresent, but immaterial:

Cosí si svela prima di legarsi / a immagini, a parole, oscuro senso / reminiscente, il vuoto inabitato / che occupammo e che attende fin ch'è tempo / di colmarsi di noi, di ritrovarci...

Another point, the "punto morto" of 'I limoni' is the flaw in Nature that will provide a clue to Montale:

Vedi, in questi silenzi in cui le cose / s'abbandonano e sembrano vicine / a tradire il loro ultimo segreto, / talora ci si aspetta / di scoprire uno sbaglio di Natura, il punto morto del mondo, l'anello che non tiene, / il filo da disbrogliare che finalmente ci metta / nel mezzo di una verità.

This point is beyond time, or at least not subject to it, but only a fleeting privilege, at best, to mortals who are mired in calendric time: "Ma l'illusione manca e ci riporta il tempo / nelle città rumorose dove l'azzurro si mostra / soltanto a pezzi, in alto, tra le cimase." This point is a rift in the fabric of phenomenal reality which reveals the void. The void is the "punto dilatato" of 'Voce giunta,' which is a metaphor for the infinity of the holographic universe.

It also brings into the void a presence, and this is our concern here. This poem is a literal "punto dilatato": vertically it goes from memory to the present, but somewhere along the way, it stops and expands horizontally to give Montale, and the reader, a poem which is a presence in absence. Poetry approximates the process of materialization and dematerialization in the phenomenic world made of "attimi di una mostruosa opera d'arte sempre distrutta e sempre rinnovata" ("La solitudine dell'artista..."). Therefore, it is almost ironic for Montale to say, in the last stanza of 'Voce giunta,' "cosí si svela prima di legarsi / a immagini, a parole, oscuro senso / reminiscente," for he was linked to the *scatto* of memory and the feeling of the void in one moment of poetic significance. In 'Il balcone,' I believe he hinted at this by saying he could not change the nature of the "arduo nulla," but he could add to it his most recent "motivo":

Pareve facile giuoco / mutare in nulla lo spazio / che m'era aperto, in un tedio malcerto il certo tuo fuoco. / Ora a quel vuoto ho congiunto /

ogni mio tardo motivo, / sull'arduo nulla si spunta / l'ansia di attenderti vivo.

Memory stands as the artistic challenge of representation; metaphors of memory become art itself – a cinematic montage, at that. Obviously, to remember, to use memory, means to project a moment that is currently absent; lost in Swiss time, but present in internal folds of time. That is, memory creates a presence in empty space and yet the space, because of the immaterial nature of memories, remains physically uninhabited. Ultimately, from where does the projection come? Is it invisible and latent until it is perceived on the photoreceptors of the eyes?

A poem like 'Vecchi versi,' could be a late motif which will fill his void. If the lines of this poem are typed in a particular period of time, then they are recent to that time, but they speak of something old or past if based on a memory. Therefore, by the very title 'Vecchi versi' ('Old Verses'), we are presented with a complex moment in determining the temporal relationship between Montale, the poem, and the event that he recalls. If they are "old verses," is this an old composition? Or is the composition harking back to old ways? They are automatically old because, for Montale, the universe exists as a complete whole recorded once for all.

Though it is an "occasione,"the poem 'Vecchi versi' does not seem to be one of Montale's latest motifs, as the opening poem of the *Occasioni* implies. Rather, perhaps because of a "scatto," something suddenly clicks or registers – as in a memory – and we are quickly back in another time or place in our mind. The *Occasioni* reflect a "frazionamento della realtà in istanti brevemente percepiti e rapidamente consunti." I would argue that they are not "consunti";[21] rather the limits of time and human physiology impede Montale's visual or aural field from perceiving these traces. In 'Voce giunta' the memory-voice of Clizia is brought back to Montale by the call of the coots. He must wait for another such "occasione-spinta" if he wants to have another memory. The difference then would appear to be in the timing. In 'Mottetto 18' there is a perfect outward situation in reality to complement the feeling of his dissipating memory. It is a metaphoric representation of Montale's fear of entropy:

Non recidere, forbice, quel volto ... Dura il colpo svetta. / E l'acacia ferita da sé scrolla / il guscio di cicala / nella prima belletta di Novembre.

It is a moment which supplies the perfect objective correlative. The photo is a metaphor for a memory and even this is further metaphorized by the cicada shell which, like a photo or a memory, is a trace of something no longer instinsically present. The scissor cutting never physically occurs, but the outward correlative of the acacia is vivid. Here, in 'Vecchi versi,' we are given the word "Ricordo" as the opening word and we are then consumed by images from the moment remembered only to be told at the end that this "farfalla" will remain associated with the rest of the surroundings old walls, shorelines, a "tartana", embarking pines, and a small delta. To return to that mnemonic locus means to re-experience the inhabitants of it.

Poi tornò la farfalla dentro il nicchio / che chiudeva la lampada, discese / sui giornali del tavolo, scrollò / pazza aliando le carte – e fu per sempre / con le cose che chiudono in un giro / sicuro come il giorno, e la memoria / in sé le cresce, sole vive d'una / vita che disparí sotterra: insieme / coi volti familiari che oggi sperde / non piú il sonno ma un'altra noia; accanto / ai muri antichi, ai lidi, alla tartana / che imbarcava / tronchi di pino a riva ad ogni mese, / al segno del torrente che discende / ancora al mare e la sua via si scava.

In fact, it is the moth that becomes a reference point in the swelling point of memory that conjures up the memories of his domestic adolescence. Here, he juxtaposes memory with images of continuity ("ad ogni mese," "che discende ancora"), the same memory which raises or cultivates these events in it, much as the present continues as he is remembering the past inside an expanded point, or "punto dilatato." This infinite regression and expansion in motion recalls Zeno's arrow: at any "given moment the arrow occupies a space equal to its volume and simply is where it is."[22] Each infinitesimally fractioned moment is present as space outside of time. Hence, the reader is left with a somewhat contradictory impression of Montale's notion of memory and its function. Though he speaks of fleeing memory and fogs of memory, in 'Vecchi versi' he speaks of "le cose che chiudono in un giro / sicuro come il giorno, e la memoria / in sé le cresce, sole vive d'una / vita che disparí sotterra," which are "dotati di una loro oggettività autonoma, in sé conchiusi come il giro del sole e (insieme ad altri rari 'depositati': i volti familiari di chi è ora lontano, di luoghi in cui siamo nati) indelebilmente custoditi e cresciuti nella memoria."[23]

From the first word we are thrust into memory as if we had walked in suddenly on a private moment, and perhaps the reason he remembers is not formulaic for it is never the same, but it will be a precise landscape, a particular juxtaposition of exterior life. One could perceive this as a memorial hallucination because of the perfect juxtaposition of material objects being reflected on the visual receptors of the poet's eyes; one could additionally imagine this as reality glimpsed as holographic instants. There are the old walls, freestanding and resistant to time. Next to them are the shores which are both eternal and yet subtly ephemeral and are subject to water erosion. There is the "tartana" that runs its regular, constant course; a material creation, perhaps resistant to change. The final image is the torrent which seems to flow perpetually and descends "still" ("ancora"). It is as persistent as time, but even in the persistence of time, memories will return regularly, like "tartane" at the sign ("segno," perhaps a delta-like indentation in the shorescape) of this "torrent that carves out its own route down to the sea."[24] Time is part of the illusion of the entropic world. Montale cannot know yet that his moments – present or remembered – are all part of the predestined memory: without realizing it, he has lived his life platonically, merely recalling what had already occurred. For Plato, the world is memory awaiting recollection.

This image of memory is contradictory to the image of a forever fleeing memory in 'Mottetto 18' ("Non recidere, forbice"). In fact, memory re-evokes absences so that they become, in the void of presence, a temporary presence; one that could conceivably return "ad ogni mese" like the boat's imbarcation of pine trees. The trees and the movement of the "tartana" have a feeling of the dynamism of the everyday, which seems to flow freely with memory, even with the image of death, offered by the death-head moth ("al dosso il teschio / umano"). The harvesting of trees for lumber even becomes a necessary destruction which appears to contrast the lopping off of the top of the acacia tree ('Mottetto 18') which is associated with the loss of memory; the worst of any possible fates for Montale. This is the great polemic of the father in 'Voce giunta':

> *What the tenor of the conversation between the two 'shades' is the poet simply has to guess, and he conjectures that while Clizia is tormented by religious doubts, his father is troubled by an ever stranger fear: by a belief that each memorial recall of which he is the object will weaken the "larva di memoria" remaining of him in the minds of the living and hasten his regression into the passive memory.*[25]

What Clizia says is what Montale puts in her mouth for the sake of the poem – during its composition, he reflects upon it. In the hologram, he sees two sides of the same spatio-temporal moment: two separate moments (that of his father and of Clizia) are, in actuality, connected like "atomi equivalenti."[26]

'Vecchi versi' also appears to contrast imagery and memory in the context of revisitability which is lacking in 'Non recidere.' The latter, 'Mottetto 18,' is intoned with the stasis of a photograph and any movement seems to be fleeting, negative. Whereas in 'Vecchi versi' Montale gives us an image that, even as a memory, opens up to us a world of dynamic movement (the fluttering of the moth and its bridging of the interior room and the exterior landscape). The moth, associated with death, moves among the elements of ordinary life (a card game, sleeping children, a lamp with "conterie," or the hanging fringe of glass beads). The moth also brings in two themes: flight and the interior-exterior interplay.

If a photograph, generally, is a static memory, one that only seems to dissipate with the passage of time, the moth of 'Vecchi versi' is not only movement, but also a reminder of a memory to which Montale can come home to again and again. The most curious detail, and certainly one of the most difficult to interpret, is the image in the third stanza, verses 35–37: "e attorno dava se una mano / tentava di ghermirlo un acre sibilo / che agghiacciava" (and around it, if a hand tried to grab it, it let out a sizzling hiss that chilled the veins). The lines leave us with some possibilities.

Perhaps it is a simple image of what actually happened in the moment being remembered. The moth fluttered within the shade of the lamp, to whose light it had been instinctually drawn. If it was the lamp that caused him to recall the moth and the associations of it, it would be in keeping with the themes of the "barlumi," quick flashes of light that jostle the mind to recall. His reality might simply be that which he felt physically, as well as in the electronic impulses which stimulated his retinal cells. The "barlumi" are the intermittent lights of Vernazza's port and remind us of the poem "Cigola la carrucola" where one experiences "the very Montalean theme of the schism between the present and the experience of an earlier, different self, the impossibility of recapturing the past in the gray, washed-out, tired memory, except in rare glimpses."[27] It is important to take into account the photo-cinematic aspect of Montale's experience: illumination is essential in revealing latent images. As an image exists invisibly in the frame of the photo gram, when illuminated, it dilates in its projection onto a surface: whether an actual screen or the retinal screen. If someone – Montale, even – tried to catch the moth, it may have reacted by sinking deeper into the recess of the shade; closer to the hot bulb, creating a burning, crackling sound. This is logical enough to accept, but perhaps it is more complex. It is complex because it could have a different meaning which is not rooted in the reality of the moment, but rather in an extremely subjective, fantastic impression of the moment, or even the poet's own present impression filtered through the memory of his immediate impression in the past. In the first case he has constructed a poetic subjective correlative of his inner feelings (or, fears) of this "insetto orribile." In the second case we have revisited the event, distanced by time, and linked by memory. Montale alternates between his past events and his present mindset, as if he can go back and reconsider his reactions in the past, thereby using an objective correlative, not of immediate reactions, but of his own dialogue with the past. "In his view a total emotional recall adds a somewhat mysterious aura of consolation to a past experience."[28] In his later works, Montale will reveal an awareness that there is no appreciable difference between the present and the past in the holographic world of the mind – or, the holographic mind as a universe. Though the prior two assumptions would be arguments for how strong memory is and its importance to Montale, the third hypothesis would be an argument for flow of life, death, and personal impressions through a non-static memory; a permanent, predestiny recorded in the universe. Though the holographic universe is 'static', Montale registers an evolutionary memory: visual stimulus becomes interfered in the overlap of images in the many folds of the universe. This interference produces what Montale perceives as a unique movement-image.

Past presence and present presence have an interchangeability reminiscent of the interchangeability and simultaneousness of the present and a dream in the present. In either case, memory or dream, a distinct presence is created that accompanies Montale in "Il sogno del prigioniero." In this 'provisional conclusion' of the *Bufera*, we first rely on Montale's feeling of existential isolation and a flight motif similar to that of 'Vecchi versi': the starlings outside are his only wings, but wings nonetheless: "Il zigzag degli storni sui battifredi / nei giorni di battaglia, mie sole ali." Late at night he fuses dream and desire with a memory of Clizia who is far away. While dreaming, he can be at her feet if he believes it, if he wants it enough, memory, in subconsciousness, will furnish the rest, creating a distinct sensation of presence in absence. All of this occurs in immanence when Montale's experience in the present is produced by a sensation equal to one from the so-called past. The one sensation seems to span two moments, like the flavor of Proust's madeleine: "It seems that it [the flavor] contains a volume of duration which extends it through two moments at once."[29] It is as if Montale has associated a "schermo d'immagini" around him with screens of images both imagined and remembered. The screen seems to be one and the same: the visual screen on the locus of the mind where images are received and reshaped. In this infinitely regressing and expanding point, experience is a juxtaposition of traces and electrical impulses from the ocular photoreceptors. Each experience leaves a latent trace on the brain's screen of images. They are impressed on it the way words and sings are impressed and compressed into each other on Freud's 'Wunderblock.' In much the same way as the moth – in memory – has guided the reader and Montale through memory's inventory which we could call the "schermo d'immagini." Then, at the end of 'Vecchi versi,' Montale links to this to a present "schermo d'immagini":

Poi tornò la farfalla dentro il nicchio / che chiudeva la lampada, discese / sui giornali del tavolo, scrollò / pazza aliando le carte – e fu per sempre / con le cose che chiudono in un giro sicuro come il giorno.

The last strophe, set off by a hyphen, testifies to the continuous association and interchangeability between past and present screens of images. If they are pressed into the same plane of mental 'wax', then they are but one juxtaposition of coexistent images in the poet's visual field. The poems give memory a form in the present, that is, the present of the poem.

This is not as clear in the case of 'Mottetto 6.' The title alone speaks of seeing the beloved physically, but also through the presence of memory. In 'Vecchi versi' the last stanza's imagery of the things closed in a "giro sicuro come il giorno" is relevant to the association of the moth he conjures up, in this 'Mottetto' it is not clear if the "schermo d'immagini" is closing in, positively, or closing out, negatively. It is not clear if it is projection, protection, or barrier (good or bad), nor if the screen is outside of the poet or in the back of his eye where images are focused on the receptive cones and rods. In fact, the only positive reassuring quality that is communicated within the "screen of images" around him is some of Clizia's presumed light in the strange, chance, occurrence of the passing of the two jackals.

While ordinary, banal image-scape around Montale in 'Vecchi versi' is calm, perhaps even consoling, the images around him are in a sense equal to the image of the "farfalla" of 'Vecchi versi.' They may be re-experienced through the moth. It is not a relationship of past-image-to-present-image, but one of image of death to possible image, albeit refracted, distorted or incomplete, of a sign of Clizia. Either way there is a slipping towards emptiness, not fullness or presence. The jackal image could be a consolation, justification, or an allaying of his fears in order for him to deal with the uncertainty of whether she is present. It appears to him to be too linked to Clizia not to be a sign of her. It has stimulated the part of Montale which receives visual impulses in such a way that his mind has experienced her. Whether the screen is internal (the poet's brain as a hologram) or external (the universe as a hologram) is irrelevant. Montale perceives her in a virtual space. "Memory is not in us," Deleuze argues, "it is we who move in a Being-memory, a world-memory."[30]

In this sense one is – by the time one has gotten into the 'Mottetti' and beyond – already progressing past the harsh, terrestrial images of the *Ossi*. By contrast with certain *Ossi* poems, the reader can truly see how Montale's poetry has developed by moving from simply confronting the objective world to conceiving of other metaphysical – and metaphorical – possibilities. In 'Marezzo' (*Ossi di seppia*), Montale has nothing before him but presence and yet it does not, in the end, offer him any solutions to his existential condition. 'Marezzo' differs from the poems of the *Occasioni* in the scope of the poetry. It is a poetry not based primarily on occasions or the absence of a Clizia-like character, but on the presence of Montale's search for a clue to existence; a secret of the universe. 'Marezzo,' therefore, resides in a basic present. Montale presents to the reader a void that comes from a static life, so static there is little difference between past and present; thoughts are undone in being alone ("si struggono pensieri troppi soli"). Life is reduced to still photo grams between which the poet feels he can find the real truth in the void onto which they are projected – an intuition posited in 'Forse un mattino andando.' Memory is eroded; not the memory of a particular past, but the concept of memory has no chance to flower here: "Parli e non riconosci i tuoi accenti. / La memoria ti appare dilavata. / Sei passata e pur senti / la tua vita consumata." The "sei passata" is a conceptual reference to the given that time has passed, but from this past it appears life has little accumulation in memory: "e pur senti la tua vita consumata." It is consumed, not put into a past that is somehow alive in memory. Where the life of even the inanimate seems to grow or change around him, "a scatti," all he seems to find is the vanity/futility of life: "Ah qui restiamo, non siamo diversi. / Immobili cosí." With no change there is, in a sense, no separation into past and present. One is driven away from hope, from meaning, from memory, and into a pure moment where all that is meaningful (or meaningless, even) is the physical aspect ("tu riprovi il peso / di te"). Life has no ulterior expectations. Instead the stronger presence of memory in *Le Occasioni* reflects the hope he puts in Clizia. In turn, a constant verticality of hoping, waiting, evoking of Clizia is analogous with a faith he puts in his search for a truth; though he has little faith in an objective truth per se. In Clizia's conspicuous absence, the poetry that relies on her as interlocutor and savior becomes more cinematic. Like an editor, Montale forces voluntary memory to interpose and collide images so as to produce a resultant third image on his visual receptors.[31]

Having contrasted the different poetic mindsets between 'Marezzo' (*Ossi*) and 'Mottetto 6' (*Occasioni*), one can begin to appreciate the ultimate overall direction which Montale's poetry takes in its voyage from 'I morti' (*Ossi*) to 'Voce giunta' (*Bufera*), and then to *Farfalla di Dinard*. One can see the trajectory of Montale's consideration, through memory, of hope and faith. Through the absence of a significant personage, be he/she living or dead, Montale considers both the eternal "male di vivere", specified in 'Spesso il male di vivere ho incontrato' (*Ossi*), and the same sentiment shared ironically – in the sense that the dead no longer live (*vivere*) – as the dead and living are equally dependent on memory; equally fixed into folds of memory. It becomes, then, interesting to compare the "fissità" ("fixity") of the former ('I morti') and the "distaccarti" ("detachment") of the latter ('Voce giunta') in regard with the themes at hand: Confrontation with an immovable world that is eternal and highlights – by its very existence – the insignificant mortality of the poet and the possibility of transcending – if only through memory – the limits of time and the harshness of mortality. "Events do not just succeed each other or simply follow a chronological course; they are constantly being rearranged according to whether they belong to a particular sheet of past, a particular continuum of age, all of which coexist."[32]

Interestingly, both 'I morti' and 'Voce giunta' – one the beginning of Montale's memorial parabola; the other its endpoint – weave wonderful tapestries of the natural world into the poetry with a concise and powerful language. An example of this in 'I morti' comes from the second stanza:

reti stinte che asciuga il tocco tardo / e freddo della luce; e sopra queste / denso il cristallo dell'azzurro palpebra / e precipita a un arco d'orizzonte / flagellato.

From the second stanza of 'Voce giunta,' equally present is the poetic language which balances the content of the poem:

l'ombra non ha più peso della tua / da tanto seppellita, i primi raggi / del giorno la trafiggono, farfalle / vivaci l'attraversano, la sfiora / la sensitiva e non si rattrappisce.

Part of this attention to the external world, while concerned with the internal workings of the mind and memory, is created by the dynamics of interchange between the levels of memory, absence-presence and death. 'I morti' begins with the sea as a protagonist that carries memories, separates them, and offers only negativity as entropy. It is a sea that is agitated and calmed and in this way seems to reflect an outward correlative of the heart's status. It ends also with an image equally as cruel: it will somehow filter memory, spiritual existence even in the afterlife, and even submerge the flight of the dead. It leaves off with the ellipses to suggest a continuity of this negative spiral where we are never relieved of the "male di vivere." While the sea has moments of calm and of "bonaccia," humans have a constant spiritual tempest that even the power of memory cannot overcome. For even those recently departed – "da noi divisi appena" in 'I morti' – are soon engulfed by the sea, drawn to it and entrapped like a tub-gurnard trapped in a net, in a cold deadlock: "come la gallinella / di mare che s'insacca tra le maglie."

In 'Voce giunta' Montale creates tension built on a preconception of a stronger, more efficacious memory. The whole reasoning for the dialogue between the absent (Clizia) and the dead (Montale's father) is predicated on a strong memory which is not fixed in a deadlock, and the poet's narrative credibility is key. It interchanges, along with the dead, in an environment that is in constant evolution:

> *Ho pensato per te, ho ricordato / per tutti. Ora ritorni al cielo libero / che ti tramuta. Ancora questa rupe / ti tenta? Sí, la bàttima è la stessa / di sempre, il mare che ti univa ai miei / lidi da prima che io avessi l'ali, / non si dissolve. Io le rammento quelle / mie prode e pur son giunta con le folaghe / a distaccarti dalle tue. Memoria / non è peccato fin che giova. Dopo / è letargo di talpe, abiezione / che funghisce su sé ...*

Through Clizia's message to Montale's father, one discovers that the ghosts of the past can go through stages, perhaps like the "smaterializzazione" in 'Sul limite' in *Farfalla di Dinard*. Through the distant spirit of Clizia, both the poet and his dead father learn that the memory which only suggested a dead end for hope and for the afterlife is a contiguity. In the physical body, vision is received in a virtual locus so that in the dead, who are equally virtual, no difference in sensation occurs. By basis of comparison with the sense of being closed in an uncaring landscape, the poetry of the *Ossi*, i.e., 'I morti,' can only lead Montale to believe that absence is a final step in the entropic death of time, and memory can only lead one to think of these ghosts, tortured by their own human memories ("ricordi umani"):

> *Cosí / forse anche ai morti è tolto ogni riposo / nelle zolle: una forza indi li tragge / spietata piú del vivere, ed attorno, larve rimorse dai ricordi umani, / li volge fino a queste spiagge, fiati / senza materia o voce / traditi dalla tenebra.*

In *Farfalla di Dinard*, we see an example of a character who loses these traces by virtue of having passed over to the afterlife. He is no longer trapped in his mind's fear of death and forgetting. Rather, he will require the holographic film of his life in order to inform himself of his past. For Montale, being caught within one's mind would be like being caught in a hologram which renders each reminiscence equidistant and potentially simultaneous. Commenting on Proust's *A la recerche du temps perdu*, Shattuck reveals a holographic vision avant lettre: "The act of Ultimate recognition removes all images from the stream of time to set them up temporally equidistant in Time, equally available to our consciousness."[33] Cambon reminds us of Montale's world of memory and we see just how it pertains to his father's world in the beyond:

> *l'anima non ha scampo, e si ritrova soltanto nell'estrema intensità con cui vive gli avventi dell'attimo e della memoria. Rifiutando la dispersione di un calendario ufficiale, si inoltrerà sempre più nel labirinto dell'interiorità sofferta, sognata e interrogata di continuo.*[34]

They have moved into the wholly cosmic realm but cannot find complacency due to their being still tied to their human expectation. The mind is virtual and is connected to an equally virtual soul. In this sense, the mind leaves the corporal part of the human after the corporal has died, as a spiritual matter, not a temporal one. However, if the abstract, conceptual mind is the same in the body as in the afterlife, then the souls of the dead cannot know they are dead and will insist on conceiving of themselves in temporal terms. These temporal terms are still tied to human intervals of time, mortal time broken up into units known as Swiss time. And the spirit does not know that it has entered a realm where human intervals of time no longer pertain; time is non-existent in this eternity. This is why Montale's alter ego in 'Sul limite' fears revisiting the movie of his life. He still thinks in terms of forgetting and the possibility of future. He does not realize that all moments – past and present – have been removed of time and they are experienced spatially like a holographic film strip.

The "poiché" of the first verse in 'Voce giunta' sets up a simultaneous reasoning for the presence of his father's spirit and a tension which moves the poet and the reader forward:

> *Poiché la via percorsa, se mi volgo, è più lunga / del sentiero da capre che mi porta / dove ci scioglieremo come cera, / ed i giunchi fioriti non leniscono il cuore ma le vermene, il sangue dei cimiteri, / eccoti fuor dal buio...*

A poem beginning with the English equivalent of "being that" seems to be establishing a following, an expectation of a "then." In this case the "then" corresponds to the "eccoti fuor dal buio" as if to say that since the "via percorsa, se mi volgo, è piú lunga / del sentiero da capre che mi porta" ("since the road journeyed, if I turn back, is longer than this goat path that leads me"),[35] it is not surprising that you, father, should appear from the afterlife. The "via percorsa" is the literal way of arriving at the cemetery, but figuratively it is a way of saying that there is more behind us as time passes. With more behind us, Montale has more material in his memory from which to draw. The past accumulates to outweigh the prospect of the future; and he is like Borges' Funes (from 'Funes el memorioso'). Yet, oddly, it is the existence of the memory, and history, which mark a distance between the present and transpired present, which is now in the past, clearly argues for the coming of a future.

Memory is not fixed in the past into a single form, and neither is life fixed – finished – when it moves to the heavens in immaterial, voiceless forms (a concept familiar to anyone who has read Dante's *Paradiso*). Not being material, memory cannot lose its physical attributes the way a human can by sloughing its corpse and freeing its soul, and it will certainly not extinguish itself as the father fears. It accumulates and, ironically enough, can even become lethargy and abjection that grows like mold on the mind if it does not change or evolve as humans do. Neither is memory a sin as long as it pleases us. In fact, the beauty of memory is that it is an abstract with no concrete limitation or boundaries. In this sense, it approaches Leopardi's concept of infinity. Montale failed to recognize the "arduo nulla" in 'Il balcone' as the boundlessness of the undefined, or the infinite.

Memory is the "oscuro senso / reminiscente" ('Voce giunta') which is immediately associated with the "vuoto inabitato" (v. 53). In being mysterious, abstract and even pre-linguistic (expression), it is like the afterlife in that it appears to be a void, non-presence. On the contrary, it is "reminiscent" of an uninhabited void before we were brought into the world and into which we will return, in the afterlife. This will be the noumenal world behind the phenomenal world of illusions. Perhaps they are in the same void which remains so until we occupy it with our visual field, as in 'Forse un mattino andando.' But because memory is invisible and abstract, conceptual mental imagery, even when it "occupies" a point, does not physically occupy it and therefore, the "vuoto inabitato" is the "unlived-in void." It is a thing that can be conceivably infinite and yet never occupy physical space. Indirectly, death and absence are seen as negative, and the ellipses at the end of 'I morti' leave the reader with an image of submersion: extinction into the nothing that follows the ellipses.

Instead the very presence of absent figures through memory is as much a testament to memory and hope. Harping on memory can lead to abjection. Embracing the past and the present, memory, death, and moments of absence as a continuum which was begun before we were even living, as a concept, in the void before our actual presence, can only lead to consolation of the "male di vivere" even if a truth, per se, is unquantifiable or impossible to qualify. The very presence of people who are physically absent compounds this. Montale is not looking to a time (in the absolute past) when he and a tu-interlocutor cast their anxious hope ("quivi / gettammo un dí su la ferrigna costa, / ansante piú del pelago la nostra speranza!") as if it ended there. In 'Voce giunta' the hope cast once is hope present now. They are the same moment viewed from different angles. In the *Farfalla*, we will explore Montale's intuition of the world as multiple, not singular. 'Voce giunta' reveals that we are greater than our physical form:

Il vento del giorno / confonde l'ombra viva e l'altra ancora / riluttante in un mezzo che respinge / le mie mani, e il respiro mi si rompe / nel punto dilatato, nella fossa / che circonda lo scatto del ricordo. / Cosí si svela prima di legarsi / a immagini, a parole, oscuro senso / reminiscente, il vuoto inabitato / che occupammo e che attende fin ch'è tempo / di colmarsi di noi, di ritrovarci ...

If the "vuoto inabitato" is relative and seen as something that can be filled, or occupied, as suggested by "colmarsi di noi" (v. 55), then Montale sees that we no more or less occupy it than the dead or a memory do. It is merely a matter of shifting our expectations from the worldly to the abstract. And memory, like the presence of ghosts, can cohabitate with us until we return to a spiritual form which is, like the flash of memory, present, albeit in a form that reveals itself "prima di legarsi / a immagini e parole" ("before it is linked to visual images or words"[36]). (The dialogue between the absent Clizia and the dead father cannot be heard by the poet, and yet he recognized that they were conversing. This calls to mind the surreal fancy of the 'Gerti' poem where in dreams sounds are understood, though not communicated. The sounds are "spogli," v. 17.)

What remains important is the voyage, or journey, from 'I morti' (*Ossi*) to 'Voce giunta' (*La Bufera*) and then to *Farfalla di Dinard*. In the midst of this parabola, it is in the *Occasioni* that the greatest changes in perceptions of death, absence-presence and memory occur. Particularly in the 'Mottetti' one sees the external world in two ways: the exterior/external world which clashes with the interiors (structural and mental) and the external world of the "schermo d'immagini" where the poet is isolated in absence which, through speculation, becomes the locus of presence and life.

'Mottetto 20' is one in which "the brevity of life allows a measure of doleful submission."[37] It is important to trace the so-called parabola of the poet, who, in the *Ossi*, finds only the "male di vivere" ("Spesso il male di vivere ho incontrato"), in the 'Mottetti' finds hope in awaiting an epiphany; finds an eerie, mysterious consolation in 'Voce giunta'; the consolation of infinite absence-presence. Then in the *Farfalla di Dinard*, which defines that absence-presence as the 'virtual' film of life, art itself becomes the greatest analogue of memory. Memory is itself a presence in an absence of its original form. Yet, if the world is a holographic projection, it never truly had form except for that which was attributed by the sensitive mind of the poet. The consideration of form plays an inextricable part of a total process of remembrance-transference into the essential alphabet, which will serve to communicate the incommunicable, giving *figura* to the *res*:

> *Lieto leggerò i neri / segni dei rami sul bianco / come un essenziale alfabeto. / Tutto il passato in un punto / dinanzi mi sarà comparso.*
> *('Quasi una fantasia')*

Certain objects seem to be unrelated links to occasions of memory or epiphanies, yet it is precisely at the pre-lingual level, that of the coming together of the "essential alphabet," that all landscapes, internal and exterior, find analogies. The analogy is what causes the "scatto", and what comes out of the "scatto" will be what he conjoins to the void, as his latest motif ('Il balcone'):

> *Ora a quel vuoto ho congiunto / ogni mio tardo motivo, / sull'arduo nulla si spunta / l'ansia di attenderti vivo.*

The landscape around him is the "schermo d'immagini." Yet what is difficult about this reference (specific to 'Mottetto 6,' but applicable to the general mindset) is that one cannot say whether it is a screen of projection, of protection, or perhaps even a barrier, much like the "muraglia" of the *Ossi*. Is he recalling "i tuoi crucci" ('Mottetto 7,' v. 4) while he takes in the landscape where a *tu* obviously is no longer present, or does he see something in the landscape which correlates his relative mood with regard to "i tuoi crucci?" Could this landscape be the screen of images that causes the flash of memory? Or does the flash of memory cause him to immediately assimilate it to the things around him, projecting, as it were, his memory on a screen?

It seems as though the screen is a projection and being such it is a sort of correlative for his memory, acting as an exterior template. The template is not *the* "essential alphabet," but *an* "essential alphabet." As we first have thoughts, even abstract, and then assign them to the pre-existing words of our language, we do not necessarily have an outward, objective image that can represent our visions in memory. Memory can be described by words, but as an image it remains visual, at the pre-lingual stage. To be more precise, the image also remains an interior landscape. It is this distinction that must be addressed in Montale: the points where past and present meet, and where internal and external meet, both linguistically and spiritually.

Notes

1. From this point on all English translations of Montale's poetry will be taken from Jonathan Galassi. When the Galassi translation does not render the subtlety of meaning for my purposes, my translation will be used. Eugenio Montale. *Collected Poems (1920–1954)*. Tr., with annotation and commentary, by Jonathan Galassi. New York: Farrar, 1998. Hereafter referred to as Galassi.
2. F. J. Jones. *The Modern Italian Lyric*. (Cardiff: University of Wales Press, 1986): 407.
3. F. J. Jones. "Montale's Dialectic of Memory." *Italian Studies* 28 (1973): 105.
4. Sergio Solmi, *Scrittori negli anni: saggi e note sulla letteratura italiana del '900* (Milano: Garzanti, 1976), 194–5.
5. Eugenio Montale, *The Storm and Other Things*, by Eugenio Montale. Tr., with preface and commentary, by William Arrowsmith (New York: Norton & Co., 1987) 199.
6. Maria Cristina Santini. *La 'Farfalla di Dinard' e la memoria montaliana*. (La Spezia: Agorà Edizioni, 1989): 30.
7. Antonielli, Sergio, *Letteratura del disagio*. (Milano: Edizioni di Comunità, 1984), 200.
8. For an insightful commentary on this see Almansi, Guido and Bruce Merry. *Eugenio Montale: The Private Language of Poetry*. (Edinburgh: Edinburgh UP, 1977) 78.
9. Bruno Biral, "Il sentimento del tempo: Leopardi, Baudelaire, Montale." *Il ponte* 21.2 (July-Dec. 1965): 1173.
10. Santini 37.
11. Rebecca West, "On Montale." *Chicago Review* 27. 3 (1975): 19.
12. Galassi 459.
13. Galassi 478. Here Galassi is paraphrasing – and translating – from Giorgio Zampa, "Introduzione" to *Eugenio Montale: Tutte le poesie*. 2nd ed. (Milano: Mondadori, 1991), xxviii.
14. Eugenio Montale, *Poesie*. Angelo Marchese, ed. (Milano: Mondadori Scuola, 1991) 183.

15. Galassi 476.
16. Translation mine.
17. Italo Calvino, 'Forse un mattino andando,' in *Letture italiane in occasione dell'80o compleanno del Poeta*. Sylvia Luzzatto ed. (Genova: Bozzi, 1977) 42.
18. Eugenio Montale, *Poésies, III: La tourmente et autres poèmes, La bufera e altro (1940–1957)*. Bilingual ed. Tr. Patrice Angelini with the collaboration of Louise Herlin, Gennie Luccioni, and Arnaud Robin (Paris: Gallimard, 1966) 174.
19. Arrowsmith 199.
20. Galassi 379.
21. Santini 19.
22. Mary Anne Doane. *The Emergence of Cinematic Time*. (Cambridge: Harvard U Press, 2002): 173.
23. Dante Isella, ed. *Eugenio Montale: Le occasioni* (Torino: Einaudi, 1996) 14.
24. Translation mine.
25. Jones, 1973; 104.
26. Santini 37.
27. Pier Vicenzo Mengaldo, *La tradizione del novecento* (Milano: Feltrinelli, 1980, 2nd ed.) 41.
28. Jones, 1973; 83.
29. Gilles Deleuze. *Proust and Signs*. Trans. Richard Howard. (New York: Braziller, Inc., 1972): 58.
30. Gilles Deleuze. *Cinema II: The Time-Image*. Trans. Hugh Tomlinson and Robert Galeta. (Minneapolis: U of Minnesota Press, 1989): 98.
31. Sergei Eisenstein. *Film Form: Essays in Film Theory*. Ed and trans. Jay Leyda. (New York: Harcourt, Brace and World, Inc., 1949): 37–8.
32. Deleuze, 1989; 120.
33. Roger Shattuck. *Proust's Binoculars: A Study of Memory, Time, and Recognition in 'A la recherche du temps perdu'*. (New York: Random House, 1963): 48.
34. Glauco Cambon, *La lotta con proteo* (Milano: Bompiani, 1963) 117.
35. Translation mine.
36. Translation mine.
37. Giuliana Capriolo, "Intellectual and Sentimental Modes of Rapport with Reality in Montale's Ossi and Occasioni," in *Italian Quarterly* 13 (1969): 63.

CHAPTER 2

'Il balcone' as overture: Montale and nothingness

'Il balcone' is a fantastic poem in many ways. It not only serves as the programmatic overture for the *Occasioni* but, more specifically, for the 'Mottetti'. It is a poem that quickly changes the tenor of Montale's poetry from that of the *Ossi di seppia*; from the exterior existential quest to the inner quest where memory is explored and the exterior world literally becomes the occasion for this process. To express the specificity of certain past moments, the juxtaposition has to be ideal.

Even more interestingly, the occasions that occur externally become a present situation within which Montale hopes to express and evoke the conditions of the past; the same past that, ironically enough, is presently creating a crisis in him. In the *Ossi*, the moment is largely a present, where he ponders the possibility of breaking out of what Jones has called Montale's "remote spectral landscapes," through a crack in a wall or through a weak link in a mesh net. Therefore, the moment, though "cupo," is one of hope and of "attesa."

The same fundamental quality of "attesa" is then also present in 'Il balcone' – and the other *Occasioni* – but it is rendered more bitterly through memory:

> *Come il mare, ora la donna sta da passato nobile, positiva infanzia, e assistiamo alle sue fumose apparizioni, emersioni dalla memoria, credendo spesso di riconoscere in lei il fantasma che salva ... Seguita comunque il senso di attesa: prima, attesa dell'inno del fantasma salvatore; quindi l'ansia di attenderla vivo, la donna.*[1]

Through the memory of the past, Montale simultaneously highlights the spatial-temporal separation from Clizia, and their metaphysical separation, which occurs in a simultaneous, shared pseudo-presence that goes beyond the limits of human existence. To the extent that past, present and future are conjoined in a parallel in which, like an epiphany, experiences from the past can be re-experienced with the knowledge of the present. In 'Il balcone' (and in the *Mottetti*) Montale lives with a concrete sense of that which would be ineffable abstraction in the nothingness around him. Clodagh Brook astutely relates to this notion: "Montale's 'objects' are not just objects-in-the-world, but are also expressions of the inexpressible sense of the absolute, and also of the past and of the poet's experience of the world. As such, they are concrete correlatives."[2] In 'Infinito,' Leopardi's search for contentment goes beyond the limits of human existence and is an approach towards pure fantasy, which is, in turn, pure nothingness. Montale treats the space, intermittently occupied by those who have passed through it, as if it were an objective material fact; as a locus in which emptiness is synonymous with that which is unperceived but not necessarily non-existent: "In privileging the void, Montale illustrates the falsity of empirical knowledge, demonstrating the way in which things perceived by the senses act as a screen, hiding an ultimate, veracious reality from humanity."[3] The sensistic Leopardi goes from a materialist world into the *vago* of the infinite, while Montale sees the *vago* as part of material reality, pessimistic as it may be:

> *Pareva facile giuoco / mutare in nulla lo spazio / che m'era aperto, in un tedio / malcerto il certo tuo fuoco. // Ora a quel vuoto ho congiunto / ogni mio tardo motivo, / sull'arduo nulla si spunta / l'ansia di attenderti vivo. / La vita che dà barlumi / è quella che sola tu scorgi. / A lei ti sporgi da questa / finestra che non s'illumina.*

In the expression "pareva facile", the imperfect automatically implies that now, as opposed to then, it does indeed seem difficult. In memory Montale realizes that it should not have been so easy for him to reduce the limitless potential of the "spazio" that Clizia had offered him; now he feels regret. So the imperfect prepares the reader for a present that is more hopeless: "sull'arduo nulla si spunta / l'ansia di attenderti vivo." The "spazio" that had opened up to him when he knew her was a potential to assimilate her positive attributes. Now that she is gone he regrets having missed the obvious, turning that space into nothing. Clodagh Brook explores this aspect of nothingness:

> *In privileging the void, Montale illustrates the falsity of empirical knowledge, demonstrating the way in which things perceived by the senses act as a screen, hiding an ultimate, veracious reality from humanity... Moreover, the void itself is described in terms of spatial dimensions ("dietro di me" and "alle mie spalle") which give it position and therefore render it a thing, rather than a nothing.*[4]

Now he must fill that space. In a positive light, space could be new potential; in a negative light space could be an agonizing emptiness. With this rather hopeless situation, Montale is forced to look for some sign of her, as is the case in the 'Mottetti.' Throughout the 'Mottetti,' in particular, he looks for a sign of Clizia's presence – where she is seemingly absent – and if he finds no sign, their separation seems more inevitable and unbridgeable. However, where his memory coincides with the occasion presented to him, objective correlatives will allow Montale a conduit for expression. Epiphanies that Montale had missed in the past will not go unrecorded now, for he will have since been furnished with the proper (linguistic) tools with which to represent and, therefore, recognize the transcendent. The vague abstractions will henceforth be expressible in linguistic terms. What one may call *vago*, Montale calls form; what could pass as void, Montale calls presence. Brook addresses this with specific reference to stanzas one and two of 'Il balcone':

Here two cases of dissolution occur. In the first, space (fullness) becomes nothingness (emptiness), although this 'nulla', like voids found elsewhere in Montale's poetry, is in fact populated with things, as evidenced by his desire to see the woman stirring within the nothingness in stanza two.[5]

The important thing is that when Montale revisits a past moment with the mind of the present, he is afforded better expression, in essence, proving the presence in the void. On this ineffability of the expressible, Brook, refers to the poem 'Vasca.' Citing the line "è nato e morto, e non ha avuto un nome," she adds, "The existence that was momentarily born may have died simply because it was not assigned a name, having been too subtle or formless to be grasped and held in language."[6]

Reality expressible merely in terms of linear time and material presence is not the background in 'Il balcone' nor in the rest of the *Occasioni*. It is merely a screen of images – perhaps in an egoistic sense – onto which Montale gazes, awaiting the perfect juxtaposition of the external landscape to help him materialize his internal landscape, including Clizia and his past there, in that particular moment. Memory is the experience of life as a series of filmic – or photographic – after-images. Memory becomes the weapon used to oppose the "vuoto che ci invade" ("Barche sulla Marna"). With a materialization of what was previously abstract, he will look not into absence but at a presence – aided by memory conjoined to the images in the "schermo d'immagini" – in the void, which can be taken as a sign. Hence the concern about both the space opened up to him and the arduous nothing of 'Il balcone' with the "ansia" of seeing her again. Consequently, his every latest motif will progressively bring about an introspective poetry rooted in the template of memory, which will fight the certain inferno of 'Mottetto 1.' Each epiphany recorded within his poetry offers a contiguity of spatial events. Memory occurs in a holographic void that allows a sensation to be experienced as a connection between two seemingly separate events. The perfect reproduction of a moment is a re-experience of the senses in the virtual (here, noumenal) world behind the phenomenal world. Bergson, Deleuze reminds us, "introduced a profound element of transformation" in this regard: "the brain was now only an interval [écart], a void, nothing but a void, between a stimulus and a response."[7]

Montale's *vago* is reality – simply because it lacks a determinate quality, and does not make the uninhabited space around him any less of an object than Leopardi's hedge, in the famous 'Infinito.' Montale tries to connect the non-visual conceit of absence-presence to a correlative in his surroundings (on the *screen of images*). Both Montale and Leopardi occupy a material domain in which, as Lansing remarks, "transcendence is denied to all but a few, and forever to the poet [Montale] himself."[8] Yet, ultimately, Montale's world is more isolating: while Leopardi pertains to the whole of humanity, which is denied this transcendence, Montale lives with his negative experience, while Clizia is the one who discerns the light outside of Montale's darkness – "ti sporgi dalla finestra" ('Il balcone'). And if both poets remain confined to the physical world, then Montale will materially fill his voids with his poetics. He will literally fill the void with each successive motet; if only as a by-product of his search – he has the illusion of "the world as representation,"[9] as he called it.

Montale is objective and unsure that the world has in it anything beyond the hard reality offered in the wall and the cuttlefish bones of he eponymously titled collection *Ossi di seppia*. But even in Montale's 'Forse un mattino andando in un'aria di vetro' (*Ossi*), the poet imagines the essence behind the appearance of things themselves. What happens is that in Montale's world the Kantian phenomena (appearances, or the way that humans experience) and noumena (the true essence of things in themselves) are blurred together. For Montale, it is a question of manipulating the contingencies of space and time – as in memory.

In 'Il balcone' the emptiness of reality spurs on regret and anxiety. Leopardi's hedge paradoxically instigates a journey outward, beyond the hedge itself, as a result of introspection: "io nel pensiero mi fingo." The concrete 'siepe' causes his thoughts to rebound in onto themselves. In the material confines of the terrestrial world of Leopardi, Lansing notes of 'L'infinito':

> *The escape from the mundane is provided, ironically, by the poet's inability to extend his line of vision, while sitting atop Mt. Tabor, beyond a hedge or row of bushes. Unable to glimpse the panorama in the distance and more than but a part of the «ultimo orizzonte», the skyline, the poet is compelled to explore with his imagination the infinite vastness of space that lies beyond the hedge.*[10]

Montale's imagination creates an ideality as in the potential breaking through the "varco" of poems like 'Casa dei doganieri.' Yet it is one thing to be aware of his own plight, another to remedy it. His imagination is not enough, as, perhaps, in Leopardi. So he depends on his memory, but often it acts somewhat autonomously through the poet who is its mere medium, in a sense. (Clearly, "Iride" is a good example of Montale's consideration of himself as poetic medium.) A good example is in the early 'Fine dell'infanzia,' where even his mere recollection is not strong enough to resolve his metaphysical conflict: "Poco s'andava oltre i crinali prossimi / di quei monti; varcarli pur non osa la memoria stancata." Let us compare this to the more sublime image of creative fantasy in Leopardi's "Le ricordanze:"

> *E che pensieri immensi, / Che dolci sogni mi spirò la vista / Di quel lontano mar, quei monti azzurri, / Che di qua scopro, e che varcare un giorno / Io mi pensava, arcani mondi, arcana / Felicità fingendo al viver mio.*

Yet Leopardi's memory, perhaps one of his few consolations, is two-fold for him. "Il passato non è un barlume oppure una sequenza di immagini appiattite, ma è tempo che conserva la sua durata."[11] It is sentimental in Leopardi, albeit bittersweet. Sweet in that his memories are complete and unfading, especially since he imagines control over their recall. Any presence from the past is consoling, but frustrating in that it is completely removed and isolated from the present. In Montale, the past is no longer "ricuperabile come momento di vita in cui ci si possa immergere nuovamente."[12] The problem is based on the fact that there is a schism between perceptions of time: there is geologic time and Swiss, calendric time, but there is a difference between an objective time and a subjective time. Antonielli breaks them up into "tempo impersonale" and "tempo personale."[13] In this light, we can see how programmatic the physical window in 'Il balcone' is when we consider it as the plane between the interior (the subjective) and the exterior (the objective). Montale is on the threshold of the point that the moth of his memory was able to cross in 'Vecchi versi,' which exemplifies the general thread of *Le occasioni*, tenored by 'Il balcone.' 'Vecchi versi' is the poem, *in cui si dice della farfalla che una sera era entrata nella casa del poeta, aveva sconvolto i riflessi di un paralume sulle pareti, poi le carte da gioco alzate a due per volta su un tavolo, infine aveva compiuto il salto dal tempo esteriore e impersonale a quello interiore e personale di chi si fosse trovato, in seguito, a ricordarla.*[14]

Space in 'Il balcone' is the presence of her absence, but because this evokes in Montale's memory an image of Clizia, it burns around him as he futiley desires to fill it with the past. It is for this reason that the reader is left with a sense of contradiction in the first stanza of 'Il balcone,' that is, if one makes the assumption (*a priori*) that space is already, in its essence, complete nothingness ("nulla"). The void is an absence-presence in that the absence paired with his memory of her presence makes the space, paradoxically, a material factor: the abstract *vago* is perceived visually through Montale's objective correlatives. Using 'Forse un mattino andando' as a reference point, Brook sums up Montale's mental posture in the regard of a void being an absence/presence: "...The void itself is described in terms of spatial dimensions ("dietro di me" and "alle mie spalle") which give it position and therefore render it a thing, rather than nothing."[15] Leopardi's perspective has no room for an objective correlative. In fact, his notion is that of an exaggerated, albeit pessimistic, reduction of Kant: not the *Ding an sich*, but the thing is only itself and nothing more. It is for this reason that the reader is left with a sense of contradiction or paradox in the first stanza of 'Il balcone,' that is, if one makes the assumption (*a priori*) that space is already, in its essence, nothing ("nulla"). It is nothing because it is empty – Clizia's physical presence no longer occupies it. Leopardi, in both the *Zibaldone* and in 'L'infinito,' realizes how that which is undefined can seem not to have recognizable boundaries and is therefore confused with the infinite (*Zibaldone*, 4 gennaio 1821) and "che l'infinito venga in sostanza a esser lo stesso che il nulla" (*ibid*, 2 maggio 1826).

The second stanza doubles the sense of *adynaton* of the first. Montale does not say that he has added his most recent motif within the void, but he has conjoined them to the void, as if it were of physical substance. But what completes the paradox is Montale's third stanza. Here, in a completely present tense, he literally conjoins a memory of her to the physical room in which he finds himself: "A lei ti sporgi da questa / finestra." As Montale reminds us, the "ti sporgi"[16] refers to memory and fantasy, the something in void space which could be the object of nullification of the first stanza. And the window becomes that "schermo d'immagini" of 'Mottetto 6.' It is simultaneously the objective correlative of his feeling of obscurity, which provokes a flash of memory, and it is the screen onto which he projects his memory of her. In the window's physicality – or, its quiddity – what appears to be space can never be reduced to nothing.

'Il balcone' is quite a contrast to some of Montale's earlier works. In fact, Montale, unlike Leopardi (in 'Infinito') or the Ungaretti of 'M'illumino d'immenso' ('Mattina') is not illumined by immensity. The "male di vivere" is just as pervasive in his imagination, his memory, and his present reality. He uses, first imperfect, then present perfect (to represent something that goes for the past and for the now) and then a present which indicates not only a general tendency, but also the difference between the imperfect "then" and the present "now," which indicates a continuity of his struggle. While Leopardi's fantasy leads to temporary obfuscation and pacification from the deprivation of pleasure, Montale's poetry has a sense of constant "attesa," leading back to a memory or through a memory. It makes him a prisoner to his memory, as if the impediment to the "varco," by which to pass beyond, were within himself.

Key to our argument is the notion of illumination in 'Il balcone.' In the *Ossi*, the hot noonday sun overexposes images, leaving a void; in the *Occasioni*, the lack of light does not allow latent traces – though present – to appear. Because of this, Montale waits for "illuminating" epiphanies. What Deleuze says about this issue reveals much in the interpretation of Montale's opus:

> *There is no illuminated matter, but rather, a phosphorescence diffused in every direction that becomes actual «only by reflecting off certain surfaces which serve simultaneously as the screen for other luminous zones.»*[17]

This is why Deleuze states that the brain is a screen and nothing more.[18] Rodowick offers further comment by referring to Benjamin: "For Benjamin, the longer the interval of exposure, the greater the chance that the aura of an environment – the complex temporal relations woven through its represented figures – would seep into the image, etching itself on the photographic plate." Claire Huffman recalls how Montale "suspends feelings until he discovers both a proper vehicle for them and a very particular meaning in some very precise images."[20] Rather, the feeling will not arrive unless the proper montage of effects creates the adequate conflict; or, Eisensteinian 'conflict'. The fact that time has passed is an inevitable reality, but since he has not fully addressed his relation between his experience and his language, it is still an open moment that needs closure. It began in the past, but it is an ongoing moment; not a concluded one:

> *La poesia nasce sempre in un rendiconto del dopo, non come rappresentazione o illuminazione del presente delle situazioni. "I Mottetti" sono reinterpretazioni, riscritture di un evento spirituale accaduto prima e inteso poi, o, meglio, dopo corretto e chiarito, magari anche soltanto in una domanda o in un rinvio ad altro ancora e oltre.*[21]

This also pertains perfectly to the nature of 'Il balcone' as a programmatic poem of aperture for the 'Mottetti.' The three moments: (1) "rendiconto del dopo" in "ora," verse 5; (2) "pareva facile giuoco," a spiritual event from the past; and (3) the possibility of an "other" or beyond, in crossing over the window, the "sporgersi" to a life that gives off light, as opposed to the obscurity whether within oneself or within the physical room. Montale cannot see the absent Clizia and resorts not to his imagination, but to his memory. Later, in *Farfalla di Dinard*, Montale realizes that she was there all along, as an illumined, latent presence.

Montale's infinite space in 'Il balcone' is oppressive in its lack of a presence. The lack of presence assails him as an absence-presence. The void in the space around him is an arduous nothing – not the nothing that is infinity for Leopardi, but a hard nothing which has presence. It is so hard that the waiting is blunted upon it: "sull'arduo nulla si spunta / l'ansia di attenderti vivo." Leopardi's *vago* is imagined – it is truly abstraction unsupported by a correlation in Nature – while Montale's *vago* is real.

On top of the "sheer void" ("arduo nulla") his hopes of seeing Clizia again become "blunted"[22] and maybe the closest he will come to re-experiencing her is not in memory, but in the intermittent flashes of memory. Only in memory can the moment exist out of time, guaranteeing a longer duration of the moment of visitation, or temporary presence in the void, of the salvific one. The longer the duration the greater Montale's chances that the epiphanic fulmination will turn into a salvation. Lonardi is quite acute in his interpretation of the dream in 'Barche sulla Marna.' He imagines the absence-presence of a dream, like a hologram, as offering a virtual form to Montale:

> *La «trovata» del sogno non è del Montale maggiore, anche se si spinge almeno al sogno del prigioniero: ma è appunto a questa «forma» che Montale ricorre per aprire, entro il negativo, una durata del momento antinegativo, una durata della «fantasia di salvezza» decisamente eccezionale, per misura svolgimento analiticità, rispetto alle sue abitudini; e, torno a dire, è proprio per queste durate lunghe che in parte o del tutto si ricorre al ricordo e all'allusione leopardiana.*[23]

And all the same, the emptiness of unlimited space beyond the hedge is still giving Leopardi a sense of illumination, like the life that gives off light to Clizia. Yet the nothingness of unlimited space opened up to Montale is not too far removed from the "nulla alle mie spalle ... con un terrore di ubriaco."[24] As Leopardi is illuminated by immensity (like Ungaretti in 'Mattina'), Montale presents to the reader a window, "rispetto al quale il mottetto-manifesto di Montale marca per antitesi la propria posizione etica e poetica."[25]

As in 'Il balcone,' in 'Casa sul mare' Montale had identified how he differs from Clizia, the "creatura privilegiata che può scorgere quella vita che dà barlumi."[26] She is someone who leans out of the window, illuminated, while he is ever turning inward; a fact that can only force his mental reliance on memory: "Forse solo chi vuole s'infinita, / e questo tu potrai, chissà, non io" ('Casa sul mare'). In these two poems Montale defines a necessary alter ego, and the image is negative. For Montale, the *nulla* of "Portami il girasole" is a vanishing to pure nothingness, the "ventura delle venture." Montale's balcony solidifies a sensation of inner solitude, placing himself, in Valentini's words, "tragicamente solo con se stesso, dinnanzi alla sua coscienza disincantata che, per volgersi la vita, ha bisogno di un *alter ego*, lo specchio costituito da una donna amata."[27] And he can only reach her by reaching nothingness, which is in the void behind the world as hologram. The nothingness is the real reality in which he will find Clizia. However, being that she is absent for a large part of the *Occasioni*, he must evoke this alter ego through memory, and therefore, the poetry of the *Occasioni* becomes the intersecting point of the void ("il vuoto" or "il nulla") and the sense of past as a way of helping him cope with the present, i.e., a presence in that void. Montale views fleeting mnemonic snapshots of her: each of these is like syneddoche of the whole woman. He has yet to see the holistic image of pure spatial representation outside of time, as if to view all the moments of the Eleatic arrow, distinctly and simultaneously in a hologram.

The crisis of the present is that even the reality around him seems untrustworthy and evanescent. Certainly a good example of this would be 'Mottetto 20,' "Ma cosí sia," about which Valentini says: "Ecco le prove che la vita, tanto vertiginosa, può essere ridotta a pochi segni, piú piccoli del fazzoletto di Clizia."[28] What faith can he put in his memory of things if things, such as a shell of a cicada, are no guarantors of a concrete reality? Additionally, all the while he is convinced that a truer reality resides behind them. It is this shell, previously seen in 'Non recidere, forbice,' but also the ephemeral vision of life in 'Sotto la pioggia' that demonstrates this: "guscio d'uovo che va tra la fanghiglia, / poca vita tra sbatter d'ombra e luce." But we know that if shade only exists with respect to light, then Montale's inner state of shade is intensified by Clizia's relation to light, which we see in 'Il balcone.' There is a sense of moving forward in Leopardi's poetic works, while Montale dwells in the past. And though Leopardi too drifts into memories, they are separate as if the time in which they unfold is self-contained and not capable of bumping into the current continuum of time of the present. For Deleuze, these collisions of spatial moments within an imposed framework of time would be the past as present becoming past as past.

Clizia is drawn to, and knows, only the life that gives off "barlumi," and Montale is the opposite. So, while he was one of the "razza che rimane a terra" ('Falsetto'), with respect to Esterina, who lived for the moment, it seems Montale lives inside the moment, trying to preserve it in memory, while Clizia moves forward, beyond time and place; undaunted. This is also the case in 'Sul Llogegrat' about which Arrowsmith notes: "The poet – amateur ornithologist and professional music critic – is pedantically and professionally involved in the naming of his world, differentiating it; whereas the woman, at one with the world, is all being."[29]

She is the one, after all, who has gone beyond and returned covered with icicles from the clouds of her flight in 'Ti libero la fronte dai ghiaccioli.' But because he stays behind, and she moves beyond, he can only know her as the presence which he has evoked through memory in her absence. If shade only exists with respect to light, then Montale's inner state of shade is intensified by Clizia's relation to light, which we see in 'Il balcone.' This notion is illustrated in Montale's 'La casa dei doganieri:' "alla donna che non ricorda, si oppone il poeta che ricorda."[30] The reason he cannot change the space between him and Clizia into nothing – as stated in 'Il balcone' – is because of his inability to forget. He delineates this quite clearly with the anaphora of "tu non ricordi" in 'La casa dei doganieri':

__Tu non ricordi__ la casa dei dognaieri / sul rialzo a strapiombo sulla scogliera: / desolata t'attende dalla sera / in cui v'entrò lo sicame dei tuoi pensieri / e vi sostò irrequieto. // Libeccio sferza da anni le vecchie mura / e il suono del tuo riso non è piú lieto: / la bussola va impazzita all'avventura / e il calcolo dei dadi piú on torna. / __Tu non ricordi__; altro tempo frastorna / la tua memoria; un filo s'addipana. // Ne tengo ancora un capo; ma s'allontana / la casa e in cima al tetto la banderuola / affumicata gira senza pietà/ Ne tengo un capo; ma tu resti sola / né qui respiri nell'oscurità. // Oh l'orizzonte in fuga, dove s'accende / rara luce della petroliera! / Il varco è qui? (Ripullula il frangente / ancora sulla balza che scoscende ...). / __Tu non ricordi__ la casa di questa / mia sera. Ed io non so chi va e chi resta.

Being of the race that remains earthbound (as he had labeled himself in 'Falsetto'), Montale watches the "petroliera" ('La casa dei doganieri'). Clizia is the "orizzonte in fuga" and the intermittent light of the ships are the "barlumi." He remains on the "balza" ("crag") where a wave gathers and re-gathers "still," as if it were unchanged, constant, like the poet's insistent memory; while *she* does not remember. She is incapable of remembering as she is already a part of the hologram. Being far off on the horizon, she could not know this "frangente" ("simple little wave"). Valentini argues that waves have become, for Montale, a "simbolo di memoria campeggiante sulla nebbia del ricordo."[31] In the last lines Montale makes the distinction between his remembering and her failure to remember, and all the while highlighting the general fog of memory that comes about living in both the past and the present at the same time: "ed io non so chi va e chi resta." As the poet turns inward, lacking faith in the external world, communication with the "tu/Clizia" is synonymous with a "comunicazione intermittente con una realtà che può essere evocata ma non posseduta."[32] He holds the end of a string and feels the futility in the fact that at the other end there is no beloved. But, he implies that she might hold the other end. In so doing, she would bridge the temporal expanse to a level where two spatial moments co-exist. The string extended through two moments at once. The house associated with that memory no longer exists phenomenally. This is the case especially for Arletta, for whom it may not even be possible to remember the house. Yet, the virtual, holographic house exists like a thread extending through past, present and future. This timeless, platonic form had been demolished before their meeting and, therefore, doubly removed in memory: the memory of it before meeting Arletta, and the memory of the period of time during which he knew Arletta; remembering that she could not share the memory with him.

The reason why his "ansia" to see her again becomes blunted in 'Il balcone' is also revealed in 'La casa dei doganieri.' Their destinies are mutually exclusive because Montale continues to hold the thread in the continuum within a memory which runs parallel to cosmic time while his beloved resides in the continuum of cosmic time, not holding the end. Montale continues deluding himself in the phenomenal perception of the world, never realizing that there is no need for a thread, as he and Clizia are part of one continuum. He only sees her in memory, and the hope of truly seeing her while still of this earth is futile, especially in the face of the "arduo nulla." He lives among the things that memory grows ('Vecchi versi'). Therefore, it is logical that he would have an end of the thread, while Clizia does not hold the other end. Where is the other end? Does the thread even exist? The fact that it is even put into question cements the notion that neither truth nor proof of reality exist.

So he will not wait for her (if she even still exists) for without the other end of the thread his memory and reality are not completed; they have no basis in reality. Hence, the Pirandellian feeling of the poetry. Speaking of his own hope in the search for the truth in 'Intervista immaginaria,' Montale mentions how a "velo sottile, un filo appena mi separava dal quid definitivo."[34] She is not there, and does not pertain to his "oscurità," as far as he is concerned. Therefore, he attempts to create her existence through the surrogate of poetry, but this nothing but a series of paradoxical moments. "Essi, per lui, sono anzi i momenti in cui piú dolorosa si avverte l'impossibilità d'un'espressione assoluta."[35] That is, an impossibility of reaching a truth, for he cannot get beyond the void as absence to the void as reality over which his visual world is projected. If she does not partake in the memory, it becomes one-sided and even memory could be akin to a dream: did any of this ever exist if it cannot be corroborated by another human being? Or was it the construction of the memory that "cresce le cose in sé" ('Vecchi versi'), so that these "cose" live and grow in memory in a time continuum related to cosmic time, but not within it; rather parallel to it. In fact, Montale questions the good that has come from time shared with this special woman. How real could it have been if now it seems as if it would be more valid had he imagined it, rather than recalled it? Her presence is on the level with the same "barlumi" (here, "rara la luce" or "intermittent light") which help to define her on the metaphysical level, if he is fortunate enough to glimpse her latent image. Even *barlumi* and intermittent light both appear to come from nothing and return to nothing, which is perhaps an elaboration of the "vuoto dietro le cose" ("the void behind things") that Montale had already considered in works such as 'Forse un mattino andando' and 'Il fiore che ripete.'

In this sense, 'La casa dei doganieri' is in the same vein as 'Non recidere, forbice' within the plane of 'Il balcone.' Everything falls into the category of the 'nebbia di sempre' ('Non recidere'). Memory is the last stronghold, proof, of existence and the closest the poet will get to a truth is through the flashes, "barlumi," and other intermittent light sources. Valentini reminds us of the ultimate quality of an existence where signs of reality and truth come from such tentative, dubious sources, especially with regard to 'Non recidere, forbice.' "Cadendo, quel volto si muterebbe, da ricordo vitale, in quella 'nebbia di sempre' in quella assenza di memoria che è veramente morte."[36] But in 'Sul limite' (*Farfalla di Dinard*) absence does not exist, as our author reasserts that which he had proposed in the *Ossi*: "tutto è già stampato (.....)." For this reason, it is not surprising that Montale would treat the absent Clizia and his own deceased father as roughly the same type of entity in 'Voce giunta con le folaghe.' As long as he remembers them, absence and death are two similar states that are vital as long as the memory is vital. Yet they are both irrevocably lost – one to the afterlife, one to unbreachable distance – if his memory should fail him. In 'Voce giunta,' the message from Clizia is addressed to Montale as much as to his father. In this later work of the *Silvae*, Clizia warns Montale of his over-attachment to memory by saying, "memoria / non è peccato fin che giova. Dopo / è letargo di talpa, abiezione / che funghisce su sé." But in 'La casa dei doganieri' it almost appears that Montale finds Clizia's not remembering as the abjection, the turn towards nothingness. It is this very fear which is addressed in 'Voce giunta' through the character of the father. He is fearful that the "larva" of memory in those who survive him is so insignificant, as it is, that even that minimal trace of who he was will be extinguished at the slightest movement and become the "arduo nulla" of 'Il balcone.' If he were forgotten in their memory he will have become a perfect nothing, and life will have been lived meaninglessly. By 'Sul limite,' his alter ego has assumed a pseudo-Clizian role: he lives in a pure present. In the afterlife of this farfalla, Montale realizes that we are no better in eternity at recalling, for one cannot recall without the intermediary of time.

What is intimated about the fears of memory in the dead of 'Voce giunta' is clearly precedented in 'Il balcone' and 'La casa dei doganieri.' 'Il balcone' perhaps gives us the background of the void, while 'La casa dei doganieri' is an example of his latest motif, which he will conjoin to it. Both, however, contain the necessary elements about memory, which help to explain better a reading of 'Voce giunta,' one of his later works of the third collection, which can be appreciated best within the context I have begun to construct. The reader of Montale's 'Il balcone' will see the nothing that will be the net result of time winning a battle over memory and creating an absence. This absence is a consuming void, an "arduo nulla," as opposed to the void as noumenos in 'Forse un mattino andando.'

Notes

1. Sergio Antonielli, *Aspetti e figure del novecento* (Parma: Guanda, 1955) 61.
2. Clodagh J. Brook, *The Expression of the Inexpressible in Eugenio Montale's Poetry: Metaphor, Negation and Silence*. (Oxford: Clarendon Press, 2002) 95.
3. Ibid. 116.
4. Ibidem.
5. Ibid. 120.
6. Ibid. 34.
7. Gilles Deleuze. *Cinema II: The Time-image*. Trans. Hugh Tomlinson and Robert Galeta. (Minneapolis: U of Minnesota Press, 1989): 211. Deleuze refers here to section III of Henri Bergson's *Matter and Memory*. Trans. N. M. Paul

and W. S. Palmer. (NY: Zone Books, 1991): 176. In the English version, we see the brain referred to as an "intermediary" between sensation and movement.
8. Richard Lansing. "From Hedge to Wall: Montale via Leopardi." *Studi di filologia e letteratura italiana in onore di Maria Picchio Simonelli*. Ed. Pietro Frassica. (Alessandria: Orso, 1992): 184.
9. Montale, Eugenio. *The Second Life of Art: Selected Essays*. Ed. and tr. Jonathan Galassi. (New York: The Ecco Press, 1982): 300.
10. Lansing 180.
11. Bruno Biral, "Il sentimento del tempo: Leopardi, Baudelaire, Montale." *Ponte* 21 (1965): 1171.
12. Ibid. 1169.
13. Sergio Antonielli, *Letteratura del disagio* (Milano: Edizioni di Comunità, 1984) 197.
14. Ibid. 203.
15. Brook 116.
16. Lorenzo Greco, ed., *Montale commenta Montale* (Parma: Pratiche, 1980) 28.
17. Rodowick cites Sartre: Jean-Paul Sartre. *The Imagination: A Psychological Critique*. Trans. Forrest Williams. (Ann Arbor: U of Michigan Press, 1962): 39–40.
18. D. N. Rodowick, *Deleuze's Time Machine*. (Durham: Duke University Press, 1997): 33.
19. Ibid. 8. Rodowick cites from Benjamin's "A short history of photography," trans. P. Patton, in *Classic Essays on Photography*. Ed. Alan Trachtenberg. New Haven: Leete's Island Books, 1980. 199–216.
20. Claire de C. L. Huffman, *Montale and the Occasions of Poetry* (Princeton: Princeton UP, 1983) 34.
21. Giorgio Bàrberi Squarotti, "Lettura dei 'Mottetti'." *Lettere italiane* 49.1 (1997): 67.
22. Guido Almansi and Bruce Merry, *Eugenio Montale: The Private Language of Poetry*. (Edinburgh: Edinburgh UP, 1977) 71.
23. Gilberto Lonardi. *Il vecchio e il giovane e altri saggi su Montale*. (Bologna: Zanichelli, 1980): 75.
24. Italo Calvino, 'Forse un mattino andando.' *Letture montaliane in occasione dell'80o compleanno del Poeta*. Ed. Sylvia Luzzatto (Genova: Bozzi, 1977) 33–34.
25. Dante Isella ed., *Le occasioni*, by Eugenio Montale. (Torino: Einaudi, 1996) 5.
26. Paola Desideri, "Clizia: salvezza e perdizione nella sintassi narrativa dei Mottetti montaliani." *L'approdo letterario: Rivista trimestrale di lettere e arti* 75–76 (1976): 153.
27. Alvaro Valentini, *Lettura di Montale: 'Le occasioni'* (Roma: Bulzoni, 1975) 38.
28. Ibid. 151.
29. Eugenio Montale, *The Storm and Other Things*. Tr., with preface and commentary, by William Arrowsmith (New York: Norton, 1985) 186.
30. Valentini 164.
31. Ibid. 168.

32. Giuliana Castellani, 'Alle soglie della memoria,' *Contributi per Montale*, ed. Giovanni Cillo (Lecce: Milella, 1979) 142.
33. Montale to Alfonso Leone, June 19, 1971: "The house of the customs men was destroyed when I was six. The girl in question never could have seen it." Eugenio Montale, *L'opera in versi*, ed. Rosanna Bettarini and Gianfranco Contini (Milano: Einaudi, 1980) 917.
34. Eugenio Montale, "Intervista immaginaria." *Il secondo mestiere: arte, musica, società*. Ed. Giorgio Zampa (Milano: Mondadori, 1996) 1480.
35. Mario Martelli, *Eugenio Montale: Introduzione e guida allo studio dell'opera montaliana, storia e antologia critica* (Firenze: Le Monnier, 1982) 36–37.
36. Valentini 147.

CHAPTER 3
The *Occasioni* and the 'Mottetti': Late motifs and latent images

In the first 'Mottetto,' 'Lo sai: debbo riperderti e non posso,' the *capoverso* indicates two things. First it tells the reader about Montale's state of mind, so that one realizes why he views the exterior landscape so negatively; so painfully. Second, the "non posso" indicates an unwillingness to lose, or to forget, which will justify an odd search for a "sign," a pledge, of Clizia in a spiritually incongruous landscape of ironwork, masts and dust.

> *Lo sai: debbo riperderti e non posso. / Come un tiro aggiustato mi sommuove / ogni opera, ogni grido e anche lo spiro / salino che straripa / dai moli e fa l'oscura primavera / di Sottoripa. // Paese di ferrame e alberature / a selva nella polvere del vespro. / Un ronzío lungo viene dall'aperto, / strazia com'unghia ai vetri. Cerco il segno / smarrito, il pegno solo ch'ebbi in grazia / da te. / / E l'inferno è certo.*

The "ebbi" of verse 10 confirms that Montale is relating the present to a past, and that the "riperderti" of verse one was not a physical re-losing, but one that pertains to memory. The original "perderti" ("losing you") must have occurred not long after the moment which the past absolute recalls; when he received this "pegno," or pledge, from her.

The "screen of images," then, serves simultaneously as a reflection of his interior state, and as a landscape that offers him much poetically, but the only certainty is his general "male di vivere": "E l'inferno è certo" ("And hell is certain"). If, on a level of external landscape, Montale cannot even find one object of consolation, or one of a commensurate relatability to the prelingual image in his memory of Clizia, how can he prove that she was even there? If presence can be whisked away so easily to absence so that nowhere in the current present is there a connection with it, it would almost seem as if the meaning of life were diminished. If life can bring such delusion, death will surely bring no peace and calm. Much like the "fiati / senza materia o voce / traditi nella tenebra" ('I morti'), Montale sees life as a precursor for the afterlife, and, based on what he has seen, the "male di vivere" will become an innovation of this expression as a *male di non-vivere*.

However, this hell is not the Hades of Lucifer, per se. Rather, it is a void of heaven and a manifestation of Montale's lack of expectation based on his earthly experiences. Continuing the themes of 'Il balcone,' as they permeate the 'Mottetti' at hand, one ought to consider the words of Maria Sampoli Simonelli on the "male di vivere" of both Montale and Leopardi:

> *If Leopardi sought for the "why" of the universe and the life of man, to conclude that «perhaps in whatever form, in whatever / condition he may exist, in cot or cradle / it is a gloomy birthday for the one just born» ("Canto notturno di un pastore errante") Montale does not even bother to search, because he assumes the answer to be true from the start. What Montale asks is rather of what does this suffering consist? That is, he asks the why of the suffering, only to conclude that it is a suffering without reason and without purpose; it is an unquenchable thirst for knowledge, a painful desire or longing for something that can never be attained and which resolves itself only in nothing.*[1]

Though the first part of Simonelli's argument in regard to Leopardi does not seem perfectly probable, the second part seems to be quite appropriate and well-founded. This is, after all, a "paese di ferrame e alberature / a selva nella polvere del vespro," and Montale "is not one of those poets, mystic or pantheist, whose metaphysical anguish is allayed by the thought of communion with nature. In the rigidity of physical objects he reads his own condemnation."[2] That condemnation is the certain hell – he experiences the matter of the phenomenal world.

'Mottetto 1' tenders a tense moment to the reader. Part of the tension is derived form the general sense of *attesa* that one reads in the work. The *attesa* is formed by the fusing of the moment of memory with the present situation. "Debbo" ("I must") implies something he will have to do sometime later. "Cerco" ("I'm looking for") implies a searching, and when one searches, the duration can be unlimited, contingent on when, and if, the object of the search is found. Again, the two verbs "cerco" and "ebbi" links a remembered past with a continuous present, and between the two, the reader feels a suspense that is interrupted by the last line like a sudden epiphany, albeit a negative one.

It is within this *attesa* that throughout the rest of the 'Mottetti' the poems are written with this sense of searching: looking through his memory, he constantly tries to find an external presence that will become the medium through which Montale will recreate the presence of Clizia. If he can resist losing her again, and find her sign, memory will torment him less, as implied by the third person conjugation of "straziare" in the lines: "Un ronzío lungo viene dall'aperto, / strazia com'unghia ai vetri." With regard to the 'Mottetti,' of which 'Mottetto 1' is a prime example, Galassi speaks about a:

> ...*theme of devotion to a distant loved one ... derived from stilnovistic practice (itself a version of courtly love tradition), the great type of which is Dante's dedication to the impossibly remote Beatrice. Amor de lonh is the defining convention of stilnovistic poetry: since the beloved is often married or otherwise unavailable, the use of occult symbols, symbolic names, and other covering devices (trobar clus) becomes standard practice.*[3]

A sign, besides one of a "certain hell," would also confirm that life is not a means or an end to itself either; rather it would imply a more profound level of entelechy.

In 'Mottetto 2' the fusion of memory and the present to form the *attesa* occurs over three different planes of time:

> *Molti anni, e uno piú duro sopra il lago / straniero su cui ardono i tramonti. / Poi scendesti dai monti a riportarmi / San Giorgio e il Drago. // Imprimerli potessi sul palvese / che s'agita alla frusta del grecale / in cuore ... E per te scendere in un gorgo / di fedeltà, immortale.*

The fact that two verbal tenses (periods of time) exist literally within the poem means that the poem itself is twice a metaphor for memory: two time periods co-exist in it, not as time but as spatial entities on the page. The "many years" refer to a period in a past prior to the past moment in the poem when a *tu* brought him a sign, much like the "pegno" of 'Mottetto 1.' In the second stanza the poet is in a hypothetical present that pivots on the verb "potessi." This *attesa*, this "if only I could," which resembles the pure contingency of the first 'Mottetto,' is also highlighted by the imagery of the quest. It is precisely the image of Saint George and the dragon that lends an air of chivalrous quest analogous to the stilnovistic courtly love; the woman above, the man below in many vassalitic poems.

The accumulation of years to which he refers in a present, looking back, suggests that he was waiting for a sign even then, previous to the image in the mountains. He had already felt the void of the present next to the memory of her presence:

> *Molti anni, e uno piú duro sopra il lago / straniero su cui ardono i tramonti. / Poi scendesti dai monti a riportarmi / San Giorgio e il Drago.*

But soon it becomes evident that even this sign was the result of his memory of Clizia fused with the desire of the present to see her and the dramatic quality of the mountains. These mountains (around the sanatorium) stand tall and quiet, forcing the reference points of sight to be vertical. The sense of waiting is heightened by this verticality. This anxiousness, first established in 'Il balcone,' is then further intensified in the second stanza of 'Mottetto 2.' The "potessi" creates a horizontal tension over time and the verb "scendere" not only adds to this sense of tension based on hypothesis, but also completes the sense of vertical tension; a possible falling from above. It is the moment between potential and kinetic movement.

The second stanza reflects the theme of putting presence in the void, whether in 'Il balcone,' in 'Voce giunta,' or in the writer's virtual presence in the void of the afterlife of 'Sul limite.' Montale's wanting to imprint Saint George and the dragon – both the sign of Clizia and of his memories of Genova – on the "palvese" of his tormented heart is akin to conjoining his every most recent motif to the "arduous nothing" of 'Il balcone.' The "arduous nothing" and the meaning in relation to it of the things around him are all based on a tenuous reconciliation between the flash of memory from the past and the means for expression around him. Therefore, despite the seemingly ostensible dialogue between the dead and the absent in 'Voce giunta,' it is a case of Montale expressing his own concerns about death, absence and memory through the voice of the other two, much the way that Eliot employs a subjective first person that is not the poet himself. Eliot's 'Gerontion' uses the voice of an old man who is clearly not Eliot:

> *Here I am, an old man in a dry month, / Being read to by a boy, waiting for rain. / I was neither at the hot gates / Nor fought in the warm rain / Nor knee deep in the salt marsh, heaving a cutlass, / Bitten by flies, fought.*

Montale recounts as a character 'Voce giunta con le folaghe' and also as a witness to the dialogue between his father and Clizia, yet what Clizia says and what the father feels are reflections of Montale's own inner struggle:

> *L'una forse / ritroverà la forma in cui bruciava / amor di Chi la mosse e non di sé, / ma l'altro sbigottisce e teme che / la larva di memoria in*

cui si scalda / ai suoi figli si spenga al nuovo balzo. // – Ho pensato per te, ho ricordato / per tutti. Ora ritorni al cielo libero / che ti tramuta.

The existence of the bodiless voices, Montale's first person explains in 'Voce giunta,' was dependent on this frail environment, so tenuous that the day's wind confuses living shade (Clizia, far away) with the reluctant one (his deceased father), perhaps because in the faculty of memory they are temporally equidistant in the immediacy of the holographic screen of images:

Il vento del giorno / confonde l'ombra viva e l'altra ancora / riluttante in un mezzo che respinge / le mie mani, / e il respiro mi si rompe / nel punto dialatato, nella fossa / che circonda lo scatto del ricordo.

In a flash of an instant, memory has infinite meaning, as if it can immediately reveal myriad latent images to the virtual locus of the infinitely expandable mind: "Cosí si svela prima di legarsi / a immagini, a parole, oscuro senso / reminiscente, il vuoto inabitato / che occupammo" ('Voce giunta'). And so the "arduo nulla" of 'Il balcone' and the "punto dilatato" of 'Voce giunta' are roughly the same space. Their very oxymoronic nature seems to reflect this. A nothing, or a nullity, can be arduous, for in the moment before a concept is linked to an image or to a word, it has unlinked meaning within Montale and, therefore, it has limitless potential in terms of the words he chooses to use as his literary, semantic agent. The ardor comes from within and is symptomatic of his struggle before the absence of Clizia's presence. A point can be "dilatato," widened, to encompass the space around his memory because before it is assigned a value, be it to a word or to a correlative, it has only potential, and, therefore, only potentially infinite, space.

This particular aspect is revealed in 'Vecchi versi.' While earlier this poem was discussed in connection with the nature of Montale's memory, now it serves in a discussion of the ways his past and present come together in a timeless, infinitely expandable, virtual point which is the screen of images as it receives intermittent visual manifestations of holographic world. In 'Vecchi versi' Montale speaks of a moth that was ("fu") forever "con le cose che chiudono in un giro / sicuro come il giorno, e la memoria / in sé le cresce":

Era un insetto orribile, la farfalla, un grave monito come da un altro mondo, ma quello che ora importa è che nell'attimo di fissarsi nella memoria del poeta, traeva con sé, nella dimensione di un'altra vita, tutto un insieme di particolari, una complessa circostanza di paesaggio, un esterno e un interno, volti familiari, l'ora del tempo e l'avversa

> *stagione, il segno tenace di un torrentizio scavo della terra in direzione del mare. Qui Montale compone una pagina di originale poesia, generalmente, seppure variamente, apprezzata, rende non fenomenico, come è stato detto, il fenomeno [cfr. R. Assunto, "Per una teoria della poesia di M.," in Omaggio a M., a cura di S. Ramat, Mondadori, Milano, 1966.], ma compone anche con estrema attenzione e in significativo crescendo la storia segreta di come si forma un oggetto che possa servire, in un secondo tempo, alla scoperta della realtà vera o profonda. La farfalla di Vecchi versi è una madeleine che invece di esserci presentata mentre funziona da rivelatrice in una tazza di tè, di tutto un paese, lo sia al momento in cui si carica della virtú che le consentirà la rivelazione. Genesi di un oggetto idoneo a una futura «intermittenza del cuore.» Ogni volta che il poeta richiamerà il quadro di quella sera, quel mare, quella stanza, quella lampada, quel tavolo con intorno la madre, i nipoti, lui stesso, tutto fino a quel segno di torrente che fra l'altro sarà il segno etico-letterario di tutta una vita.*[4]

This is the Bergsonian notion, which Deleuze explicates in *Difference and Repetition*: "each present present is only the entire past in its most contracted state."[5] Memory preserves moments of the so-called past in the universe as hologram. The momentary projections of the present are the external commotion around Montale, but Montale cannot see them as being connected. Everything is experienced as then and now:

> *Insieme / coi volti familiari che oggi sperde / non piú il sonno ma un'altra noia; accanto / ai muri antichi, ai lidi, alla tartana / che imbarcava / tronchi di pino a riva ad ogni mese, / al segno del torrente che discende / ancora al mare e la sua via si scava.*

This external landscape is walls, "tartane," torrents, etc. But those external words and images become simultaneously used as a means for expression and closed in the "giro sicuro" along with the other things that fall into memory's custody. So memory is the "punto dilatato" of 'Voce giunta': infinitely intangible and infinitely expandable to include not just walls, "tartane," and torrents, but these things that "ad ogni mese" ("each and every month"), and "ancora" ("still") incorporate a sense of continuity over time so that memory's flash is not just a "punto dilatato," but a chronological interchange of present and infinity. It is a presence that exists in constant absence, but only in the relativity of the constant presence of the mundane continuum. In this continuum, 'Vecchi versi' also extends the discourse on absence restored through memory to the realm of death as simply a form of absence, though in this case not final: "insieme / coi volti familiari che oggi sperde / non piú il sonno ma un'altra noia" (and we ask ourselves if "noia" is not synonymous with death). Of course, this is later fully developed in the personification of dialogue between the concepts of physical absence through separation and absence through death in 'Voce giunta.'

In the regard of semantics, says Rodowick, each "sign acquires meaning only through its interpretation in another sign and so on ad infinitum."[6] As with Funes of Borges' eponymous 'Funes el memorioso,' one sign could contain an infinity of significance built within it. "Buffalo," then, is a perfect example of the elasticity of an outwardly limited point of reference that becomes a presence in the void as it expands to accommodate Montale's individual experience:

Mi dissi: / Buffalo! – e il nome agí. // Precipitavo / nel limbo dove assordano le voci / del sangue e i guizzi incendiano la vista / come lampi di specchi.

By merely refering to that one word, he can return into a state associated with the word. In the current moment, there is much commotion about him, but something is missing, something is absent. Into his metaphysical void he launches the presence of an emotion or mindset related to the meaning that "Buffalo" had in another, past context. As a sign, the incongruity of the word is perhaps the same reason it was chosen to name the velodrome: A foreign place name gives it a sort of allure. His physically saying it, suddenly, compounds to the reader just how incongruous his memory – attached to it – is with the flow of events of the people absorbed in the current moment. Yet it widens, dilates, as if the flash of memory connected to its evocation were a doorway through which one can enter a world parallel to a past co-existent with the present, even as the present becomes the past. Although the connotation extends a presence into a void, albeit a bustling arena, it is equally empty for him until he satisfies the experience with language; and he does.

With the *attesa*, already spoken about in the other poems, I address the sense of hesitation in 'Bagni di Lucca':

Fra il tonfo dei marroni / e il gemito del torrente / che uniscono i loro suoni / èsita il cuore. // Precoce inverno che borea / abbrividisce. M'affaccio / sul ciglio che scioglie l'albore / del giorno nel ghiaccio. // Marmi, rameggi – / e ad uno scrollo giú / foglie a èlice, a freccia, / nel fossato. // Passa l'ultima greggia nella nebbia / del suo fiato.

The heart that hesitates ("esita il cuore") is followed, logically, by the surroundings or even the very objects causing its hesitation. The flash of memory is evoked in the seeming absence of Clizia ("la chiami come vuole," Montale tells us in his auto-interview)[7] by the very things and movement present in that void, apparently unrelated to him, which are aligned in a way to be commensurate to his remembrance.

'Bagni di Lucca,' after a closer reading, reveals an affinity with 'Mottetto 18,' "Non recidere, forbice." The most obvious similarity is in the action of the "scrollo," which corresponds to verse six's "scrolla" in 'Mottetto 18.' This action causes an object – a cicada shell and leaves, respectively – to fall inevitably, like the inevitability of forgetting. Then the reader notes the hesitation of line four that creates an *attesa* to set up the fall of the leaves, like a transfer from potential to kinetic energy.

The poem has the unlimited possibility of a memory, but it is explored as it unfolds, in the present. It shares the commonality of the "punto dilatato," and refers, like memory, to an instant of unlimited expandability.[8] In a flash of memory, real time continues to move forward while the poetic time stops to expand infinitely. But Montale continues to sense that there might be a "dimensione temporale in cui passato e presente sono momenti equivalenti." The poem's time progresses on a vertical axis, while the recalled, poetic, time moves on that point horizontally. So in 'Bagni di Lucca' we are presented with a poem that is immobile mobility. Real time passes, as suggested by the falling and by the passing of the herd, but a moment of hesitation becomes filled – in a flash – with all the imagery of the poem. And the poet represents it as an essential statement composed from the proper juxtaposition of all of the images around him, supplied to him ready-made as naturally occurring elements of the landscape. The same could be said, perhaps, for 'Altro effetto di luna':

La trama del carrubo che si profila / nuda contro l'azzurro sonnolento, / il suono delle voci, la trafila / delle dita d'argento sulle soglie, // la piuma che s'invischia, un trepestío / sul molo che si scioglie / e la feluca già ripiega il volo / con le vele dimesse come spoglie.

What takes eight lines to write and appears to be moving linearly along time's axis is but one flash, one instant. It is a "punto dilatato" enlarged to even include the very "essential alphabet" used to express the essential statement which will represent all that is that moment. So one reads it in real time, but realizes it is arrested, poetic time created for the sole use of the poetic moment. The air of arrested time is created by the *attesa* of the relative pronouns in verses one, five and six. The relative pronouns cause the reader to expect a complement in a dependent clause which never comes, only to realize that the relative pronouns are used as adjectival modifications and these items ("trama," "piuma," "trepestío") become part of a list. The only verbs used are those following the relative pronouns which modify the nouns and tell the reader that it is a "trama del carrubo **che** si profila," a "piuma **che** s'invischia," and a "trepestío ... **che** si scioglie." The only action verb not preceded by a relative pronoun ("che") is the "ripiega" of verse seven. It does not say what kind of "feluca" it is, but what the "feluca" does to its sails. It also explains how ("come") it folds its sails, so that all other descriptions are immediate images while the sail allusion is a simile which is less immediate and makes the reader aware of a mediating poet, as if only in the last line is he speaking, explaining ultimately a correlative of thought for the moment which is the essential statement of itself. These things can certainly be included, along with the swimmer and dachshund of 'Verso Vienna' who enter "cosí nel numero delle cose che chiudono in un giro sicuro come il giorno,"[9] which comes to us from 'Vecchi versi.'

'Carnevale di Gerti' is a supreme moment in the poetry of Montale which relies on memory to create a presence in a void. Like 'Vecchi versi,' the poem plays with time, as all is closed in the "giro sicuro" of the poem. It is appropriate for this collection, for it is an occasion about the very nature of "occasions," as it becomes in itself a presence as poetical work. When there is an absence, a separation, only the aspect of space, infinite in its uses, infinite in its possibilities, is left. 'Gerti' exploits that space terrifically, speaking of absences as presences that may have already been and questioning when they may reappear. Through memory, it is possible that they will:

> *Se la ruota s'impiglia nel groviglio / delle stelle filanti ed il cavallo / s'impenna tra la calca, se ti nevica / sui capelli e le mani un lungo brivido / d'iridi trascorrenti... / se si sfolla la strada e ti conduce / in un mondo soffiato entro una tremula / bolla d'aria e di luce dove il sole / saluta la tua grazia – hai ritrovato / forse la strada che tentò un istante / il piombo fuso a mezzanotte quando / finí l'anno tranquillo senza spari / ... È Carnevale / o il Dicembre s'indugia ancora? Penso / che se tu muovi la lancetta al piccolo / orologio che rechi al polso, tutto / arretrerà dentro un disfatto prisma / babelico di forme e di colori...). // E il Natale verrà e il giorno dell'Anno / che sfolla le caserme e ti riporta / gli amici spersi, e questo Carnevale / pur esso tornerà che ora ci sfugge / tra i muri che si fendono già.*

The very nature of the conditional "se" in the poem is telling (seen four times alone in the excerpt above):

> *Il presente stesso si rivela a volte ambiguamente incerto o giocato su diversi punti prospettici, e ne è prova l'uso frequente del se che acquista in Montale un valore tra il condizionale e il temporale, tanto che i due moduli a volte si alternano ad indicare sia circostanza concomitante sia circostanza eventuale, creando così l'immagine di un tempo insieme reale e ipotetico.*[10]

"If" is as hypothetical as the future itself which is implied, but also as hypothetical as a past that may or may not have happened in a particular way. In verses 12 and 13 the syntagm "hai trovato / forse" appears, which implies that Gerti either has or has not found the road. The present perfect implies that the moment in question has, indeed, passed chronologically. Therefore, the "forse." after a series of present hypothetical clauses, once again combines the conditional with the temporal. Montale leaves this deliberately ambiguous, where he could easily, more clearly, have written "avresti trovato" in the conditional.

Montale uses the present hypothetical to have a poetic dialogue with the one who is absent, but the present is also active as an imperfect of all the things for which Gerti wished that evening when they had passed New Year's Eve together. He conducts a virtual dialogue in a holographic universe. Imperfect verbs, by nature, are not perfect because they have begun something in an unspecified past, which may still be occurring as an action into the present. The imperfect tense's very expression implies indirectly a collision of past as becoming a present and a present becoming past. Though it is clear that this tense can be used for narrative purposes in the past, imperfect would not merit its nomenclature if it were clear at any given time that the action ever came to completion, much the same way a hypothetical "if," never brought to fruition in the past is tantamount to a hypothetical "if" in the present, in terms of any completed action.

In the first "lassa"[11] of 'Carnevale di Gerti,' a reader can see the condition common to the other poems of which I have spoken. In an effort to approximate a flash of memory, Montale needs to fill that point with all that makes up the flash; but to do that would make it no longer a flash, rather a drawn out moment. He is able to sustain this moment as singular and sudden by employing a sense of *attesa* within the single phrase. The subordinated succession of "ifs" ensures that the reader stays within that particular moment, and attempts to approximate the duration of reading the physical poem to the duration of the flash of memory.

This *lassa* could be referring to a "now" and the present perfect ("hai trovato") refers to an action completed recently. However, in the second *lassa* Montale writes "Ed ora," as if to suggest that the present tense from the first lassa was not a true present, but an iterative description of Gerti's world from the past; normally related by the imperfect, to which I alluded above. The "Ed ora" implies Gerti's presence, but she is not present. She exists only through his memory, filling the void with her presence in the lines of the poem where the "Ed ora" of verse 16 and "ora" of verse 20 cause the reader to forget the circumstances of absence and react as if he/she were following a dialogue which is unfolding between the poet and Gerti. The poem is a literary approximation of a holographic experience.

Part of the insistence that Gerti dwell in the world of "spogli suoni" is because only there, in the "immaginario fiabesco,"[12] can she, and Montale, hope to hold time still or even go back, as suggested by the movement of the "lancetta," and "(tutto / arretrerà dentro un disfatto prisma / babelico di forme e di colori...)." The use of parentheses in this *lassa* means that the reader is stepping outside the poem for a moment to discuss the true nature of geologic, or cosmic, time, which appears irreversible. This prepares the reader to better comprehend verses 55 to 58: "La tua vita è quaggiú dove rimbombano / le ruote dei carriaggi senza posa / e nulla torna se non forse in questi / disguidi del possibile."

Memory, and remembrance as a concept, become the "disguidi" of the realm of possibility. Nothing ever goes back, just as the hand on the clock will never go back. If, then, this inevitability were disrupted or reversed, surely that would be a sign of a "disguido" from this reality. Any return through memory equals a step into a perpetual moment and, therefore, a slipping away from chronological, linear time. Therefore, both subject and form (the poem itself) become "disguidi" from the natural course of things.

Something in the wheels speaks to him of her. The fact that they are wheels "senza posa," calls to mind their motion, like time rolling forward "irrefrenabile," and I cannot deny this fact. At the same time a moving carriage wheel evokes an illusion seen also in 'Mottetto 15' ("Al primo chiaro"): this is the sense of illumination "a tagli." Perhaps the "disguidi" are the invisibility of the wheels as they turn. Yet, they are there, despite the optical illusion. If this is the case, then the universe as hologram may be ever-present despite any "disguidi" that our poet might have with:

Al primo chiaro, quando / subitaneo un rumore / di ferrovia mi parla / di chiusi uomini in corsa / nel traforo del sasso / illuminato a tagli / da cieli ed acque misti.

This 'Mottetto' refers to the train tunnel going through the area of the Cinque Terre where one goes from darkness to light, occasionally catches glimpses of light and external images streaked in between the cement pillars, as they whoosh by. To the "non coscienza" these slices of illumination enter the tunnel giving hints of understanding. This illumination speaks of cinematic projection and the intermittent movement of celluloid frames. As my study aims to move the discourse to the *Farfalla di Dinard* aesthetic, I can point to two examples for which the *mottetto* at hand is a precursor. Though I will discuss them at greater length in a later chapter, it is worth mentioning them now. The first is 'La casa delle due palme,' a poem replete with the narrator's cinematic vision of the world. From the train, on which he arrives, all "appariva e spariva"[13] as if in the cuts of montage; all was intermittent and unclear until "un lampo non gli illuminò il cervello."[14] Additionally, Montale further develops the cinematic illumination in the *farfalla* 'Sulla spiaggia': "un lampo illumina la mia mente, un vero lampo nel buio."[15]

In 'Carnevale di Gerti,' however, the poet remains still while the vehicle passes: it moves forward, without rest, simulating time's inevitability, and in the spiral of its turning the wheels give the illumination "a tagli" of what it passes, or what the poet may see while looking through them. The fact that the carriage brings the object of his fancy away from him seems painfully inevitable, and perfectly applicable to Montale's second book of poems, which is thematically about separation.

These "tagli" of illumination are, in turn, flashes of understanding, or perhaps flashes of memory. If these 'cuts' are representations of memory, then memory's analogue is clearly cinematic. Cinema is a 'grand illusion': "Cinema works by obliterating the photogram, anihilating that which is static. It appears to extract a magical continuity from what is acknowledged to be discontinuous."[16] Continuity from the discontinuous implies a further connection with the void: the phenomenal reality is but a discontinuous projection behind which is the screen, or void, of which Montale spoke in 'Forse un mattino andando.' This implies a persistence of image, or after-image, which stretches all moments into one moment. In this regard, Montale's cinematic aesthetic bears an affinity to the theories of C. W. Ceram: "Cinematography is technically based on the phenomenon of persistence of vision – the capacity of the retina of the eye to retain the impression of an object for the fraction of a second after its disappearance."[17] One may think of Eliot's concept of getting the better of words for a thing one no longer has to say. But at the same time, the most subtle message from the denseness of the last *lassa* of 'Carnevale di Gerti' is how little it takes in the "schermo d'immagini" before him to reproduce the presence of Gerti in the void of her absence.

In 'Verso Capua,' the flash of memory evokes a past situation. It brings Montale to a virtual point. That point then opens up – "dilata" – as if in a holographic portal, a doorway to what that point offers. In 'Verso Capua,' Montale communicates that point. The introductory ellipses highlight the sudden nature of the flash of memory *in medias res*:

> ... *rotto il colmo sull'ansa, con un salto, / il Volturno calò, giallo, la sua / piena tra gli scopeti, la disperse nelle crete ... e tu in fondo che agitavi / lungamente una sciarpa, la bandiera / stellata!, e il fiume ingordo s'insabbiava.*

With one flash of that point in memory the reader can see and feel all that acted on Montale in that moment. But, as a poet, Montale materializes the point for the relative perspective of who is reading. From without it seems a point – for it is a conceptual bookmark, pagemarker, for a past moment – and from within it offers to the reader the continuum and the variety from that moment which seems limited now because it has passed. The reader interprets the moment as a continuum of moments that may still be unfolding, rather than as a singular one. Montale exhibits in poetry what Bergson had stated abstractly: "Practically, we perceive only the past," which would consist of divisible moments of reality into which the reader would become distracted, losing sight of the fact that the "pure present" is "the invisible progress of the past gnawing into the future."[18]

The ellipses of the first line of 'Verso Capua' give the reader the impression of being thrust into a situation which had preceding moments. It is typical of Montale to immerse his reader in the suddenness of the flash of memory which overtakes his own interior mental landscape and immerses him, as well. The reader, like Montale thinking back in the past, steps out of real time into that expansive territory which is compressed infinitely into the virtual points of his memory, as in Bergon's folds. Here, however, with the use of so many descriptive imperfect tenses mixed with the concise past absolutes, the moment becomes part of a protracted time, not a single still-life snapshot:

> *Laggiù si profilava / mobile sulle siepi un postiglione, / e apparí su cavalli, / in una scia di polvere e sonagli. / Si arrestò pochi istanti, l'equipaggio / dava scosse, d'attorno volitavano / farfalle minutissime. Un furtivo / raggio incendiò di colpo il sughereto / scotennato, a fatica ripartiva la vettura.*

Time within this memory is moving along in a parallel to the real time of the surroundings in which Montale stops to ponder. This separation is tantamount to creating parallels of time – past and present – so that the poet will move in relative time within the memory and become distanced from the past. It is a Proustian paradox; or, as Poulet states it: "The simultaneity of the successive, the presence, in the present, of another present: the past."[19]

Thematically 'Verso Capua' fits perfectly into the *Occasioni*. It does not describe the moment of departure in a present, rather it already considers departure a past. So, clearly it is a poem about the separation which creates the very absences in the *Occasioni* onto which Montale projects a presence: mentally, as memory; and physically, with the poem as the material artifact of his every "tardo motivo" ('Il balcone'). The "bandiera stellata" ("star-spangled banner") is a reference to the destination of Clizia in America, leaving Europe as a Jew fearing religious persecution. This is a prehistory of a moment like the one expressed in the second strophe of 'Mottetto 4,' "Lontano, ero con te." The distance between them, the trans-Atlantic separation, is clear, and, despite this distance, Montale is able to be with Clizia through his remembrance of her. Time is removed to the order of a unified space, through which their togetherness need not rely upon an intermediate space. Typical of Montale's poetry, the lines from 'Mottetto 4' cause the reader to wonder "for what?" when reading "per questo": "Il logorío / di *prima* mi salvò solo per questo:" then in the next line the reader sees "for what": "che t'ignoravo e non dovevo." It is as if the present suddenly gives the past a new meaning it never seemed to have. It is typical of Montale because though it is a statement it might as well be a question pondering the nature of existence and truth: for what? Why? The strong caesura of the colon after "per questo" forces the reader not only to stop and see the connection between this line and the next line, but also to explore any other more metaphysical meanings beyond the obvious. It is, in the words of Cambon, "una dichiarazione per la spiritualità che sconfisse la assenza reale."[20] Each presence in the absence is a Proustian re-emergence of a place: they are "wading places"[21] with no calculable movement; rather they are simultaneous and equidistant to the poet.

'Verso Capua' is one of those Montalian moments that tend toward an encapsulation of memory. As previously mentioned, the ellipses give the reader a feeling of interruption into the fact, *in medias res*. Then, at the end, comes the moment of salutation, which could have ended the poem, that is with "...la bandiera / stellata!" However, the last phrase is "e il fiume ingordo s'insabbiava" ("and the greedy river sunk into the sand"), and this resembles the "monte di sabbia" of 'Ezekiel saw the wheel,' which, Cambon says, "la clessidra del tempo aveva ammassato in cuore."[22] One gets the sense of continuing time within the memory itself; the unity of space implies the plurality of time.[23]

This is also another example of the "punto dilatato." Infinitely enlarging, and enlargeable, is this point of time and memory in its particular chronological plane. Logically, if this moment were to continue, it would abut with the present moment in which Montale is pondering it as a Bergsonian past. Yet it remains distinct, like a point, and encapsulated so that there is that moment inhabited by them (Montale and Clizia), and looking back it becomes an unlimited void in relation to the present moment. Perhaps it explains the 'Mottetti' better, or helps us understand their creator's mindset.

It is necessary to examine the setting for Clizia's departure. The river, the Volturno, "calò, giallo, la sua / piena tra gli scopeti, la disperse / nelle crete." Then a furtive ray of sun "incendiò di colpo il sughereto / scotennato." And, of course, the river (in a verbal imperfect-descriptive tense) "s'insabbiava," perhaps the same sand of 'Proda di Versilia' that is not fertile for memory: "Sabbia che non nutre." Then in the absence of her, later, after she had departed, in this locus, why then could he not, with similar conditions, believe she is somehow still present in the void, in her absence? This is rather like the opposite of the film projection; and similar to the wheel in 'Gerti,' which in turning appears to disappear. When Montale writes in 'Mottetto 1,' "Cerco il segno / smarrito, il pegno solo ch'ebbi in grazia / da te," it would be as if he were saying in reference to 'Verso Capua,' "where is that river that sank into sand, at least the physical proof related to your existence?" Likewise, if the cork-tree forest of 'Verso Capua' were gone, he might assume that hell is certain, as in 'Mottetto 1,' for if he thought enough of them to include them in his correlative of thought, then their disappearance would be significant, as the presence was a sign for him.

The 'Mottetti,' by their very title, imply a brief musical moment. The brevity of each of the twenty pieces is lucid, and as such, exemplifies the very nature of the *Occasioni*; moments, of which the 'Mottetti' are a central part. Isella, appropriately referred to this section as "topograficamente centrale," and also as the "sede di una concentratissima memoria poetica."[24] They are, in this quality, the instant, immediate artifact of an ineffable mental state; a state solidified by concrete language for abstract notions. The poems represent the fusion of Montale's current state with a past situation shared with another (let us call her Clizia, though certainly a senhalic Arletta in the first three) but in the *ambiente* of *her* absence. (In fact, all but one, 'Mottetto 17,' have the inclusion of a far off *tu dialogante*, or a memorial representation of a Clizia.) They seem to be, more than the other poems of the *Occasioni*, reminiscent of the thesis in 'Il balcone,' is that these are literally his "ogni tardo motivo" conjoined to the "arduo nulla." And as such the reader is forced to see the nothing of the present as a corollary to a something of the past readdressed through memory. Therefore, in these poems, as in much of his opus, the poet is not living in the moment, for the moment. He is searching the present to find a remnant of the past. Every occasion is an inevitable motivation to remember, to re-think the past; every memory of the past is a motivation to rethink the present.

Perhaps one could even speculate on the musical implication. In this regard, one could accompany this speculation with the notions of Eliotian objective correlative. It is a sort of formulaic expression of a particular emotion so that private emotion becomes accessible to a reader. Yet, whereas Eliot's is a correlative aimed at universal conditions, Montale's seems to be employing a more subjective correlative:

> *È con le Occasioni, e cioè già in area ermetica e "dantesca" che, mentre la rescissione è riconosciuta in modo inderogabile, il "correlativo soggettivo" si specifica come tentativo di una presa di coscienza oggettiva, attraverso le occasioni, cioè attraverso le coincidenze di tempo con ciò che avviene, coi "luoghi" dell'evento, dell'alterità della fenomenologia naturale, e quindi si fa fondato il desiderio di captarne soggettivamente l'entità oggettiva, per proiezione omologica dell'io, e di annettersene il valore oggettivo, quasi per una tentata terapeusi di "ciò che non siamo, ciò che non vogliamo," cioè attraverso ciò che può affermarsi anche con un discorso negativo, come nella Verneinung freudiana, in cui è la negatività che afferma ciò che non è altrimenti affermabile.*[25]

If that were the case in Montale, then each musical piece could be a variation on the same musical theme – a Proustian occurrence seen, not through time, but in a fixed locus from various perspectives in infinite multiplicity – like a hologram. In this case, each represents a different facet of Montale's remembrance of the past. Each one acts as a subjective correlative of the fusion in his memory between the past and the surroundings of his present. The brevity results from the need to concentrate as much emotion as possible into as few words and objects from his environment to do two things: approximate the sudden flash of memory; and reduce the fusion of the external world and the internal world of Montale into a compact portable linguistic expression, which serves as a Proustian compact locus, which Poulet describes as follows:

> *[T]he Proustian novel takes its points of departure in a place as narrow*

as possible and comparable to the miniscule volume of a cup of tea; but it is to transform it immediately into a place spacious enough to contain a village, a church, some gardens, an adjoining countryside, that is, a vast space, which, howevver, had contained, like the maximum in the minimum, an initial space most restricted.[26]

The greatest asset of a poet is his/her economy of language, and in the 'Mottetti' Montale has created single expressive units that act as semantic envoys of his abstract memory. In these wonderful, "musical" moments, there is subjective memory and experience aided by the objectification of his own states of mind. It is as if memory rediscovers itself in material objects, signs of an occult-like meaning between Montale and his dedicatee. Clair Huffman reminds us that "words are experience; a way of becoming conscious."[27]

Because of the nature of the *Occasioni*, as opposed to the nature of the preceding *Ossi*, the style needs to become as compact and terse as a distinct 'Mottetto,' in order to treat more economically the subject matter of memory and absence. Recreating the environment around himself, Montale is less inclined to use the "ansante e infruttuoso elenco di apparenze estratte dalla realtà"[28] and in the *Occasioni* even all that is actual nature "non è impressione ma allusione."[29] The world is intuited semiotically. The poem becomes the catalogued name for a moment; a tangible artifact of a past for which the poet previously lacked an appropriate linguistic symbol. Montale had not missed the moment previously, but until now, like Eliot in 'East Coker,' he did not have a language with which to record it:

Because one has only learnt to get the better of words / For the thing one no longer has to say, or the way in which / One is no longer disposed to say it.

But unlike Eliot, Montale has "learnt to get the better of words for the thing" which he clearly wants to express, while Eliot would perhaps "no longer [be] disposed to say it."

In the first motet, Montale refers immediately to the emptiness created without the presence of Clizia. He uses what could be deemed hermetic, or even abstract, terms to join the past and the present with regards to Clizia's past presence and her current absence. He uses the lost sign (vv. 10–11) which served as a pledge ('pegno,' v. 11) of grace or salvation. It is obscure and completely abstract, yet is has a particular designation; so specific in meaning to Montale that the sign served as a pledge then, the absence of which, now, guarantees his hell, his doom as clearly as it guaranteed salvation or grace in the original moment. It is as if he had a template of the original situation and one of the current situation; he superimposes one to the other and they are practically identical, except for the lost sign. He superpositions one moment on the other; as with a Proustian 'magic lantern', which projects cinematically an image on a wall; or, as Poulet states it, "The image and the wall appear simultaneously, the one under the other."[30] And that is enough for him to lose hope of seeing her again. In fact, one could argue that the original sign was no less fleeting and fragile as the contingency of the poetic moment. Montale's verb "riperdere" of 'Mottetto 1' calls to mind the very existential cycle illustrated in 'East Coker' by Eliot: "there is only the fight to recover what has been lost / and found and lost again and again." Montale frames memory less in terms of time, and more in terms of Proustian spatial positioning.

The "spiro salino" is essential to 'Mottetto 1,' as it pertains to Montale's work, in general, in a thematic way. This "salty breeze" seems particularly *à propos* to the intangible nature of memory, as climatic conditions such as wind and saline air are intangible and yet affect our senses in many ways. Memory is an abstract which creates a presence, which is, in its essence, not tangible; it is as much allusive as elusive. Though wind is a physical phenomena, it is completely and utterly invisible. One feels and sees its effects and yet one can never experience it visually per sé. The wind, here, is present as a motif of ineffable and fleeing memory and it also literally carries the salty attribute of the sea (of the *Ossi*) which strengthens the moment of epiphany for Montale: it brings the sea with it. It is a memento, as it were, synonymous with a souvenir, not unlike memory itself. As memory is a spatially projected remnant of experience, so is heavy, salty air a remnant of the sea, carried to a physically different place or time. It is as if the wind were an abstract subjective correlative that simultaneously inhabits both the physical and the metaphysical worlds, as does the poet in his mind. In a poem like "Noi non sappiamo qual sortiremo" (*Ossi*, 'Mediterraneo 6'), tradition carried on to posterity, Montale implies, is carried on wind (air); even the very words one speaks move through air, carried invisibly on its medium, much like the wind itself:

> ...*un poco del tuo dono / sia passato per sempre / nelle sillabe / che rechiamo con noi, api ronzanti. / Lontani andremo e serberemo un'eco / della tua voce, come si ricorda / del sole l'erba grigia / nelle corti scurite, tra le case. / E un giorno queste parole senza rumore / che teco educammo nutrite / di stanchezze e di silenzi, / parranno a un fraterno cuore / sapide di sale greco.*[31]

I cannot but help imaging the 'eco' which stands as a compliment to the air motif – an echo is a sound, which loses its force gradually, but does it truly disappear? Or, is the slow dissipation an indication that it never truly disappears? In theory, it may still be floating in space. This transcendence of time is akin to the "libeccio" of 'La casa dei doganieri' that is not *a* wind, but *this* specific wind that is the same wind which for years has been lashing the old walls of the house.[32] From the fragment, "altro tempo frastorna / la tua memoria" ('La casa dei doganieri'), one could surmise that wind is associated with time as a derogator of memory. Then, there is the image in 'Mottetto 2': "Imprimerli potessi sul palvese / che s'agita alla frusta del grecale in cuore." It is a painful image of memory, but more important is the notion of imprinting, fixing something into an object in constant motion.

'Mottetto 2' is predicated on the accumulation of years over time and the inability of memory to render these images to the poet in a concrete way. They are not concrete and Montale cares to imprint them upon an escutcheon or banner as visibly as a commonly recognizable image of Saint George and the dragon. But most of all he would even sacrifice himself like a chivalrous Saint George, fearlessly, if he could have an immutable faith like that of Clizia, who believes in the continuum of the material and the spiritual. Montale lacks the faith and sees all as a mere phenomenal illusion; not the world of Maya in a deep spiritual sense, but a world as hologram. He uses "immortale," in my estimation, not only to refer to faith as unchangeable and firm, but also immortal in the true sense: outside of linear time as mortals know it, into a world where past and future are irrelevant. It is one perpetual present where memory would be superfluous. Or perhaps memory is Montale's perpetual present.

In fact, it is the very nature of life in a sanatorium – 'Mottetto 2' – that is in a sense isolated or hidden as seen more explicitly in the poem 'Dopo una fuga' (*Satura*):

C'erano le betulle, folte, per nascondere / il sanatorio dove una malattia / per troppo amore della vita, in bilico / tra il tutto e il nulla si annoiava.

With solitude and separation from Clizia in the *Occasioni*, a general change from exteriors to interiors, as suggest by 'Il balcone,' the sanatorium of 'Mottetto 2,' which resembles that of 'Dopo una fuga,' is apt. After all, in the enclosure of a sanatorium, shut off from the outside world, all that remains is contact with the outside world through memory. Isolated within a world of memory, it is conceivable that one could be "in bilico / tra il tutto e il nulla"

('Dopo una fuga'). It is precisely this state that lends meaning to the *Occasioni*. Meaning in the world of absence and separation causes Montale to turn inwards, to memory; a subjective world where there is absence ("nulla") or presence ("tutto") through memory, and in order to pertain to the objective world he is forced to live "in bilico."

In terms of the world of memory outside of time, there is the 'Mottetto 3,' 'Brina sui vetri.' Within the theme of the sanatorium, the "brina" ("frost") calls to mind the fog of memory present in 'Mottetto 18.' This time the separation is not only one of distance but it is within an interior, and even the minimal communication is fogged or frosted. Isella speaks of the mountain sanatorium where "la vita in comune acuisce l'incomunicazione. Sospeso il tempo, assente in tutta la quartina anche come categoria verbale."[33]

Much as memory already implies a separation – that of a present-become-past and the present – the panes of glass in a window offer a barrier for the interior world separated from the exterior. The fog of memory implies a more profound sense of separation in time – literally a fading of the image, albeit in the medium of memory – and the hoar on the physical barrier of interior and exterior makes the pain of separation worse in the insecurity of blindness.

The beauty of the poem hinges on the card game motif. Montale employs literal and figurative meanings of the cards to create an integral subjective correlative for the actual past experience, a metaphor for that experience and then a correlative as motivation in the present for the flash of memory. In the seminal moment from the past, the cards represented a physical experience but they were figurative in terms of the chance involved; that salvific moment. How would Clizia escape a closed-in, uncommunicative, melancholic existence of the sanatorium? This makes him see the parallel of contingency in his own experience: survival on the war front.

In the present Montale fixes on a card and from that instant he immediately thinks of Clizia's cards (perhaps haruspicate) in the sanatorium which triggers the association with his own past travails. And at the same time the feeling of no communication and despair in the present mimics that of the past. Both are conjoined in the last couplet, and this is based on his delineation of poetic time in the verses as opposed to real time. In memory, a remote past can seem like just one moment ago, and the present is separated from the past only by the time it takes for something, anything, to allow the poet to leave the active present to access the past.

This process functions on two parallels in 'Mottetto 3.' On one level, Montale sets up a pre-memory in the *passato remoto*. The present card is a semantic link to her past. From the poet's present point of view, her past motivates his return to his own past in a parallel plane of time. Now, Montale places himself in a more recent past where something recalled would be described not by a *remoto* but by a *prossimo*. He concludes in the memory, as he does now, that this is not her fate. He seems to be unknowingly rejecting Eliot's notion of all time being "unredeemable" ('Burnt Norton,' 1.15). He revisits the past in such a way as to give new meaning to his present and also to his past, as if time were a mere angular perspective rather than a physical law.

'Mottetto 3' ends with: "È scorsa un'ala rude, t'ha sfiorato le mani, / ma invano: la tua carta non è questa." One would conclude it is one of the cards from "lunghi soliloqui" and the very card he has in front of him. It is *this* card ("Questa") in the present moment, as well as in the past. Figuratively, this card refers to the destiny predicted in tarot cards; physically this card refers to the games one plays to pass time in solitude.

Unlike Eliot, Montale finds time redeemable, given that, for the latter, time is purely relative; a construct of convenience for ordering spatial events in a digestible way. For Eliot, as well, there is "sudden illumination – / We had the experience but missed the meaning" ('Dry Salvages,' 2. 44–45). However, Montale's sudden illumination is the "harsh wing" ("È scorsa un'ala rude," ('Mottetto 3')), which offers him understanding; renders present and past as an interconnected moment. It is an understanding of the meaning which he had missed in the original experience. He gazes back on this poetic moment, in which he says that "this card is not yours." Needless to say, Montale might disagree with Eliot that "time is no healer" ('Dry Salvages,' 3. 8).

'Mottetto 4,' 'Lontano, ero con te,' once again, revisits the meaning Montale may have missed in the past. And in this rejoining of the past it may be,

> *possibile intravedere una realtà diversa o una diversa disposizione della realtà, di afferrare un senso, un rapporto imprevisto e imprevidibile. Istanti solenni, cui è da attribuire, per la loro pregnanza un significato religioso, capaci di conferire all'effimero, riscattandolo, sembianza di eterno.*[34]

This is, in fact, one of the closest definitions of memory itself that one could give. From the solemn moments we may assign semantic value to one's past. These semantic values can be carried forward even into a present and into the future, much as language moves along:

> *Lontano, ero con te quando tuo padre / entrò nell'ombra e ti lasciò il suo addio. / Che seppi fino allora? Il logorío / di prima mi salvò solo per questo: // che t'ignoravo e non dovevo: ai colpi / d'oggi lo so, se di*

laggiú s'inflette / un'ora e mi riporta Cumerlotti / o Anghébeni – tra scoppi di spolette / e i lamenti e l'accorrer delle squadre.

Only in the present could Montale look back and speak in relative terms of that which was unknown to him in a past situation. Only now, looking back, does he see greater meanings in his experience on the front with the 158th regiment. He could not have realized that Clizia's and his destiny had been on similar paths until he re-examined his past. Exploring the meanings of the current crisis – that of mourning Clizia's father – he existentially questions what universal plan could have preserved him presciently, for this pain. He almost 'images' the pre-recorded hologram of life as providing an artistic creator with an artistic predestination that appears to him as memory. This and that pain, or "logorío," are established as implied demonstrations based on the word "prima" from verse four which allows the reader to infer a before and an after. The "questo" of verse four further implies a "quello" (that one). Pain and anguish of the moment, create a flash of memory; that of his anguish and pain from another time. The reader may wonder why he does not think of Clizia (in a moment when she was with him) or even of his own relative whom he had possibly already mourned. It is a question of resultant and not categorical memory, for as Hartnack – in his essays on Wittgenstein – says: "There is no difference between the two statements: 'It is the same sensation that I had before' and 'It is not the same sensation I had before.'"[35] Therefore, the similar sensation he feels does not necessarily bring him to a memory of a similar event, but of a similar sensation; the sensation being within the rhyme of "squadre" and "padre" that solidifies "la fine col principio, la minaccia della morte con la sua presenza."[36] Returning to the separation, isolation and anguish of the war – the connection he makes to this sensation – he concludes that Clizia was with him even before he knew it. They had coexisted in a spatial plane, regardless of time, as if they existed in two overlapping film projections. Now it seems that she was with him before he had even met her. She had to have been there at the front, for what else could have kept him alive, preserved him, for a moment such as this, painful and yet seemingly futile in the scheme of things?

The line "ai colpi / d'oggi lo so" pulls the reader into the poetic-mnemonic present typical of Montale where spatial and chronological parameters come together to place the reader simultaneously in the past and the present. The word "colpi" plays a double role in this matter and it becomes the link for both poetic moments. With the semantic value of the implication of "colpi" there is a link with which to put the presence of a past into the current void. The link connects Montale to that which is separated from him by three thousand miles, and to that which occurred over 20 years earlier. It is as if Montale edited the predestined film of his life to make the two moments sequentially, and spatially, connected.

Without Clizia as his salvific, guardian angel, unbeknownst to him at that time, he would not have been "saved for this." But being "saved for this" forces him to make an extrasensorial connection between the two moments: the connection between that salvific force and Clizia. Memory has served as a filmic montage, creating presence in his current sense of absence, but it has given new meaning to the past. Through memory, Montale has edited time, rendering it redeemable. He has got the "better of words" to express something, it seemed, he may have no longer wanted to say – because of that very semantic/linguistic crisis – and he becomes 'disposed' once again to say it. He has added his latest motif to the void of experience both in memory and in the present. Perhaps here, more than in other poems, he has maintained his promise from 'Il balcone': he has added a unit of linguistic expression-presence to a linguistic locus that had been previously empty. He has also edited presence into an absence. In the visual locus of the mind, he has stimulated his photoreceptors to react, thereby projecting the same experience into the present: it is not a memory but the same exact moment.

The line "ti ignoravo e non dovevo" is most interesting. He was unaware of Clizia's identity, and should not have been ("I did not know you but should have" (trans. mine)). But poetically he was unaware then of all the things that she represents now. Having been introduced to her, he can look back and say that he did not recognize faith and hope in a time of crisis or war, but he should have, if he had been more like Clizia. It is a circular logic that wholly depends on the function of memory. The fact that he was saved from the war for this, "questo," is evidence of this. He was ignorant because he was not supplied with the correct semantic language to deal with it, and yet he feels that he was remiss in not conjoining meaning to experience. Now, since his meeting with Clizia, with all that he attributes to her, she becomes the perfect semantic word (in a stilnovistic way) for all that then was unknown to him. It seemed that all "le ansie e i rischi della sua ['of his', speaking of himself in the third person, as "Mirco," one of his poetic alter egos] vita trascorsa convergessero verso quella Clizia allora ignota."[37] Everything prior to meeting Clizia seemed to converge on the very same Clizia, unknown to him then. Though he did not perceive her presence next to him during the war, she was physically there. He should have possessed her qualities. Thus, syllogistically, he should have been aware of her, known her.

'Mottetto 5' is the pre-"schermo d'immagini" 'Mottetto,'[38] in the sense that it comes directly before 'Mottetto 6,' "La speranza di pure rivederti" in the structure of the 20 'Mottetti':

> *Addii, fischi nel buio, cenni, tosse / e sportelli abbassati. È l'ora. Forse / gli automi hanno ragione. Come appaiono / dai corridoi, murati! //* .... *// – Presti anche tu alla fioca / litania del tuo rapido quest'orrida / e fedele cadenza di carioca?*

The first two lines introduce the classic Montalian *elenco di cose*. Then he claims "È l'ora" ("Now is the time"). For what? For whom? Perhaps now seems like the time when Clizia herself departed, and these images act like a simultaneous recollection, or correlative, for the sentiment he felt under those conditions; the correlative which stimulates his optic nerves to produce the same presence, which he perceives as memory. Within four lines he is already immersed in a spontaneous, yet familiar, dialogue with Clizia. Mengaldo, speaking of the bipartition created with the ellipses, postulates a "risoluzione *ex silentio* delle possibili mediazioni tra i due momenti esistenziali."[39] It might be given motivation or explanation in the poetic sense, but it is not resolved in terms of Montale's overall crisis. Observing him lapse into a personal dialogue with a Clizia who is absent, the reader may postulate that he has either brought her to the present from the past, or he has momentarily left the present to go to the past. Yet, perhaps he has edited the two spatial moments so that they overlap. In either case the current situation at the train station is the fulcrum of the two experiences. The lack of resolve here is in his inability to simply look objectively, to simply observe his environment. He knows that the world is phenomenal, so he chooses his own illusions to project on to the void.

He is not the other people – "gli automi" – nor does he associate himself with them. However, given the separation, or exclusion, he wonders if the automatons may be correct in lending themselves to the brutal monotony of the objectified, albeit phenomenal, world. Montale implies this in the dialogue in which he asks Clizia if she also lends herself to it. And this is why Montale cannot simply observe 'reality' or experience memory: he wants to see these things objectively, but he is inevitably drawn into personalizing the experience of the screen of images, wondering if it is the semantic value that will invariably and always represent that particular past experience, much like Funes. Only Funes catalogues the world as it unfolds. For Montale, all has already been imprinted for him to neoplatonically recollect, or edit, in a proper sequence. They – "gli automi" – may be right because they do not separate themselves from the world of images of which they are equal parts or members. Montale does not see himself as one of the images in the list or on the screen. Instead he excludes himself from them, assuming he can find his essential alphabet in them. But, Martelli proposes,

> *non fa forse l'uomo parte integrante di quello stesso mondo che vorrebbe conoscere oggettivamente? ...Una conoscenza oggettiva può essere ritenuta possibile solo partendo da una concezione dualistica dell'uomo, ammettendo cioè che l'uomo sia costituito da un corpo, appartenente alla terra, e da un'anima che, distinta dal corpo ed eterna, si sollevi al di sopra del mondo.*[40]

In this detachment Montale sees the world also subjectively, but he cannot find it impossible to ask a question to a dedicatee three thousand miles away. He does not wonder if "she" is acting like these "automi"; rather he asks her directly: "do you?"

In other words, he is not "walled-in" like the other men, albeit separated from Clizia. In fact the rhyme "abbassati/murati" is a connection of two images: lowered and closed in. These two images are the antitheses of Clizia when we consider lowered to also figuratively mean terrestrial, and closed in is the opposite of her detached, ethereal spirituality. But, if she is how Montale describes her, she cannot pertain to the phenomenal world of illusion. She lives beyond them, in the void, able to project herself into any conceivable moment as if through a secret corridor of time – perhaps, a worm-hole of time. The train station is a perfect subjective correlative for his memory. He remembers Clizia by observing the objects, as if they were syneddoche of her whole; mere points in a union of virtual overlap. The objects in the poem serve to evoke the memory of Clizia in terms of acting as a correlative for his subjective separation from not just Clizia, but the other women in his life. Yet, they do not evoke memory; rather they reveal a spatial continuum. Montale's poetry is the very idiolect composed by the "essential alphabet" of the present for a greater understanding of his past. His poetry is bound to its own time through which he revisits and assigns more precise words and meanings to the experiences he has undergone.

Perhaps, however, it is not the present train station which causes him to ask Clizia in the present – wherever she is – if she pertains to those men (cf. also "di quella razza che rimane a terra" ('Falsetto')) who lend themselves to the "carioca." Instead it may be literally what he said to her in that situation. Yet, in either case, it is precisely the timeless world of Montale that creates poetic time which can be revisited; and the past can address the present and the present can address the past interchangeably. Presence is always a memory away: because of his phenomenalist view of the world he is no more a part of the present than he is of the past. The use of suspending ellipses dramatizes that there is a separation between two moments. Yet, the fact that these moments do not appear incongruous testifies to the timelessness that can only exist in memory or in poetry itself. Ironically, memory exists precisely as a process of time, so in Montale's poems, time does not exist; rather there is pure presence – suspended animation of a spatial juxtaposition. Hence the dual world of real (cosmic) time and poetic (memorial) time.

The "automi" suggest habitual regularity as if this particular scene were now as it was then, when Clizia left. Because of its unchangeability the scene is simultaneously a metaphor of memory, as well as a report of memory itself. Perhaps this query, offset by ellipses, is what he had not thought to ask her then, but does now. It goes for here, where Montale is, as it does for there, where Clizia is: the poet questions whether Clizia is one of the "automi" or not. It is relevant as a redeemable moment in time, redeemed through memory and as a carry-over of the angelic, salvific presence from 'Mottetto 6': perhaps Montale experiences her as if she were physically there. Her presence is acknowledged through a flash, and thus she is there. He does not experience a flash of memory but an illumination which causes a latent image on the film of life to become visible.

More interesting is the aspect of the "correlativo soggettivo" as defined by Bigongiari. The *elenco* of the so-called "schermo d'immagini" appears in the first stanza, suggesting an objective stylization of emotions as seen in Antonioni films where the landscape becomes an extension of the inner world of his characters' minds and the director relies upon objects that have a particular emotional value for the character. The objects in the first stanza of 'Mottetto 5' create an image that suggests a general feeling of departure; an ordinary enough situation, objectively speaking:

Addii, fischi nel buio, cenni, tosse / e sportelli abbassati. È l'ora. Forse / gli automi hanno ragione. Come appaiono / dai corridoi, murati!

Then there is a pause, through the use of ellipses, as if to say that this is how the objective, phenomenal world functions, and one realizes – by the second stanza – that the "automi" are designed as a contrast to Montale's very personal, subjective view. (He is not, by virtue of the implicit contrast in the statement, one of them.) He completely refuses to make this objective view a symbol for his own metaphysics. Regarding this, Galassi examines Montale's demeanour, referring to how his:

disdain for "men who don't look back ('Forse un mattino andando')" or for the "other shadows" of 'Ti libero la fronte' intensifies through his career. Humanity is divided into two categories: the small circle of those who feel (and suffer) and the rest, who are not truly alive.[41]

Perhaps those who look back are also those who have a special sensitivity for the past, and an intuition that there is a more real reality behind the film projected on the phenomenal world.

The first line of 'Mottetto 6' automatically creates poetic tension and personal strife between the disconcerting image of the future and the sure image of the past, which, at best is only an image in a memory:

La speranza di pure rivederti / m'abbandonava; // e mi chiesi se questo che mi chiude / ogni senso di te, schermo d'immagini, / ha i segni della morte o dal passato / è in esso, ma distorto e fatto labile, / un tuo barbaglio: // (a Modena, tra i portici, / un servo gallonato trascinava / due sciacalli al guinzaglio).

The verbal tenses proffer a present subject looking back to a past moment in which he was summoning the past, for the future (or at least his present situation) was uncertain. The poem, now, becomes the artifact of the past, and yet in the present it fills what would otherwise be a void. But even in the original moment of this experience, Montale questions if in the seeming void of Clizia's absence she was not present, for in the illusory world of phenomena, an absence may be hiding a truer presence. Even Montale did not know if the screen of images around him projected a vision of the past, a death vision of her future, or a current hallucination. The very confusion is interesting in this respect. One might argue that the image in memory of her is strong enough to make him question his senses, but the form and content become fused in the fact that it is clearly this type of unnerving doubt that motivated him to feel his hope fleeing him, a hope in yet seeing her still.

Intratextually speaking, the "segni" (signs) of verse five bring us back to the first motet. In that one, the lack of a sign, or a pledge, was a sure indicator of the lack of hope. The only certain conclusion in the situation mirrors the one concrete, indisputable fact of living; that of inevitably dying in the entropy[42] of the universe. Now, in 'Mottetto 6,' the very presence of a sign is a possible signal of death, or maybe something more – it is hard for Montale to discern. Words such as "distorto" and "labile" and the "speranza" that was fleeing him (in the imperfect tense) represent a time that is never still and for which perhaps a static expression would be ill-suited. This moment, from the point of view of feeling and from the point of view of some sort of semantic sign, exemplifies the argument of turning back time to redeem it with the reflection of the present which produces a more apt expression of it. To live time without memory is to live without hope, for the distance that separates the present from a past is logically what separates this moment from a future when the past will look back on it as a past. The very possibility of future is proven by the presence of the past. The perspective of the poet, both as an individual and as poet, depends on his memory. Otherwise his experience will belong to the moments in which "piú dolorosa si avverte l'impossibilità di un'espressione assoluta."[43] In *Farfalla di Dinard*, an "absolute expression" becomes the eternal cross-correlated images of the perfect artistic creation: the film of all lives.

'Mottetto 7' address the thematics of separation. The actual topos of the station ("scalo") is the place to which one arrives or from which one departs. Perhaps Clizia has left for good, perhaps she will return, but certainly she is not present with the poet physically. The idea of this separation is quintessential *Occasioni* material. Further, the structure of the stanzas, which divides existential moments, is typical of the 'Mottetti,' especially 'Mottetto 5' ('Addii, fischi nel buio') which is, incidentally, also set in a railway station:

Il saliscendi bianco e nero dei / balestrucci dal palo / del telegrafo al mare / non conforta i tuoi crucci su lo scalo / né ti riporta dove piú non sei. // Già profuma il sambuco fitto su / lo sterrato; il piovasco si dilegua. / Se il chiarore è una tregua, la tua cara minaccia la consuma.

Obviously, Montale finds himself in a "scalo," or station, which is implied, as Isella observes, by the use of elder bushes as landscaping along railway tracks,[44] though it could be a pier for embarking on a ship. But more important is the image of the swallows. The rhythmic flight of the swallows, now exposing their white undersection, now diving and swirling, revealing their dark upper section, must have been a terrific image. Beyond that, its utility as an image of beauty is short lived, for the journey of the flock of swallows from the pole to the sea immediately reminds him of Clizia: the alternation of light from dark to white on the swallows stimulates his optical senses to produce her there.

Hence the first strophe serves him as the flash of memory, which will reveal the "crucci" that are on her mind. But the second strophe serves as a correlative of the content of his mind. In fact the very structure and syntax of the verses link together form and content. Speaking of the rhyme and meter of the poem, Isella notes a timbric richness "che esalta la felicità ritmica, sottolineata anche dalla esposizione in rima tronca delle preposizioni (sull'orlo del verso iniziale di ciascuna strofa, senza l'appoggio del nome). Senonché la prima ha suono squillante, chiaro; l'altra, chiude la curva del mottetto, cupa."[45]

The outside world suddenly sets off the *scatto* of memory in the first stanza. But the scene does not comfort Clizia's agitation. That is, it does not bring her back to where she is not ("dove piú non sei"). Where she is not is physically at the station. The second stanza comments on his emotion resulting from the net process of the external world affecting him as a trigger of visual imagery – here, experienced as memory. From exteriors the poet turns to interiors. Yet, here the external does not affect his interior; rather it is a correlative of it.

The first image is the perfumed scent of an elder bush. Already, the image is one of an invisible, intangible element which affects the poet, and that could be a description of memory as well. His olfactory awareness heightens because a storm has cleared, and he is granted a moment of "chiarore." (Only in a moment of truce could his senses of sight and sound be given a reprieve long enough to concentrate on a subtle, simple aroma.) But this reprieve for the poet to appreciate mundane pleasures has an ephemeral duration; it will last only until the storm interrupts it. His thinking of her absence creates new agitations that do not comfort and they threaten this peace: "Se il chiarore è una tregua, / la tua cara minaccia la consuma." Perhaps, once again, he lives in memory as the rule, and moments in which Clizia's threat (maybe even a threat she had made upon having to leave Italy due to the antisemitic racial campaigns) does not consume that moment of repose are the exceptions: "ma il pensiero dell'assente consuma, «cara minaccia,» l'istante di eccezione."[46] As such, once again, Montale resounds Borges' line "Sólo una cosa no hay. Es el olvido," from 'Everness.' Looking retrospectively from *Farfalla di Dinard*, I believe Montale does not live in memory (as a rule) but in the noumenal void behind the phenomenal world.

A similar theme is exposed in a later poem of the *Bufera* cycle, 'Su una lettera non scritta.' To bettter appreciate this work, it is important to recall how the *Occasioni* are presented differently from the *Bufera*. Zampa explains that the "*Occasioni* sono dunque gli istanti fatali dell'esistenza, quando in un baleno è possibile intravedere una realtà diversa o una diversa disposizione della realtà, di afferare un senso, un rapporto imprevisto e imprevidibile."[47] In "Il saliscendi bianco e nero" the moment is an exception. The poet is not provided the luxury of seeing the world objectively, rather the objects and phenomena around him are not afforded the privilege of Eliot's roses which have the look of roses being watched. The external world, or "schermo d'immagini," causes his introversion into memory, and thus becomes his subjective correlative. In 'Su una lettera non scritta,' one perceives the change in Montale who becomes more extroverted where his poetry is less concluded in himself and more in a universal offering to a participating audience. In fact, his senhals and memory become actual tools for greater, more objective discourses, as seen in 'L'anguilla' where past allusions in his poetry are not used to examine the past but are brought into an active view of the contingency of current events. They are more effective because they are charged with the past and recycled semantic value. In the words of Rodowick, "a sign acquires meaning only through its interpretation in another sign and so on ad infinitum. Of course, this is in keeping with Deleuze's own philosophy: 'The present designates the most contracted degree of an entire past, which is itself like a coexisting totality'."[48]

The lines "Oh che io non oda / nulla di te, ch'io fugga dal bagliore / dei tuoi cigli. Ben altro è sulla terra" ('Su una lettera non scritta') give the reader an indication that the poet does not want a "cara minaccia" to affect his current view of the world around him. "Il ricordo-assenza della donna è un aspetto della negatività del presente."[49] He wishes himself a life where the present, objective world is the norm, and the memories that would consume that world are only the exception and not the norm of the *Occasioni*. Greco makes a comment about two poems from the *Occasioni* and the *Bufera*, respectively, on this: "In 'La speranza di pure rivederti,' la realtà valeva solo come schermo d'immagini, qui ['Su una lettera non scritta'] nonostante l'assenza della donna, il poeta non rimane indifferente di fronte alla vita."[50]

Earlier, in the *Ossi*, complete images of introversion spoke of disappearing as the adventure of adventures ('Portami il girasole'), but even elsewhere in the *Ossi* one sees precursors of Montale's inversion into the mind in the *Occasioni*. In 'Casa sul mare' he ponders negating the external, phenomenal reality of the world to reside in the intimate chasms of his memories, as if they were the real noumenos: "Tu chiedi se cosí tutto vanisce / in questa poca nebbia di memorie; / se nell'ora che torpe o nel sospiro / del frangente si compie ogni destino." He wonders if one locus can preserve infinite spatial projections in memory even as the phenomenal world dissolves in the 'now', a word which Cortázar calls a lie in 'Las babas del diablo': "qué palabra, *ahora*, qué éstupida mentira."[51] Montale realizes he must abdicate ("cedere"); he is not as strong as others of Esterina's proportion who can exist in the now. He takes nature's indifference personally, rather than being indifferent to its illusions. Esterina, or perhaps even Clizia, would have had a lasting "tregua" during which to enjoy the elder perfume after the squall. The poet cannot cannot enjoy the present, either convinced of its fiction or absorbed in the plane of memory which precludes him from the present. Memory is the "cara minaccia" to the present.

This "sweet threat" implies that memory is bittersweet; that it threatens the complacency of the here and now, forbidding Montale from resigning himself to the world of phenomena. The threat ushers in the presence of someone, a woman, who would normally not physically be there. She is welcome, then, but also unwelcome. She is a reflection of the noumenal world – the predestined memory – which he can only glimpse as syneddoche through his fog of memory. 'Mottetto 8,' is a clear example:

Ecco il segno; s'innerva / sul muro che s'indora: / un frastaglio di palma / bruciato dai barbagli dell'aurora. // Il passo che proviene / dalla serra sí lieve, / non è felpato dalla neve, è ancora / tua vita, sangue tuo nelle mie vene.

Clearly 'Mottetto 8' makes a reference back to the first of the series with a hint at the motif of the sign. One finally gets close to a concrete, externally existing, free-standing description. It would seem a flash of subconscious memory in the abstract mental image which meets its corollary in the external world. It is finally something Montale's reader can physically examine. For a moment, the real world behind the projection is representable through his "existential alphabet"; in their particular juxtaposition in the landscape the letters form the image of the sign. "For once the epiphany coincides immediately with its occasion, and the poet knows a fulfillment."[52] The letters are innerved on the wall as if a cinematic projection which is part of the wall as much as it moves over its surface. The wall is guilded by this and by the "crenellation" ("frastaglio") of the palm frond, and the dazzlingness of dawn adds a notion of an epiphanic reality. Light has written an image as if in a Proustian hologram: "What will the Proustian novel be...if not an immense landscape whose turning light makes successively multiple aspects appear?"[53]

All of these letters of his existential alphabet have spelled out perfectly the sign. In 'Vasca' there is an unrealized, unrecognized sign, which was "born and died and never had a name." Here, the unnamed *it* is recognized and has a name. In Montale's visually experiencing his sign, Montale's environment has confirmed that Clizia was present all along in the infinite layering of phenomenal imagery. "As in a dream when a presence that has come from the profound depths of memory somehow remains and makes itself known and is wonderfully transformed into something completely unexpected,"[54] here the sign made itself identifiable under the form of an unexpected juxtaposition from the "schermo d'immagini." The possibilities are many: (1) the object motivated the flash of memory; (2) the object is a visual marker for the memory (as with Funes); (3) the eternal noumenal world behind the projection revealed itself; (4) his memory is a reflection of the platonic noumenos, where all is written, or inscribed, before time. In the last case, a memory would be a re-collection of true reality. In any of the cases, "the coincidence of a certain, actual sensation and a certain former sensation determines a raising up of memories."[55] This phenomenal screen of images would seem a juxtaposition, but the noumenal world is one complete void with infinitely 'superposited' images: "Superposition requires the disappearance of the one so that the appearance of the other may take place."[56] But in Montale's holographic cinema, there can be simultaneity, which causes interference. This explains why, to the poet, the presence of Clizia is rather sporadic or intermittent.

If Montale is predisposed enough and obsessed enough, his searching for a sign to confirm that Clizia accompanies him in a noumenos transcendent to the phenomenal. He is akin to Antonio in Calvino's 'L'avventura d'un fotografo.' Antonio seeks a remnant of presence, constantly pondering when, or what, to photograph: the photographic remnant is a presence that indicates an absence. When does the landscape coincide with the disposition of the photographer? "Per fotografare quanto piú si può bisogna: o vivere in modo quanto piú fotografabile possibile, oppure considerare fotografabile ogni momento della propria vita. La prima via porta alla stupidità, la seconda alla pazzia."[57] Galassi mentions how experience and meaning have coalesced here: "The lost sign of the first motet is now dazzlingly present: in an intimation from nature."[58] But is it an intimation from himself or from nature, ultimately? Is he considering every aspect of every moment of life as conceivable material for acknowledging Clizia's presence in the void? Or does he, *a priori*, have a set idea of what that sign should look like while setting out to find it? Like Calvino's Antonio, Montale questions whether to frequent significant landscapes where the occasions would be likely to occur, and also if such places exist. The answer is that there is no one sign or expression that corresponds *a priori* to affirm that Clizia – though physically a continent away – is somehow not entirely absent. In this particular instance, the world may have aligned itself perfectly to give an external form to the abstract, ineffable image of what he remembers of her. Or, perhaps the poet, who can only briefly glimpse the noumenal void behind the screen of images, does not see Clizia's true presence for what it is. "Ecco" is an exclamation connoting recognition of someone's, or something's, location. The possibility of this one miraculous moment has always been there, but only as a possibility; not a reality. For the Montale of 'Sul limite' (*Farfalla di Dinard*), the possibility was not there eternally: the moment itself had been eternally stamped before time; the only hint of chance is that his visual field managed to discern a layer of the noumenos underneath the phenomenal projection, thereby separating the projection from the screen onto which it is visualized.

Perhaps Montale, like Eliot, is "forced" posits David Spurr, "to devise means of approaching discursively what his visionary imagination creates intuitively, the idea of language itself as the primary weapon of the intellect comes under increasing attack..."[59] The language of Montale's poetry manifests the noumenal world through the tools of the phenomenal. The "signs of art," in Montale's works are like those in Proust's, which "force him to think: they mobilize pure thought as a faculty of essences."[60]

But existing language and external images can help Montale to put certain things into perspective even if only for himself. From the *Occasioni* onwards landscape is not a primary impetus as with the landscape of the Romantics, which is a "description of outer landscape [which] leads to an inner process of memory, vision, or reflection... [where] the speaker then returns to the outer scene with renewed perception resulting from his meditative experience."[61] Montale's external experience could very well be a manifestation of his internal visual perception in the photo-electric impulses of his mind.

Is it a step from the greenhouse in 'Mottetto 8' that Montale imagines because he can hear his own heart beating, or is it a real step that he tries to explain as somehow pertaining to him? Is this sign, then, the "punto dilatato?" That is to say, is the one sign a doorway which, once crossed, leads to infinitely expandable connections. Each of his poems represents a particular duration of experience: duration is neither linear nor chronological. Rather, it presumes at each instant an unceasing opening onto an indeterminate future. One can read 'Mottetto 9' with linear duration, but what Montale describes therein is the pure potential for a moment which exists outside of time, outside of human perception:

Il ramarro, se scocca / sotto la grande fersa / dalle stoppie – // la vela, quando fiotta / e s'inabissa al salto della rocca – // il cannone di mezzodí / piú fioco del tuo cuore / e il cronometro se scatta senza rumore – // . . . . // e poi? Luce di lampo / invano può mutarvi in alcunché / di ricco e strano. Altro era il tuo stampo.

In saying what she is not, Montale acknowledges the poverty of images. Nothing on the screen speaks to him of Clizia's true presence. In not recognizing her there, Montale relies on a recollection of her essence. He has a distinctly pathological, ingrained notion of who she is and what can be associated with her, and the distance between the screen of images and the void behind it is memory itself. He employs the imperfect "era" to establish a past conception in contrast with the present motif. He imposes the distance cinematically.

Because Clizia is not present, Montale relies on his memory to place her in his present world. As personal memory, the images – and all that is connected with them – are greatly internalized so that, in a way, the only Clizia he now knows is the one he carves within himself. He can only be with her in his memory of her; a memory so much a part of him that the sound of footsteps in the snow and that of his heartbeat are nearly indistinguishable. His heartbeat is a cue which motivates him to imagine another possible source of the sound. Or, rapt in the epiphany of the moment of this sign on the wall, Montale may realize that he hears not the cadence of footsteps in the snow, but his heart greatly excited and leaping up. Perhaps, then, the image of the burning and the palm frond were so symbolically tied to her in his memory that he had truly felt her presence and reacted accordingly with coursing blood.

The rhyming connection of "cuore/rumore" (heart/noise) is clear in 'Mottetto 9.' Yet in that stanza Montale merely says what her heart is not. The poet compares the heart to the sound of a noon cannon going off, but is it to make a correlation between Clizia's heart, or does he merely use the imperceptible beat of a heart to highlight just how far off and muffled the sound of the cannon was? In this particular poetic scene her heart is not the noon cannon – it is stronger. Nor is it the stopwatch – it is too quiet. Clizia is also not even the light of a "lampo" which "cannot change you into something rich and strange" – she is of a totally different mettle. This "lampo" motif is also interesting to the reader, because in the next 'Mottetto,' Clizia is the "folgore" ("lightening") that may or may not "leave her cloud." With his senses so heightened and aware of even the most minimal movement and sound, the poet is ready to accept an epiphany of Clizia, but it is not something the poet can force, like a Proustian memory, and he leaves off without saying what her heart is like, only indicating that its corollary is not here: "altro era il tuo stampo." The exact timbric sound was produced by falling footsteps in the snow in 'Mottetto 8,' but here if Clizia is present the poet is not fulfilled in individuating her.

One could argue that the poet misattributes the source. He cannot see Clizia eternally there in an infinitely dilatable point of a world-brain, or brain as hologram: pure essence, not momentary presence. In 'Sulla spiaggia' (*Farfalla di Dinard*), the poet insinuates an infinity of perspective that comprise the continuum of the world as memory. He is unaware that another character (Anactoria) has a memory of him, and, though it exists unbeknownst to him, it is another point in the holographic world-brain. Then it is in that point in his mind – the "punto dilatato" – that is not truly a physical point. It is an abstract concept used purely as a reference: "[*Farfalla di Dinard*] ci offre la situazione inversa: la memoria ch'è viva nell'altro e non nell'io...la scoperta, infine, che il passato non solo è reale, ma plurimo."[62] If this is the case, it means that each of these moments is unjoinable to time but coexists spatially as if in a hologram. It is an arbitrary location for the storage of that memory that only truly becomes a point – if at all – the moment of the evocation, or dilation. In 'Mottetto 10' there seems to be a "punto che ti chiude":

> *Perché tardi? Nel pino lo scoiattolo / batte la coda a torcia sulla scorza. / La mezzaluna scende col suo picco / nel sole che la smorza. È giorno fatto. // A un soffio il pigro fumo trasalisce, / si difende nel punto che ti chiude. / Nulla finisce, o tutto, se tu fólgore / lasci la nube.*

To this curiosity I refer to Montale's own thoughts on this in a letter to Bobi Bazlen:

> *A me succede spesso (e spesso volontariamente) di essere equivoco in questo modo. P. es. nel mottetto della donna che sta per uscire dalla nuvola [Perché tardi? Nel pino lo scoiattolo...]: «A un soffio il pigro fumo... (?) / si difende nel punto che ti chiude» ...è chiaro che 'nel punto' [v.6] può avere due sensi: nel momento che e nel luogo che, tutti e due legittimi. Per Landolfi questo dubbio è orrendo; per me è una ricchezza. Certo, in questo caso l'equivoco è inconscio, spontaneo; nel caso del teatro è un po' cercato.*[63]

Whether it is at the moment or in the place, how does a moment-place-point cover her? How does it hold her in? Is it a reference to the "punto dilatato?" Perhaps the very self-professed uncertainty of the poem, which is the artefact of the experience, is a reflection of the whole experience. Thus, it would not be a physical point that contains her but a visual external object-event that calls her to his mind; the *scatto di memoria*. In this sense it contains her figuratively. That point becomes the poetry itself in 'Mottetto 8' and 'Mottetto 9': it figuratively encloses her. In 'Mottetto 10,' however, it is just possible that, beyond the figurative sense of his carrying her with him in memory, she is present in the most metaphysical of ways. In 'Mottetto 4' Montale made the connection between all he should have recognized before he met her, and that which, upon looking back after having met her, becomes more significant in retrospect. He sees the world as infinitely editable film footage, shot once and for all. He did not know her because he read the holographic photograms in time-dependent succession. Behind the human world of visual perception, in the void, he will understand that they both occupied the same plane as two superposed images on it. In the *Ossi* he was waiting for a break in the net or a gap in the stone wall, but he was alone in this and the possibility of a miracle seemed more like an exercise in futility. Here, her presence – like an angelic figure – gives him comfort. He is not alone and she is with him, even if her image is visually latent, unilluminated.

However, the poet is earthbound and bound by the only world he knows: the phenomenal. Through the association of memory to external objects he recreates her presence in the absence. Then he logically concludes that perhaps other times, previously, when she seemed absent, she was there – as a representation of all the concepts associated with her (cf. 'Mottetto 4') or as a sort of angel watching over him, or as the faith or beliefs that he should have had. When existence is so tenuous, when it is based on perception, when no thing is more sure or objective than the next – in reality or in memory – there may be no sense of finality. If the customs house of 'La casa dei doganieri' could have meant so much to him, but nearly nothing to Arletta, how strong, or real, was its existence? Montale will never find the truth for which he was looking in the *Ossi*, but in the *Occasioni*, specifically the 'Mottetti,' he believes in the need to search nonetheless. In the search he finds external connections that he associates to his memories of her until she is present. The testament to memory in this poem is not a mention of the past, but that she is present enough for him to ask her in the present tense why she delays. Memory is but recollection of the predestined film of life. This is a completely analogous situation to 'Mottetto 5,' "Addii, fischi nel buio," where presence and absence are one and the same.

In 'Mottetto 12,' there is the continuation of the cloud motif (the crossing of the "alte / nebulose") and the poem also speaks of the subjectivity of perception and memory itself. In fact, it reinforces a meta-poetic memory – not just the evocation of her presence in an absence through memory, but a memory in the sense of a recycling of the same metaphors of expression which return in his poetry loaded with meanings specific to the context of Montale's poetry itself as meta-language:

Ti libero la fronte dai ghiaccioli / che raccogliesti traversando l'alte / nebulose; hai le penne lacerate / dai cicloni, ti desti a soprassalti. // Mezzodí: allunga nel riquadro il nespolo / l'ombra nera, s'ostina in cielo un sole / freddoloso; e l'altre ombre che scantonano / nel vicolo non sanno che sei qui.

Whether it is the "nube" in 'Falsetto' that "poco a poco in sé ti chiude" or the "nube" in 'Mottetto 10' from which the beloved may descend like lighting, Montale regenerates a cloud motif in 'Mottetto 12.' In this poetic metalanguage Montale is not only re-evoking Clizia's presence, but also the poetic means from his past (as a poet) to help him express better, more integrally, his past (as a human being). In fusing his use of a language from the past to a moment in the present he also creates two strophes that in form corroborate the content. Montale fuses poetic time with real time, the result of which is noumenal time, which is neither linear nor chronological.

In the first strophe the poet imagines Clizia has returned to him from a distant past; perhaps in some salvific form, like an angel from the "alte nebulose." He implies the angelic form through the reference to crossing the heavens, but also through the mention of the "penne lacerate." She is present in a cosmic form. To return to him in this state she must either be an actual angel or an evocation from the mind, a presence projected into the sky out of the resultant combination of hoping for Clizia's return and the burning memory of her in his head. And so Montale records the poetic moment with wing imagery and cyclones as a meteorological representation of the hope of her return despite the turbulent times, for which she had returned to America. The turbulent socio-political situation of 1938 Italy is not just an obstacle to tear at her wings, but the very reason for the current situation of separation.

Then, the real moment in time arrives. Noon strikes and suddenly the two strophes share a commonality. What is frozen photographically in memory must join the flow of time, which is ceaseless, relentless. For every moment the poet spends in the memory of a frozen instant he pertains less to the lives of those around him. Yet, ironically, it is those around Montale who cannot offer to him what even a mere memory of Clizia can. They are the automatons convinced in the reality of the world. On a more personal level, he describes perfectly the subjective impressions of memory, the very process of memory where to spend time with the absent means to step out of time's continuum, and away from those who function in it. But one cannot step away forever and so it is fitting that a noonday cannon brings Montale's gaze to those around him who function in the very flow of time which drew his attention from his internal world to the external world.

The other "shadows" exist in contrast to Montale. They are not aware of his own subjective world of memory, which the poet sees as an extension of a world-memory, or a perfect, noumenal present. In fact what Montale gains in the dimension of memory he loses in resolution to the things around him. Memory, then, in consoling his solitude, only creates more solitude with respect to those around him who can not possibly comprehend what he comprehends. Furthermore, those around him are "shadows"; they are mere transparent beings, with respect to the concrete images of Clizia, though she is a projection in the void of her absence. Shadow is only produced as a result of a material form meeting a source of light. Light gives it being, and the shadow is the space where light is impeded, as if the others can only be perceived in relation to Clizia, and yet they block the progress of her light. I refer to Clizia as the light source because it is a "sole freddoloso" that hangs in the sky.[64] The sun, which should be warm, has a cooling effect. Yet it is not necessarily the pale sun that the others do not notice, it is the fact that Clizia is here, reclining restlessly in Montale's bed after the harrowing trip ["ti desti a sopprassalti"] that they ignore: they do not possess his moral, though restless, yearning and awareness. It is not a progenitive sunlight which allows growth, rather it places the emphasis on that which is illuminated and that which is darkened, or shaded. Experiencing a cold sun is a pseudo-experience, much like the memory of a person. The memory of sun focuses on the light of the sun but not its heat, much like the memory of a person is a focus on an image and not the actual presence of that person. So, the fusion of hope and memory with his surroundings produces a perfect correlative of his experiences with the others of the world. While Montale is intimately affected by the sun, the others are merely struck by its light and do not notice that which it has illuminated beyond the screen of images.

In 'So l'ora in cui' and 'Forse un mattino' Montale feels that there is a possibility of there being more in his space than that which is visible. Yet because his words betray him, it is not expressible and his greatest consolation is to be satisfied with rising above the crowd that does not scrutinize existence as he does. In 'Mottetto 12,' he has turned suddenly as in 'Forse un mattino' and sees Clizia present. But her presence is beyond the usual existence of the rest of the world. At best, he can try to relate his personal experience to the general experience of those around him, but he will not have a sufficient language with which to relate it to those around him. In fact, the moment of the "compirsi" of a miracle suggested in 'Forse un mattino' is ephemeral and based on his hope for the miracle itself and the strength of his memory. Consequentially, he once again steps out of the flow of time, out of the flow of living, and the clock, or noon-day cannon, suddenly pulls him back: "Mezzodí." His sight is now returned to the common experience of all: the medlar tree, a sun above, and shadows of people coming and going down narrow streets. He has turned, in a sense, and seen the miracle of Clizia's presence but it still remains unrelated to the other shadows who do not even know she is there. The sun's illumination projects rays at just the correct angle to produce holographic images. The poet can only see these as part of his past, rather than the revelation of a pure present. Yet the "morso secreto" of 'So l'ora in cui' and the "miracolo" of 'Forse un mattino' were not based on his past. Rather they refer to a general search for meaning within his environment, a hope for some epiphany that will reveal a truth to him. Now, in 'Mottetto 12,' the present is conditioned by the past – remembrance of Clizia – and instead of simply waiting for nature to reveal her secrets, he can focus his hopes on Clizia. This recalls 'I limoni' from the *Ossi*:

Vedi, in questi silenzi in cui le cose / s'abbandonano e sembrano vicine / a tradire il loro ultimo segreto, / talora ci si aspetta / di scoprire uno sbaglio di natura.

He had not known what the miracle would even look like before in order to identify it when he saw it. At best, he will find a sign so subjective that meaning cannot be entrusted to any linguistic medium, as is noticeable even as early as the poem 'So l'ora in cui' of the *Ossi*: "Voi, mie parole, tradite invano il morso / secreto." So he walks off quietly among the crowd, dissatisfied with the impossibility of what he needs to express.

One who resides continuously in memory and views the present through memory's template will ultimately feel this distinction from the rest of the world, yet here it is not necessarily a condition of solitude for our poet, but one of a certain superiority in how he views the world. In relation to the poem 'Falsetto' from the *Ossi*, Montale offers not only common terminology, but a change in how he perceives his situation. In 'Falsetto,' contrary to Esterina's condition, he remained of the "razza / di chi rimane a terra." Esterina represented his disharmony with the illusory world; Clizia represented a break in the screen of images. Now, though there is still the contrast of sky-borne and earth-bound, he is not looking with envy at Clizia, rather as a source of faith in his search for truth. He is not deprived of flight as he was with respect to Esterina. In the *Ossi* he felt more helpless as if his fate depended purely on an uninviting Nature. If there is no flaw in Nature to be revealed, and Nature is metaphorically the stone wall, then Clizia is the equivalent of the break in the wall.

The Montale of the *Occasioni* is not the Montale of 'Antico, sono ubriacato' where, with regards to the sea, he felt the "fermento" of his heart to be no more than a mere moment for the sea, which was timeless. Though a stone along the shore was immortal and, therefore, shared the sea's timelessness in which Montale's time was a mere moment, Montale projects into the stone a need to break the ceaseless flow of time; to not be part of something "vasto e diverso / e insieme fisso." (Vast in its greatness and diverse in the changes that seem to be fantastic for human intervals, and which are quite inconsequential in geologic time that it seems fixed or unmoved.) Time, in its relative fixedness is like one extended moment – a perpetual present. In fact what keeps humans from living that way is the sense of hope for the future and a memory of the past, and past can only exist because of the function of memory. The only way for Montale to give greater meaning to an existence which offers him little objective truth is to relive past moments in memory. Thus, he can scrutinize them, and revisit them, finding small epiphanies that he may have not noticed if he had only lived them once. Now he resides in a world of memory that can only exist with respect to time. Paradoxically, as Montale lives in his past, he is the "scheggia fuori del tempo" ('Avrei voluto sentirmi'). In fact for most of the 'Mottetti' he resides outside of time, and it is only occasionally that he joins the flow of actual time.

Concentrating on defying time, he gains dimension in space. By gaining the spatial-image dimension of memory he stops time, poetically speaking, as if looking into a photograph. One can only re-examine a photo which had been previously exposed and developed from an original moment. Therefore, even the poetic moments dealing with the present are exhausted with detailed imagery that loses the dimension of time and gains that of spatial imagery. 'Mottetto 19' comes to mind: the offset hypermeter of the last line seems to stand alone, balanced on a fulcrum to counterweight all that had been said in the previous 12 lines. The last line represents the continuity of the whole moment, a "maximum-in-the-minimum":[65]

> *La canna che dispiuma / mollemente il suo rosso / flabello a primavera; / la rèdola nel fosso, su la nera / correntía sorvolata di libellule; e il cane trafelato che rincasa / col suo fardello in bocca, // oggi qui non mi tocca riconoscere; / ma là dove il riverbero piú cuoce / e il nuovo s'abbassa, oltre le sue / pupille ormai remote, sole due / fasci di luce in croce. // E il tempo passa.*

From the reed that sheds its red flabellum to the two shafts of light forming a cross, Montale abruptly leaves the reader with the only possible objective conclusion: "E il tempo passa." That is the only truth, or sure thing; all else is still an object of his search. With a consciousness of time passing, one cannot help relying upon memory to fight this process, as seen in 'Mottetto 18.' But perhaps the similarity of the two syntagms "E il tempo passa," and "E l'inferno è certo" is too convenient. Perhaps they are synonymous or analogous. If time's passing leaves one conclusion, that hell is certain, then only in memory can the poet receive succor. That is, memory is the only fight against the certainty of hell which is as certain as the passing of unceding, irredeemable time. The hell is certain, unless the poet can break through to the timeless void where memories live not as past but as spatial moments. On this Singh comments that "the fear of hell is connected with the loss of memory – the memory of the world of childhood – as well as with uncertainty about the future."[66] Of course, there is no hell, theologically speaking, in 'Sul limite.' That is, one does not lose memory. Rather, the poet's mind joins Deleuze's "being-memory."

Regardless of this, Montale lives between the memories, until he uncovers the truth of the universe and refers to the entropic hell. 'Mottetto 13' exemplifies the great value of memory in Montale's life and work:

La gondola che scivola in un forte / bagliore di catrame e di papaveri, / la subdola canzone che s'alzava / da masse di cordame, l'alte porte / rinchiuse su di te e risa di maschere / che fuggivano a frotte – // una sera tra mille e la mia notte / è piú profonda! S'agita laggiú / uno smorto groviglio che m'avviva / a stratti e mi fa eguale a quell'assorto / pescatore d'anguille dalla riva.

The first strophe is a list of all the events occurring in the flow of time as a past flows into the present. Not feeling included in the association to these things, Montale sees himself as outside of time. In fact, in the second strophe he highlights time's indifference to itself that only humans cannot ignore. It is one night, but it passes indiscriminately in the flow of time as any other night. Calling his current night deeper, he means deeper than for those who are around him. Again, Montale separates his situation from that of others; perhaps like the other shades who neither perceive Clizia, nor do they turn around to some occurrence in the split second of happenstance. Montale lives on a different level, in his poetic world. As the poet uses the words "piú profonda," he tells the reader that he is on a different level of perception. He is apparently startled by an eel-fisherman's movements. Then, he associates himself with the "assorto / pescatore d'anguille." The absorption of the eel-fisher in his task makes him as detached from the flow of other events as Montale is in his memories. If the eel-fisher had not stirred him from his meditative state, Montale may have remained there intent in his remembrance.

In 'Mottetto 14' Montale relies so strongly on memory as to suggest that his recollection derives more from a reflection of the noumenos than from a resignation to the phenomenal world. The current situation – whether a storm of salt or hail – was somehow invoked or awakened by Clizia. In the screen of images, he has edited frames. Yet, in the overlap of images in the void, they may have a spatial connection, when time is removed from the quotient:

> *Infuria sale o grandine? Fa strage / di campanule, svelle la cedrina. / Un rintocco subacqueo s'avvincina, / quale tu lo destavi, e s'allontana. // La pianola degl'inferi da sé / accelera i registri, sale nelle / sfere del gelo ... – brilla come te / quando fingevi col tuo trillo d'aria / Lakmé nell'Aria delle Campanelle.*

The morphological similarity of "campanule" (bellflowers) and the aria of the "Campanelle" (bells) is deceptively present so that a reader is not sure if it is the phonic quality of the two words that evoked an image of Clizia in his mind, or if it is mere coincidence.

Interestingly, the phonic relationship reveals the individual nature of the two verbal protagonists. The bellflowers are part of the flow of time, irrevocably part of the daily birth, death and rebirth of Nature. The aria of the bells is a role; it is fixity; it is a platonic form. Each time the role is played it is a re-enactment of its original designation. Clizia is fixed – in his memory as she is in the role of Lakmé, which in turn is a fixed character. But, if the character does not present itself externally, Clizia is absent for Montale.

Though musical imagery abounds – not unexpected in a 'Mottetto' – the image of hell is tied to the rhythm of time. Hell ("l'inferno"), is the only true certainty based on the notion that time's passing is the only certainty. More importantly, it is a "pianola" (a player piano) that plays by itself, separately and indiscriminately from any pretense of time that the poet has. Regardless of what Montale may do, he has no effect on the distinct, autonomous entity of the pianola. It is on a certain course, despite Montale, and his only recourse is to reconcile the ineffable passing of time through an indifferent nature with images from his past, fixed into his own certainty – that is, how he remembers them. The pianola rises like warm air to the icy spheres. Montale gives a poetic-allegorical explanation for a meteorological consequence; the hail. Clizia resides up above in the heavens where the sound of the pianola rises to meet her "sfere del gelo." She is so high that in order to use anything commonplace to relate this he relies on her singing attributes which could achieve extremely high registers. This highlights the role of "aria" (air) in this poem.

The poet mentions air twice but, he implies more meanings. While speaking of climatic phenomena, Montale considers the icy spheres, which are not true spheres but a level at which air changes its property to water vapor and hence ice. So he leaves the reader with the meteorological air, and a connection of Clizia's own airiness of form. She manipulates the very air by singing her *aria*, or 'Aria delle Campanelle.' It is fitting that the memory of Clizia should be in the role of Lakmé; not because of any attributes of Lakmé per se. Rather it is the function of a role to be fixed, to return over and over again, despite any subtle changes in its interpretation. Therefore, Montale does not remember Clizia but her form is externally fixed like a platonic ideal. His memories are versions of that form.

The role is a point that is only "dilatato" when occupied by the player. Songs and arias are much the same: they are comprised of set, fixed musical phrases that only come alive when sung by a singer. But what happens to Montale is the reverse. He experiences the musical phrases in other forms, not occupied by players: "su fili, su ali, al vento, a caso, col / favore della musa o d'un ordegno." Clizia becomes a fixed memory that others and other things enliven. He hears the insistent "do re la sol sol..." in 'Mottetto 11,' but it is on the level of that which is carried, intangibly on the air (we recall the *aria* pun of 'Mottetto 14') that this occurs. It is a metaphysical epiphany where the sounds created in the instant evoke the memory of Clizia fixed with the sounds, but because a sound is not visual or tangible, even Montale himself questions whether the sounds are not extensions of Clizia's airy, angelic presence. It is at this level that memory and absence-presence are completely fused, indistinguishably to Montale. Perhaps Clizia communicates to him as a disembodied voice: "La tua voce è quest'anima diffusa." Perhaps that which gives Clizia's disembodied voice presence now was always there, before he knew her, before he could assign all that is Clizia, as a person-concept, to the media around him, much like in 'Lontano, ero con te,' where he did not realize how connected he and Clizia had already been. If Montale pondered the "schermo d'immagini" in 'La speranza di pure rivederti,' perhaps in these motets he ponders an aural version of this phenomenon.

When the sounds come together just right, or are a reproduction of a melody associated with Clizia, Clizia has a de facto presence for him. Perhaps if he could turn quickly enough, he would see her there in the void field just before his eyes reach it, as in Calvino's interpretation of 'Forse un mattino andando.' Calvino makes a terrifically interesting comment:

> *Il protagonista della poesia di Montale riesce, per una combinazione di fattori oggettivi (aria di vetro, arida) e soggettivi (ricettività a un miracolo gnoseologico) a voltarsi tanto in fretta da arrivare, diciamo, a gettare lo sguardo là dove il suo campo visuale non ha ancora occupato*

*lo spazio: e vede il nulla, il vuoto.*⁶⁷

She is a diffused soul. She is transparent spirituality. She is a nothing, a void of presence, so if he could turn quickly enough to see the "nulla," the "vuoto," perhaps he could catch a glimpse of her instead of simply implying her presence. He could do more than intimate a cognizance of Clizia by merely breaking himself and others into two categories: those who feel her there and those who do not. The screen becomes distinct while images from a cinema are projected over it. Further, one recalls how in viewing a film, there is a space (small voids) between frames: one is not seeing a continuous image. Montale sees in between the frames and spies the void, the break in the stone wall⁶⁸ that is the phenomenal world. He names the others as shadowy silhouettes (for example, verse seven of 'Mottetto 12'). This means that he and those around Montale have only the vaguest awareness of each other. He is absorbed in his memory, and they in the tasks of the day.

The world as it truly is can only be viewed in immanence. To see it is to think, but to think is to remember. For thinking is a return, in a platonic sense, Douwe Draaisma asserts, to the "laws and abstractions...present in our memories from birth."⁶⁹ 'Mottetto 15' discusses how much he lives his life within his head and outside of it. He discusses his absorption into his thoughts and into his memories. And this absorption occurs on many levels:

Al primo chiaro, quando / subitaneo un rumore / di ferrovia mi parla / di chiusi uomini in corsa / nel traforo del sasso / illuminato a tagli / da cieli ed acque misti; // al primo buio, quando / il bulino che tarla / la scrivania rafforza / il suo fervore e il passo / del guardiano s'accosta: / al chiaro e al buio, soste ancore umane / se tu a intrecciarle col tuo refe insisti.

Montale talks about the great cyclical nature of the earth in the night and day. To this he adjoins other cyclical intervals, but they are of no great import for they are merely human: the workers commuting by train; the etching on the desk in the twilight. The one human group works the day, and the other the night, as if to suggest, as Ong has, that "for working purposes night and day have disappeared."⁷⁰

Time is the great barrier to perfect understanding and communication. Montale advances past this impediment, if only in immanence, realizing that time is only a by-product of the attempt to experience limitless space in any meaningful way. Memory is an additional residue of these attempts. "Memory is representation itself; time its inconceivability."⁷¹ Memory is, in essence, an after-image of the spatial, cinematic frames. To view them contemporaneously would mean to be part of the being-memory. To view them in order means to view them in linear succession; from which time and movement are born in a static, noumenal world of platonic forms. The cinematic illumination of the above poem ("illuminazione a tagli") is Montale's way of demonstrating his awareness of the rift between the noumenal and phenomenal. Yet, because he is still terrestrially bound to the limitations of the body, his eyes can only perceive the world as cinematic after-images. It is important to highlight that, though we use our eyes to see, we do not see with them. We see them in the mind, which may be part of a whole holographic universe.

Further, Montale highlights a nocturnal scene where a guard presides over prisoners while they sleep, but he draws a correlation between the current 'Mottetto' and 'Mottetto 4.' By using the line "chiusi uomini in corsa," the poet immediately calls to the mind of the reader the automatons of 'Mottetto 4': "Forse / gli automi hanno ragione. Come appaiono / dai corridoi, murati!" The closed men might be automatons as in 'Mottetto 4,' but they may also refer to a more existential statement about how isolated, closed off and shut into his own world the poet is. Clearly Montale does not belong to the cosmic, or geologic, time of the universe, but at the same time he is more closed than the closed men he mentions. His hermetic objective correlatives within the "schermo d'immagini" tend to insulate the poetry from time, and if his poetry is his inner communiqué then he too will be insulated.

Montale passes his life trying to fill the space, or void, around him with images of his beloved, though she exists in the noumenal void beyond the screen of images. But, because of this intermittent illumination, when he achieves meaning, Montale will have had the meaning but left the experience in the past where all it can redeem is the time in his memories; not cosmic time. This is very much at issue in Eliot's *Four Quartets*, and Montale thrusts himself into his memories where poetic time and cosmic time are opposed. Poetry tends to isolate a pure moment, in an epiphany, but the cosmos continues on with a pattern of its own: "And the end and the beginning were always there / Before the beginning and after the end" ('Burnt Norton'). The fact that Montale puts day before night in the poem is insignificant to a cosmos that does not see one as necessarily before or after the other. So, Montale creates a poetic world full of the correlatives to which he can entrust his poetry to somehow overcome the inevitable passing of the epiphanic moment of understanding. In this world he tries to review the facts and search for truth at his own pace, but his constant turning to his memories often hampers him from viewing the present in an objective way:

> È allora che le visitazioni dei ricordi frustrano l'attesa di conoscenza oggettiva, rivelandosi come elementi negatori di comunicazione, mentre per converso li evidenzia il regime sempre piú dichiaratamente solipsistico in cui l'io può ancora sopravvivere.[72]

Montale is left dissatisfied, and separated from the present, so-called objective world, because of the insulating nature of his poetry.

There is a constant, though subtle, battle that goes on in Montale's head: the battle between the absorption into his memory or the joining of the life around him that moves in the continuum of time (cf. 'Mottetto 13'). By choosing the latter, he lives in a world of fleeing time which only makes his memory more necessary and, as a consequence, his poetry is about memory. One witnesses an objective correlative of memory with the forget-me-not flower in 'Mottetto 16.' The very flower used to relate his poetry is a figurative and literal harbinger of memory. Yet at the same time the flower is not memory itself, nor can it compete with his memories which seem more vivid even than the flower at hand. Its colors are not as 'happy' or as 'clear' as the space between Montale and the beloved. The flower, as part of the "schermo d'immagini" around him, is still external and therefore not an internalized part of him like memory. Therefore, the nothing – the space between them – says more to him than any external object. The space here, like that of 'Il balcone,' is everything or nothing, at the same time. It is what reminds him of the separation between himself and his beloved. And in this seeming nothing he loses himself in thought to memory. It is more lucid and clear to him, as such.

Much as in 'Mottetto 13,' the poet is once again absorbed in the memorial, metaphysical part of existence only to be startled by a member of the active, physical world around him. Suddenly, the creaking from the funicular draws him from pondering the absence in which he fills the void with the presence of memory. Ironically, the very thing that startles him is both a figurative and literal reminder of his situation. *Per eccellenza* the funicular cable car can physically take him across, making the distance between himself and the one side greater as it pulls away. This metaphor highlights the distance between them much like in 'Il balcone,' in which the poet is incapable of achieving Clizia's illumination. Whereas in the phenomenal world, one tends to order time linearly, in Montale's holographic cinema of memory, the two sides between which the funicular travels are both present in a world of possibility.

One can see how the poet is awoken by the "cigolío" and that the space of the first strophe is in the limitless "punto dilatato" of his memory. He speaks of "tinte" (colors) being happier and more clear in the first strophe, and in the second strophe he mentions how the overwhelming blue will not return, as if to imply that the blue was the "tinta" from the space of his memories. By further implication, only in his memory does he have clarity, for as a result of being awoke it is an almost visible haze that accompanies him on the funicular ride. Memory and the noumenos are real, while that to which he awakens is illusory. This haze almost immediately recalls the fog of 'Mottetto 18.' This nebulous state of the air around him is the objective correlative of his greatest fear: that his memory should be dissipated by time. Time, which is constantly fleeing and has no predetermined notions of clear beginning and end, in its infinity, is the enemy of his poetic moments and epiphanies. And all the while it is time which moves endlessly making every present immediately a past.

'Mottetto 18' is one of the most important poems of Montale's repertoire in terms of his thoughts on memory:

Non recidere, forbice, quel volto, / solo nella memoria che si sfolla, / non far del grande suo viso in ascolto / la mia nebbia di sempre. // Un freddo cala ... Duro il colpo svetta. / E l'acacia ferita da sé scrolla / il guscio di cicala / nella prima belletta di Novembre.

The poet uses the imagery of a photo (whether real or envisioned in his memory) to create the very poem which is a treatise on absence-presence. Memory is like a photo, and vice-versa. A photo is a presence of a moment, which is frozen and locked against cosmic time. This presence, because it is of one moment, while time moves along, points to an absence. To be within the moment is to be fixed outside of time; outside of the living of life. Montale experiences photographs in quite a Deleuzian way. Deleuze maintains that photography, "if there is photography, is already snapped, already shot, in the very interior of things and for all the points of space."[73] Montale seeks the illumination to allow himself a perfect holographic experience where the noumenal photograph – one spatial moment like one of Zeno's infinite arrows – can be sustained; otherwise he must depend on the after-image of memory which, rooted in movement and in time, is subject to entropy. The second stanza associates a falling cold and a lopping axe-blow as rather analogous: both cold, unforgiving and certain. Both are associated with the cold, gleaming metal of a scissors cutting a photo, virtual or actual. "The cold sweeps down on the poet's world of sentiments and memories, bringing about precisely what he was afraid of."[74]

In this regard, Montale's rememberer-photographer approximates Calvino's from 'L'avventura di un fotografo.' For the photographer, only what exists as photographic images is real; as that which is recollected is real. But every instant is composed of an infinite juxtaposition of eleatic instants: a perfect hologram. From the "mobile continuità" of cosmic time, Montale imagines temporal slices of the "spessore d'un secondo"[75] in a cinema which he can rewind, fast-forward, and edit if given the proper epiphany. The photographer tries to capture distinct moments of perfection, but this sort of perfection implies its existing outside of, or being removed from, any realistic context. It is an absolute, a means to an end in a world that is constantly becoming, not simply being, which is fixed. It also reinforces Deleuze's notion that all is already 'shot'. Ultimately, the rememberer and the photographer exist in a world of spatial proportion to the rest of the "mobile continuità" and not in a temporal one. Peavler, writing on this paradigm in relation to both Cortázar's short story 'Las babas del diablo' and Antonioni's film *Blow-up*, speaks of the reversal of the "photographic process so that the photographer, not the photographed, becomes eternally immobilized, while the photographed, not the photographer, goes on its way."[76] If I substituted *remember* and *remembered* for *photographer* and *photographed*, this statement would be extremely valid to the description of Montale's practically paralyzing, isolating sense of memory, which occurs when he imagines the infinite noumenal world behind the illusion of movement and time.

Offering a certain irony with respect to 'Mottetto 20' is 'Mottetto 19,' which reads as follows:

> ... *ma così sia. Un suono di cornetta / dialoga con gli sciami del querceto. / Nella valva che il vespero riflette / un vulcano dipinto fuma lieto. // La moneta incassata nella lava / brilla anch'essa sul tavolo e trattiene / pochi fogli. La vita che sembrava / vasta è più breve del tuo fazzoletto.*

The irony consists of a life more vast than a handkerchief. The simple, mundane, inanimate "fazzoletto" is of the phenomenal world of material objects that in their integrity offer more physical, visible proof than even the most fulfilled life of someone who is not present. What many would consider a fixed point, Montale changes into a "punto dilatato." He does not see the seashell and that which is painted (fixed) on it as one entity; rather on the shell he sees a world functioning in a temporal continuum of its own. He is Funes el memorioso, Borges' character who does not see the wine in the glasses but all the shoots, clusters and grapes of the vine that produiced it.[77] The volcano continues to smolder and burn. Yet like the fixed coin in the lava, this too is a physical souvenir, an item bought to remind one of one's visit to a place in a specific time. These items are also the visual objective correlatives for his memory. What seems like a fixed image no greater than *your* fazzoletto contains in that one point a vast life if one recognizes the image as a reference point to all that preceded and succeeded it: this is the "Bergsonian idea that each present present is only the entire past in its most contracted state."[78] But the smallness, the brevity of what seemed to be a vast life can only be dilated to include the vast life if it is a reference based on something he experienced in the past which is now a part of his memory. Therefore, the irony of 'Mottetto 19' becomes even more apparent:

La canna che dispiuma / mollemente il suo rosso / flabello a primavera; / la rèdola nel fosso, su la nera / corrente sorvolata di libellule; / e il cane trafelato che rincasa / col suo fardello in bocca.

The first strophe, from the "canna" to the "fardello in bocca," represents an external screen of images. Yet, though the scene is verdant and alive, it is not for him to recognize, as he claims in the beginning of the second strophe: "Oggi qui non mi tocca riconoscere." Recognizing implies having originally met or known. That of strophe 1 is not reminiscent of anything, so for all of its vividness it does not hold his gaze. Rather he gazes into a point that is more cloudlike, or nebulous, where his memory can mould a malleable scene into something with greater personal meaning. He is searching for a sign:

La speranza di salvezza non può essere piú affidata, come in successivi lanci di dadi, all'enumerazione di fantasmi assurdamente privilegiati, aleatori rinvii all'Oggetto amato (di cui i vv. 1–7 forniscono ancora un ultimo prezioso specimen); occorre scrutarne, ormai, i segni impenetrabili "oltre lo sguardo dell'uomo" ('Palio'), là dove le "pupille remote" di Clizia indirizzano, fra abbacinanti riverberi, gli occhi del suo fedele.[79]

But casting his eyes at a point where he expects a sign, and finding nothing, he is casting his gaze into hope, or perhaps he has unwittingly glimpsed the void behind the screen of images.

"E il tempo passa," Montale tells the reader at the end of 'Mottetto 19,' but the poet has not recalled anything. He has not recognized or recollected. As he lives in after-images of the noumenos, time passes. He has found nothing in the vastness around him that has sufficed to conjure up a presence in the absence, but ironically it is in the very fixity of the seashell painting and of the coin mounted in the lava that he recognizes something. Montale's poetry accords the object a great value to him in the moment. Here, in 'Mottetto 20,' in a room, amongst immobility, he recognizes material for expression, whereas in the exterior of 'Mottetto 19' he recognizes nothing.

In the last two lines of 'Mottetto 20,' the poet makes an interesting choice of words – "vasta" and "breve" are used to refer to temporal and spatial dimensions simultaneously in a synaesthesia: "La vita che sembrava / vasta è piú breve del tuo fazzoletto." Vast was all that he now remembers, all that fits, now, in one point of his mind; brief because it is now a memory, not an ongoing present. The best his poetry can do is select a thin slice of the mobile continuity of geologic time.[80] His 'Mottetti' are the linguistic equivalents of painting a volcanic scene on a seashell or mounting a coin in hardened lava, which once was fluid, hot and glowing.

This lesson that he has taught himself seems to be what he knew all too well in his earlier poetry. A life transcribed into poetry, or poetry rooted in memory, is but a scene reduced to one flash onto a seashell: art exists, like memory, despite life's vicissitudes. Rebecca West clarifies this by saying that "art seeks to go beyond...seeks...to defy death and to live beyond the immediate circumstances of its creation. Yet, paradoxically, art – and poetry especially – is imbibed with an awareness of time, of limits, of death."[81] Though the image is clear, the problem of the inexorability of time persists for, as a human being, the poet can not change his nature. In the *Ossi* he spoke to the timeless sea directly, and the poet spoke for himself. Now, at the end of the 'Mottetti,' the objects of the *Occasioni* speak for Montale.[82] Where he had direct experience in the first collection, he now seems to speak through the filter of memory and the objects around him as a way of transcribing that memory. Perhaps Eliot stated it best: "To be conscious is not to be in time / But only in time can the moment in the rose-garden, / The moment in the arbor where the rain beat, / The moment in the draughty church at smokefall / Be remembered" ('Burnt Norton').

Notes

1. Maria Sampoli-Simonelli, "The Particular Poetic World of Eugenio Montale." *Italian Quarterly* 3.10 (1959-60): 45.
2. Arshi Pipa, "Memory and Fedelity in Montale." *Italian Quarterly* 10.39-40 (1966-67): 67.
3. Eugenio Montale, *Collected Poems (1920-1954)*. Tr., with annotation and commentary, by Jonathan Galassi (New York: Farrar, 1998) 496.
4. Sergio Antonielli, *Letteratura del disagio* (Milano: Edizioni di Comunità, 1984) 203-04.
5. Deleuze, 82.
6. Rodowick, 39.
7. It is important to remember that though the poetic only-begetter is often

referred to as Clizia, it is more a Petrarcan amalgam of Clizia-like characters: "Ho completato il mo lavoro con le poesie di Finisterre, che rappresentano la mia esperienza, diciamo cosí, petrarchesca. Ho proiettato la Selvaggia o la Mandetta o la Delia (la chiami come vuole) dei Mottetti sullo sfondo di una guerra cosmica e terrestre, senza scopo e senza ragione, e mi sono affidato a lei, donna o nube, angelo o procellaria," in Montale, Eugenio, 'L'intervista immaginaria.' *Il secondo mestiere: arte, musica, società.* Ed. Giorgio Zampa (Milano: Mondadori, 1996) 1483.

8. Santini 37.
9. Eugenio Montale, *Le occasioni. Dante Isella,* ed. (Torino: Einaudi, 1996) 34.
10. Elisabetta Graziosi. *Il tempo in Montale: storia di un tema.* (Firenze: La Nuova Italia, 1978): 62.
11. Isella 38.
12. Ibidem.
13. Eugenio Montale. 'La casa delle due palme,' in *Farfalla di Dinard.* (Milano: Arnoldo Mondadori, 1960): 49.
14. Ibid. 50.
15. Ibid. 231.
16. Doane 176.
17. C. W. Ceram. *Archeology of the Cinema.* (New York: Harcourt, Brace and World, 1965): 24.
18. Henri Bergson. *Matter and Memory.* Trans. N. M. Paul and W. S. Palmer. (New York: Zone Books, 1991): 150.
19. Georges Poulet, *Proustian Space.* Tr. Elliott Coleman. (Baltimore: The St. John's U Press: 1977): 94.
20. Glauco Cambon, *La lotta con Proteo* (Milano: Bompiani, 1963) 119.
21. Poulet 12.
22. Cambon 127.
23. Poulet 52.
24. Isella 77.
25. Piero Bigongiari, "Dal 'correlativo oggettivo' al 'correlativo soggettivo'." *Montale e il canone poetico del novecento.* Ed. M. A. Grignani and R. Luperini (Roma-Bari: Laterza, 1998) 425.
26. Poulet 67.
27. Claire L Huffman, "The Poetic Language of Eugenio Montale." *Italian Quarterly* 12.47–48 (1969): 114.
28. Gianfranco Contini, *Una lunga fedeltà: scritti su Eugenio Montale* (Torino: Einaudi, 1974) 87.
29. Ibidem.
30. Poulet 93.
31. Mengaldo suggests "api" to be in apposition with "noi" and not with "sillabe." Perhaps this is implied by the "ronzanti" – "senza rumore" relationship. Pier Vincenzo Mengaldo, *La tradizione del novecento.* 2nd ed. (Milano: Feltrinelli, 1980) 15.
32. Houses are associated with memories in the *Occasioni,* as a motif, because of the

interior nature of houses and the interior introspection of memory.
33. Isella 82.
34. Eugenio Montale, "Introduzione" to *Tutte le poesie*. Giorgio Zampa, ed. (Milano: Mondadori, 1984) xxxvii.
35. Justus Hartnack, *The Philosophical Investigations: Wittgenstein and Modern Philosophy*. Tr. by Maurice Cranston (New York: NYU Press, 1965) 94
36. Isella 84.
37. Ibidem.
38. The reader should be reminded not to overplay its immediate connection with Carducci's 'Alla stazione in una mattina d'autunno,' for Carducci's aim is a disection of the world of modernity and progress of which the train and the telegraph are clear signs.
39. Mengaldo 91.
40. Mario Martelli, *Eugenio Montale: Introduzione e guida allo studio dell'opera montaliana*, storia e antologia critica (Firenze: Le Monnier, 1982) 99.
41. Galassi 498.
42. Entropy itself will be seen, in retrospect, as something less negative and less final as a dissipated thermodynamic stage. In fact, Montale will later discover – *a posteriori* – that his fear of entropic devastation was unfounded. It could be seen merely as the still point of the world as hologram, in which all parts contain the whole and vice-versa; i.e., that entropy means not destruction but lack of distinction. Mary Ann Doane, in her book, *The Emergence of Cinematic Time*, offers insight into this. "When energy dissipates, it changes form so that it becomes unusable – that is, unable to produce work. This transformation levels differences so that, for instance, the flow of heat to a cooler space will in time cause equilibrium (according to the theory [of entropy] this will eventually lead to the death of the universe, its absolute stasis). Usable energy – that is, energy capable of producing work – is therefore defined in terms of critical presence of differences. The gravitational energy in water is usable – it will turn the wheel of a mill, for instance – only if there is a difference of levels so that the water falls from one height to another. The gravitational energy in a body of water – a lake or the ocean – is unusable without these differences. From this point of view, entropy can be defined as the annihilation of difference" (Doane 116–117).
43. Martelli 37.
44. Isella 92.
45. Ibid. 91.
46. Ibidem.
47. Zampa xxxvii–xxxviii.
48. Rodowick 39: The line Rodowick cites come directly from Deleuze's *Difference and Repetition*, 82.
49. Lorenzo Greco, ed. *Montale commenta Montale* (Parma: Pratiche, 1980) 102.
50. Lorenzo Greco, ed. "Eugenio Montale. Commenta a se stesso, parte terza." *Il ponte* 33.1 (1977) : 74.
51. Julio Cortázar, 'Las babas del diablo.' *Las armas secretas* (Buenos Aires: Editorial Sudamericana, 1966) 81.

52. Glauco Cambon, "Eugenio Montale's 'Motets': The Occasions of Epiphany." *PMLA* 82.7 (1967): 477
53. Poulet 82.
54. Italo Calvino, 'Avventura di un fotografo,' *Gli amori difficili* (Milano: Mondadori, 1994) 58.
55. Poulet 57.
56. Ibid. 92.
57. Ibid.
58. Galassi 502.
59. David Spurr, *Conflicts of Consciousness: T. S. Eliot's Poetry and Criticism* (Urbana: U of Illinois P, 1984) 80.
60. Deleuze, *Proust and Signs*, 164.
61. Ibid. 89. Spurr is paraphrasing from George Bornstein. For the original text cf. George Bornstein, *Transformation of Romanticism in Yeats, Eliot and Stevens* (Chicago: U of Chicago P, 1976) 156.
62. Cesare Segre. "Invito alla 'Farfalla di Dinard'," in *Omaggio a Montale, a cura di Silvio Ramat.* (Verona: Arnoldo Mondadori Editore, 1966): 300.
63. Eugenio Montale, *L'opera in versi.* Ed. Rosanna Bettarini and Gianfranco Contini (Milano: Mondadori, 1980) 930.
64. It is a referent to the oxymoron of Clizia's true surname, Brandeis, from the German brand (fire) and eis (ice), though it is important not to read too deeply into Ms. Brandeis' name, for it was carried down to her long before Montale knew her. But, on the other hand, as an astute poet, we wonder how he could not have even seen the innate symbolism in her name, from which the ironic contrast of two elements.
65. Poulet 67.
66. Ghanyam Singh, Eugenio Montale: *A Critical Study of His Poetry and Criticism* (New Haven: Yale UP, 1973) 92.
67. Italo Calvino, 'Forse un mattino andando,' *Letture montaliane in occasione dell'80o compleanno del Poeta*, ed. by Sylvia Luzzatto (Genova: Bozzi, 1977) 42.
68. A dominant thematic in the *Ossi.*
69. Douwe Draaisma. *Metaphors of Memory: A history of ideas about the mind.* Trans. Paul Vincent. (Cambridge: Cambridge University Press, 2000): 28.
70. Walter J Ong, "Evolution, Myth and Poetic Vision," *Comparative Literature Studies* 3.1 (1966): 6.
71. Doane 45.
72. Giuliana Castellani, "Tra memoria e storia," *Contributi per Montale.* Ed. Giovanni Cillo (Lecce: Milella, 1979) 159.
73. Gilles Deleuze. Cinema I: The Movement-Image. Trans. Hugh Tomlinson and Barbara Habberjam. (Minneapolis: U of Minnesota Press, 1986): 60.
74. Singh 104.
75. Calvino, *Gli amori difficili*, 53.
76. Terry J. Peavler, "Blow Up: A Reconstruction of Antonioni's Infidelity to Cortázar," *PMLA* 94.4 (1979): 889.
77. Jorge Luis Borges. 'Funes el memorioso,' in *Ficciones.* (Madrid: Alianza

Editorial, 1996): 128.
78. Deleuze, *Difference and Repetition*, 82.
80. Isella 120.
81. Calvino, *Gli amori difficili*, 53.
82. Rebecca West, "Montale's 'care ombre': Identity and its Dissolution." *Forum Italicum* 23.1–2 (1989): 222.
83. Martelli 57.

CHAPTER 4

'La casa dei doganieri': 'Memoria che giova' and 'memoria peccato'

In 'Mottetto 4,' 'Lontano, ero con te,' the poet is able to revisit the past and then, once in the past, gain an insight into an experience. This is not *intermittences du cœur* à la Proust; rather he virtually visits the past, which is the other co-existent side of the present. The two sides co-exist as part of the same moment. With the knowledge of the present, Montale visits the past and has an epiphany, and even within the poem there are two past moments which fuse to form this flash of meaning for him in the present: the moment of Clizia's father passing "into shadow" and the moment from World War I with references to "Cumerlotti" and "Anghébeni":

Lontano, ero con te quando tuo padre / entrò nell'ombra e ti lasciò il suo addio. / Che seppi fino allora? Il logorí / di prima mi salvò solo per questo: // che t'ignoravo e non dovevo: ai colpi / d'oggi lo so, se di laggiú s'inflette / un'ora e mi riporta Cumerlotti / o Anghébeni – tra scoppi di spolette / e i lamenti e l'accorrer delle squadre.

In this sense there is a doubling of meaning through the memory of the poet, and the mnemonic phenomenon of 'Mottetto 4' transpires in a similar way to that of 'La casa dei doganieri:'

Tu non ricordi la casa dei doganieri / sul rialzo a strapiombo sulla scogliera: / desolata t'attende dalla sera / in cui v'entrò lo sciame dei tuoi pensieri / e vi sostò irrequieto. // Libeccio sferza da anni le vecchie mura / e il suono del tuo riso non è piú lieto: / la bussola va impazzita all'avventura / e il calcolo dei dadi piú non torna. / Tu non ricordi; altro tempo frastorna / la tua memoria; un filo s'addipana. // Ne tengo ancora un capo; ma s'allontana / la casa e in cima al tetto la banderuola / affumicata gira senza pietà. / Ne tengo un capo; ma tu resti sola / né qui respiri nell'oscurità. // Oh l'orizzonte in fuga, dove s'accende / rara la luce della petroliera! / Il varco è qui? (Ripullula il frangente / ancora sulla balza che scoscende...). / Tu non ricordi la casa di questa / mia sera. Ed io non so chi va e chi resta.

In both poems there is a doubling of memory; a presence of a memorial prehistory. That is, the communion of a moment when it is chronologically inconceivable that the protagonists could have physically shared it. The two layers of memory in 'Mottetto 4' are as follows: Montale recalls how he was with the distant Clizia in transcendent spirit to share the departure of her father. This memory encourages him to consider his own times of pain and travail. What could have saved him during the war? Suddenly, he realizes that if he can be with her across 3,000 miles in one moment, Clizia could have been with him spiritually in a moment prior to their meeting and somehow have saved him, like an angel, for a later encounter. Cosmic time does not put conscious limits on moments; instead it is one moment of pure being. It is rather the human intervals, introduced in 'Mottetto 15' ("soste ancora umane") that give time its conscious limits: no god or supernatural force imposed time on humanity; man invented it. Calvino notes a cinematic hologram *avanti lettera* in Montale's works: "Il mondo empirico (invece) è il consueto succedersi d'immagini sullo schermo, inganno ottico come il cinema, dove la velocità dei fotogrammi ti convince della continuità e della permanenza."[1] It is neither there nor continuous; its permanence is not only illusory or relative but contradictory to the state of the holographic universe outside of time. What is infinite cannot be deemed permanent.

Human limits put emphasis on what is no longer in the present. The being-memory in the void transcends the necessarily linear movement of time imposed by human perception. If anything, it is 'linear-type' and not 'linear,' because time, being non-spatial, is not entirely like a straight line."[2] By not considering time as something perfectly linear, Montale transcends his situations, returning to other moments and ushering them into the present. Each moment is equidistant as a visually perceived projection. "Effettivamente Montale, nelle *Occasioni*, non si rassegna piú a ridurre il tutto a nulla; anzi tenta di mutare il nulla in tutto, popolando l'assenza con la forza della memoria."[3] This memory brings only goodness and awareness with it, for when one thinks of 'Voce giunta,' one recalls the specification of two types of memory: "memoria che giova e memoria peccato."[4] Understanding what makes memory a "peccato" in 'Voce giunta' is fundamental to understanding "La casa dei doganieri," and other poems, such as 'Mottetto 4.'

In 'La casa dei doganieri,' Montale revisits the customs house of his youth when he summered on the Ligurian coast; it is (now) in a state of decline and disrepair; empty but for the swarms of thoughts that dart into it and out again. In recalling what the house had represented for him in his earlier years, he realizes that even in that past the customs house was already a memory by the time he met the "tu" character. It is a virtual locus; a "punto dilatato" perfectly interconnected to every spatial-visual representation of it. In fact, any common moments shared by Montale and the interlocutor in the customs house occurred in its already abandoned stage. When Montale says, "Tu non ricordi," it is doubled: certainly the female interlocutor (Arletta) could not have remembered when the customs house was in useful service; but perhaps she has not preserved what it had already meant to Montale in his formative experience and memories prior to their meeting.

Where 'Mottetto 4' held a memory that helps Montale reconcile his past doubt as it transcends both time and space, in 'La casa dei doganieri' the memory "peccato" of the 'Voce giunta' is one that does not evolve and readdress itself; one that does not transcend both time and space. "Memoria-peccato" seeks, in a Proustian way, only to preserve the physical state of things in the past. Good memory is synchronized with higher metaphysical orders. I return to a description of the two disembodied voices of 'Voce giunta:'

> *l'una [implied to be Clizia, alive but far away] forse / ritroverà la forma di Chi la mosse e non di sé, / ma l'altro [implied to be the father, long since deceased] sbigottisce e teme che / la larva di memoria in cui si scalda / ai suoi figli si spenga al nuovo balzo.*

It is the fear of losing memory which makes Montale's father cling to his shores, and Clizia's lack of that fear which keeps her from residing only in memory in order to detach herself from her shores, to be truly freed.

'La casa dei doganieri' presents a version of "memoria-peccato." At first there is a chiding on Montale's part ("altro tempo frastorna la tua memoria"), as if his friend had been metaphysically negligent in her duty to preserve through memory. At the same time, one learns of Montale's own personal obsession with remembrance. He has the end of a string, which spans two spaces, like Proust's *Madeleine* – a volume of duration which extends through two moments at once. In Montale's case, multiple moments co-exist in a quantum universe. Without the other end – the union of shared experience – memory becomes vain, and perhaps it gathers "fungus on itself," a condition against which Clizia warns Montale's father in 'Voce giunta':

> *Memoria / non è peccato fin che giova. Dopo / è letargo di talpe, abiezione / che funghisce su sé...*

There is no Ariadne at the other end of the string to guide Montale. It is an unshared memory on which he insists, nonetheless; a "memoria-peccato." If he cannot be sure about the past, how can he have any sense of reality or truth in the present or a hope in the future? Hence, the "orizzonte in fuga" and the deflated, almost indifferent, final line: "E io non so chi va e chi resta." He becomes the negligent customs agent, not keeping track of the comings and goings for he has preserved a fragment of a past life, but it is disjointed from the present one.

The "varco" is extremely interesting. It is a self-reflexive reference of his poetry from the *Ossi* where he was looking for a break in the net, a gap in a stone wall, a way out; when he was looking for something that offered him a similar relief or liberation, if only on the level of a metaphysical truth (cf. 'I limoni,' 'Non chiederci la parola,' and 'Meriggiare pallido e assorto'). As this poem is an exposé on memory, Montale re-evokes a past concept the way one might re-evoke a scene in memory. He holds an end of the string. He is persistent, but others come and go. Though others may have forgotten – they do not recall – he still remembers. Memory to him is sacred, but perhaps this is a flaw. Montale's intense submission to his memories is analogous to the intense commitment of the eel fisherman of 'Mottetto 13' where recollection is metaphorized in the "smorto groviglio" ("blurred knot," as Galassi puts it):[5]

> *La gondola che scivola in un forte / bagliore di catrame e di papaveri, / la subdola canzone che s'alzava / da masse di cordame, l'alte porte / rinchiuse su di te e risa di maschere / che fuggivano a frotte – // una sera tra mille e la mia notte / è piú profonda! S'agita laggiú / uno smorto groviglio che m'avviva / a stratti e mi fa eguale a quell'assorto / pescatore d'anguille dalla riva.*

The "smorto groviglio" renders him equal to the fisherman in two ways: the sounds of its movement wake him from his memories so that he notices the absorption in which he was rapt and in which the fisherman was rapt; and it becomes a literal correlative of memory itself. While the night is filled with the merrymaking and masks of others, the poet, like the eeler, is destined to stand on the margins while the other people – be they shadows or otherwise – live in real time. Of course, though he feels that he has glimpsed a more vivid reality, this is no consolation. In 'Bassa marea' the "negro vilucchio" is the only thing that writhes and resists, and is, therefore, given the role of representing memory; a memory which is predetermined and absent until its reflection is projected onto the screen of images:

Viene col soffio della primavera / un lugubre risucchio / d'assorbite esistenze; e nella sera, / negro vilucchio, solo il tuo ricordo / s'attorce e si difende.

Because it is perceived as a reflection, there is per force duration: "the brain [is] only an interval, a void, nothing but a void, between a stimulation and a response."[6]

This dark plant twists and holds, metaphorically expanding the same argument of 'Mottetto 13,' though it is important not to forget the chronology of the two pieces: the motet being of 1938 and 'Bassa marea' of 1932. In both of these poems there is a tenuous line in the designation of the "smorto groviglio" and the "negro vilucchio." Are they naturally occurring correlatives, things that are already inherently symbolic? Or are they suitable metaphors which Montale crafts by observing his surroundings and trying to find outlets of expression. In other words, are they purely expressive symbols? Do they belong to the entelechy of the whole Montalean experience? Perhaps Montale used the one image as a metaphor in 'Bassa marea' and then years later it was a perfectly metaphysical coincidence that a night in Venice ('Mottetto 13') should present him with the naturally occurring version of the metaphor of his process of remembrance.

Though memory is the medium in which he passes much of his poetic experience, it is equated with black bindweed and a blurred knot which is twisted and resistant. It offers a gloomy image of the poet's own condition. His memory, even at the expense of isolating introversion, resists the cosmic flow of time, which, like the sea, absorbs the existence of everything. After all, the sea is seemingly fixed in its constancy – unchangeable mobility. It is perpetual and Montale is not, and neither is the bindweed with which he associates his struggle against the "certain inferno."

The first strophe of 'Bassa marea' presents a memory of evenings prior to the "now" (present) in question: "Sere di gridi, quando l'altalena / oscilla nella pergola d'allora." Those evenings – that time ("d'allora") – are over now because, though they are recalled in memory, in reality they do not belong to this or that time but to time in general, which inevitably passes like the "discesa / di tutto":

E un oscuro vapore vela appena / la fissità del mare. // Non piú quel tempo. Varcano ora il muro / rapidi voli obliqui, la discesa / di tutto non s'arresta e si confonde / sulla proda scoscesa anche lo scoglio / che ti portò sull'onde.

Though the poem is not about the moment remembered, it is about his own metaphysical condition in the face of passing time. Instead of simply talking about a by-gone time, or a moment he now remembers, he describes how even in this moment he struggles to not forget. Yet time is like the very landscape around him. And in that landscape is the bindweed. It is the only life that can live on the cliff as a trailing, twining plant. It works against the general falling ("discesa") or entropy of time as Montale's poetry defends against time's unravelling of the past.

Even in a discourse involving a present situation, Montale demonstrates how he hangs onto a moment, much in the way he hangs onto memories. In "Stanze" he focuses all of his energy on the intricate phenomena of Clizia's body:

Ricerco invano il punto onde si mosse / il sangue che ti nutre, interminato / respingersi / di cerchi oltre lo spazio / breve dei giorni umani, / che ti rese presente in uno strazio / d'agonie che non sai, viva in un putre / padule d'astro inabissato; ed ora / è linfa che disegna le tue mani, ti batte ai polsi inavvertita e il volto / t'infiamma o discolora.

What seems merely a pulse at her temples is more to Montale. He sees what others do not, even here. He sees more than just her, as she moves along, as if she were destined to move towards the future and he were destined to penetrate into the now (which is ephemeral). The present exists as progression; when one stops to analyze it, one no longer progresses; and certainly, the concept of a "now" is impossible, for as the moment occurs it is immediately a past. In the absence of progression, perhaps one would have a pure present, but for every moment one does not keep pace with that progression, one is automatically in the past. What Montale gains in dimension from his privileged insight – with respect to the others, even Clizia – he loses by being mired down in a time that is out of joint with the cosmic.

With Clizia he associates angelic airiness, light and ascendance. He has already equated himself with the race that remains on the ground in 'Falsetto,' and here, in 'Stanze,' the image of the bubble rising right before the last four lines is key:

Ed ora sale / l'ultima bolla in su. La dannazione / è forse questa vaneggiante amara / oscurità che scende su chi resta.

The bubble diametrically opposes the image of a darkness that descends on whoever remains. The bubble highlights not just rising, but its own ephemeral state, which will inevitably burst. The damnation which becomes his fate, as one who remains, is the fate of someone who is trapped in the futility of recreating – in memory – what once was, but is no more; of someone who ponders life instead of living it.

Another interesting aspect of this damnation is related to the poet's search for truth and understanding of the world; the secret behind the world, which is predestined, absolute reality. 'Stanze,' a poem of circa 1929, is a conceptual forerunner of the first 'Mottetto.' In 'Stanze' Montale is the opposite of a Clizia who touches the sign and crosses over it; transcending it. She somehow sees and touches what he cannot even find in 'Mottetto 1.' While her life transcends the search for truth, Montale is forever searching for a truth, a sign. With a perpetually fruitless search the only certainty is a "certo inferno." It seems that the beloved always lives life for the Esterine (cf. 'Falsetto') moment in the present constantly crossing over, leaving him only to experience her, and life, as a memory. She is an abstract form of perfection, but he experiences her as a platonic memory of an eternal abstract. This is very much the case in 'Sotto la pioggia' where it is a skipping of the record "that will allow the poet to escape into his memory of her"[7] so that he can experience her in a controlled way, on his own terms:

> *Strideva Adiós muchachos, compañeros / de mi vida, il suo disco dalla corte: / e m'è cara la maschera se ancora / di là dal mulinello della sorte / mi rimane il sobbalzo che riporta / al tuo sentiero*

Montale says how this "sobbalzo" of the record will bring him "al tuo sentiero" (to your path), and the following line speaks of him following a smoke trail (much like the wake of a ship). The beloved, like the ship, plods along into the present which ever becomes the future as it moves along, moving farther away from the past, for what is past was once briefly a present. She experiences truth, for truth is what she makes of her faith along the journey, while Montale's search for the truth is forever experienced in the wake of the present. His epiphanies, then, pertain more to his past than to his present. He has learned a lesson from Clizia, but it is through her experience, not his own, that he begins to understand the risk of the stork:

> *Per te intendo / ciò che osa la cicogna quando alzato / il volo dalla cuspide nebbiosa / rèmiga verso la Città del Capo.*

This stork conjures up images of the angelic beloved, who inhabits the "alte nebulose" ('Mottetto 12') or the "sfere del gelo" ('Mottetto 14').

There are many interwoven images of memory in 'Punta del Mesco,' where the poem treats less the relationship with the beloved, and more the process of memory itself:

> *Nel cielo della cava rigato / all'alba dal volo dritto delle pernici / il fumo delle mine s'inteneriva, / saliva lento le pendici a piombo. / Dal rostro del palabotto si capolvolsero / le ondine trombettiere silenziose / e affondarono rapide tra le spume / che il tuo passo sfiorava. // Vedo il sentiero che percorsi un giorno / come un cane inquieto; lambe il fiotto, / s'inerpica tra i massi e rado strame / a tratti lo scancella. E tutto è uguale. / Nella ghiaia bagnata s'arrovella / un'eco degli scrosci. Umido brilla / il sole sulle membra affaticate / dei curvi spaccapietre che martellano. // Polene che risalgono e mi portano / qualche cosa di te. Un tràpano incide / il cuore sulla roccia – schianta attorno / piú forte un rombo. Brancolo nel fumo, / ma rivedo: ritornano i tuoi rari / gesti e il viso che aggiorna al davanzale, – / mi torna la tua infanzia dilaniata / dagli spari!*

The presence of the mine smoke recalls 'Sotto la pioggia,' but also the general fog of memory in the poetry which culminates in 'Non recidere, forbice.' Memory is forever fighting, becoming smoke, fog or haze. Here, in the moment, the quarry smoke clears, and Montale suddenly has a more clear vision of the sea. Yet, he cannot observe it for what it is, rather for what memory of the beloved it may have to offer. The sea is best defined not by how it appears in and of itself, but by how Arletta's feet used to splash at the shoreline. Suddenly Montale sees the present landscape, as it was in the past. He sees himself like a restless dog on the path. He describes the image of the path, concluding that nothing has changed; it is all the same ("tutto è uguale"), which leads him out of memory and back into his surroundings. From here the figureheads ("polene") bring him a hint of her, though the allusion is quite cryptic in that it is highly doubtful that boats with figureheads would have appeared in that setting, let alone ones that rose out of the sea and were reflected on it.[8] It is as if from the moment he compared memory to the present and realized they were identical, Montale has experienced two separate spatio-temporal moments as co-existent. In fact, whereas her presence – only in memory – was related in the imperfect "il tuo passo sfiorava" ("that your footsteps used to trace"), in the third strophe her gestures and her face return to him in the present tense. In the first strophe, when the smoke cleared, he first saw the boats and the sea. Now, when the smoke of the last blast clears, he sees Arletta, as if a series of photographs were super-positioned in the same plane.

The most interesting part about what he sees of her, despite the smoke, is her "dawning at the windowsill." The image recalls 'Il balcone' – also of 1933. Like the life that gives off light from a window, which only "she" can discern. Here, she "dawns" like a sunrise on the windowsill. Suddenly, in the empty space of a frame around a window, she appears. What appeared to be pure absence of the beloved becomes, through memory, the presence in the void. From this, Montale wonders whether all presence in the void is not equally a phenomenal projection, perceived not in the mind but outside of it.

Though the sea had played a rather large part in the *Ossi*, it has not been dominant in the *Occasioni*. Where it has been present ('La casa dei doganieri,' for example), it serves as a setting rather than as protagonist in the *Ossi*. In 'Eastbourne' (*Occasioni*), however, the sea plays an active role. This player, in its grandiose, unmovable indifference, both indiscriminately destroys memories and brings them back. The sea brings all or nothing in such a seeming banality of a tide rising and falling. This is, indeed, not the first time Montale does this. In 'Eastbourne,' Montale focuses on an occasion of re-evoking an absent loved one, while in 'Crisalide' (*Ossi*) he and the "tu" are part of the overall process of nature's vicissitudes (most clearly seen in the changing chrysalis), yet the two poems share the commonality of the sea and memory. In fact, in 'Crisalide,' the poet weaves the metaphor of sea and memory so tightly that in the second strophe, the imagery of waves and the sea is problematic. Does Montale use sea imagery as a metaphor for memory, or is the sea physically present? Perhaps it is irrelevant, for the sea offers an undeniable quality as the perfect naturally occurring symbol for memory. In the second strophe the most outstanding feature of this is the "risacca" ("undertow"), seen in the following extract:

> *Ogni attimo vi porta nuove fronde / e il suo sbigottimento avanza ogni altra / gioia fugace; viene a impetuose onde / la vita a questo estremo angolo d'orto. / Lo sguardo ora vi cade su le zolle; / una risacca di memorie giunge / al vostro cuore e quasi lo sommerge. / Lunge risuona un grido: ecco precipita / il tempo, spare con risucchi rapidi / tra i sassi, ogni ricordo è spento; ed io dall'oscuro mio canto mi protendo / a codesto solare avvenimento.*

Again, in 'Eastbourne,' the physical sea is both fixed and immobile next to the mortality of humans, while it serves as a perfect metaphor for the comings and goings of memory:

> *'Dio salvi il Re' intonano le trombe / da un padiglione erto su palafitte / che aprono il varco al mare quando sale / a distruggere peste / umide*

> *di cavalli nella sabbia / del litorale... Bank Holiday ... Riporta l'onda lunga / della mia vita / a striscio, troppo dolce sulla china. / Si fa tardi. I fragori si distendono, / si chiudono in sordina.*

There is a distinction between the poetic time, which aims at the recovery of the past in order to hold onto the present through poetry, and the cosmic time of the universe's own inanimate, inhuman passing. The sea represents cosmic time and the footsteps are the poetic, human intervals. The sea brings a "risacca di memorie" in 'Crisalide' that drowns the heart of Montale with pathos, but when the tide ebbs away, sucked through the shoals, the memories disappear as time speeds past. Even the moment in which one remembers a past occasion becomes itself a memory, and invite the reader to keep in mind this has already been introduced at the beginning of this chapter. In 'Eastbourne' the creation of the hoof prints in the sand is the original occasion. When the sea washes them away they are relegated to the past and can only be revisited as a memory. Ironically, it is the same unfeeling sea that washes away the prints in the sand which brings more memories, but even these fade away to become memories of a memory. The footprints in Montale's poetic world have not disappeared. They are merely latent photographic images still etched on the virtual surface – like Freud's 'Mystic Writing-Pad.' It recalls the footprints of 'Crisalide' as well:

> *Ah crisalide com'è amara questa / tortura senza nome che ci volve / e ci porta lontani – e poi non restano / neppure le nostre orme sulla polvere.*

The vanishing footprints of 'Crisalide' are not washed away by the sea, but they part of the whole general theme here. Just like in 'Vasca' ("è nato e morto, e non ha avuto un nome"), here there is something – a torture – that comes and goes without even having a name, and the ephemeral footprints in the dust are greater than the net result of trying to break through the "gran muraglia." What is present today, he tells the reader in 'Eastbourne,' perhaps will seem a dream tomorrow, much like the footprints. Dreams are like memory in that they are the presence of some moment now absent; an absence-presence as seen, for example, in Borges' 'Ausencia':

> *¿En qué hondonada esconderé mi alma / para que no vea tu ausencia / que como un sol terrible, sin ocaso, / brilla definitiva y despiadada? / Tu ausencia me rodea / como la cuerda a la garganta, / el mar al que se hunde.*

The experience of a dream is an absence-presence. Its being implies only virtual presence on the visual receptors of the brain. But the dreams exist in an infinitely expandable "punto dilatato." Memories, like dreams, are infinitely contained in the mind. They pertain to the one who remembers and, yet, they are not in the one remembering. They are on the screen of images in the holographic universe: the brain is a receptor for holographic cinematography. They are below the surface, in the mind. Once again, the surroundings only serve as correlatives to aid him in materializing his all-too-subjective thoughts and memories. His poems are atemporal transcripts of the juxtaposition of object-words from his existential alphabet. He writes them so that "le immagini non stiano di per sé, ma siano circondate da un alone di memorie."9

Montale depends upon his surroundings, which are a subjective, existential alphabet that he uses to transcribe his thoughts and memories. As such, the image of the revolving door ('Eastbourne') is disconcerting. His external environment confuses him as each object in the "schermo d'immagini" flashes by like the glass panels, each reflecting and being reflected in the next. The screen of images around him sucks everything along with it like the sea; like the "lugubre risucchio / d'assorbite esistenze" ('Bassa marea'). Despite all that is turning around him, Clizia comes to him as a voice. Once again, Montale places himself on a different plane from the rest of the world – perhaps in the void where everything co-exists spatio-temporally. First he talks of the whirling, like a revolving door of a hotel; then with a semicolon he adds his state – "in ascolto." Suddenly there is an explanation for the previous stanza's "E vieni / tu pure voce prigioniera, sciolta / anima ch'è smarrita;" for that which he hears and recognizes is Clizia. Unlike the case of 'La casa dei doganieri' ("né qui respiri"), here he does recognize her presence; he has proof of it.

It is not simply a process of remembrance, but a struggle with entropy and a downward pull of chaos, despite which he will recall her, and thence her presence in the void is not spontaneous in and of itself – it requires the active mnemonic mind of the poet, not to mention the correct juxtaposition of external images and activity. Montale recognizes Clizia's breathing and, therefore, for all intents and purposes, she is present there as part of the whole. The notes of the English anthem, so close to those of the American version, are the return of Clizia, as the "voce prigioniera." As in 'L'anima che dispensa,' she returns on a song which is associated with her. Segre comments on women in Montale's poetry whose "apparizioni soprannaturali e abbaglianti restano (invece) confinate [hence "voce prigioniera"] nelle liriche …i riflessi dell'esperienza musicale su quella poetica sono ragguardevoli… noteremo la sensibilità ai rumori."[10]

The voice is imprisoned because it is reliant upon a melody, or other particular medium, to bring it to a point of communicability. It is freed from the body, like a spiritual form, but because it is constrained by the serendipity of notes, it is lost and restored over and over, by the whimsy of musical phrases. It returns to him in an intermittent fashion, by now familiar as the recollection, recognition, or illumination "a tagli" that Montale experiences at the point where his memorial world and the real world intersect. The music, "mia patria," suddenly cries out about Clizia's presence in the absence and Montale rises ("mi levo") to greet her. The "anch'io" implies others who rise like Montale. The others appear to rise out of reverence for the anthem, while the poet – predictably not part of the world of the men seen as shadows – is rising to meet Clizia, whose breath confirms her presence: "e il giorno è troppo folto" ("and the day is too full"). All the cosmic time around him halts for a flash, but in that instant in his memory, a simple moment becomes infinite enough to occupy the whole day, as if the point in his memory – the "punto dilatato" – opened up to accommodate her. The poet lives this moment as a playback of a film which exists outside of time and place, as an encapsulation of time, each moment fixed as a potential projection.

As with the jackals of 'Mottetto 6,' it is unclear whether Clizia sent the music or a senhal of herself.[11] The protagonists appear briefly to share both ends of the string from 'La casa dei doganieri.' Yet his words are distressing: as he had not known "who left and who remained" while the horizon was ever-fleeing, in 'Eastbourne,' Montale reveals how,

> *Tutto apparirà vano: anche la forza / che nella sua tenace ganga aggrega / i vivi e i morti, gli alberi e gli scogli / e si svolge da te, per te."*

All memories will be whirled away in a "carosello che travolge / tutto dentro il suo giro."

In 'Barche sulla Marna' Montale gives the reader a more defined version of his personal ideality in the face of reality. The ideality is presented through memory and the reality is presented as a world where one cannot help but rely on memory. As mentioned above, to live in the present is impossible, for every *now* immediately becomes a *then*. The world is not a pure being but a place where progression to a future automatically implies a leaving behind of a past. As with the movement of time and the movement of celluloid over a light source, any particular photo-image leaves the poet forever in a wake of after-images.

> *A un capo e all'altro della poesia, la constatata fuga del tempo (il*

negativo leopardiano) e la continuità indifferente o ostile della natura, e invece, nell'ampio solco aperto a mezzo della lirica, ma destinato a rinchiudersi, il sogno che restaura un tempo finalmente fermo, un «giorno [...] quasi immobile».[12]

The cork of 'Barche sulla Marna' is left to the current, happy in its ignorance, as if to remind the poet of potential bliss for those who live unselfconsciously in the flow of time:

Felicità del sùghero abbandonato / alla corrente / che stempra attorno i ponti rovesciati / e il plenilunio pallido del sole.

The cork, in contrast to Montale's lack of bliss, forces the poet's thoughts to an awareness of time gone by, as on a flowing river. So he asks where the seasons of the past have gone. How could it be that things that took so long to accumulate in the past – even the interminable duration of waiting – could no longer have any bearing on that which is around him? The images are fleeting, as in 'La casa dei doganieri' or 'Eastbourne.' But here, in 'Barche sulla Marna,' Montale provides the description of a reflection on the water where the flow of the water – dynamism – is constant but the image on it is still unchanging mobility:

E altro ancora era il sogno, ma il suo riflesso / fermo sull'acqua in fuga, sotto il nido / del pendolino, aereo e inaccesibile, / era silenzio altissimo nel grido / concorde nel meriggio ed un mattino / piú lungo era la sera, il gran fermento / era grande riposo.

Montale posits a temporary, albeit oniric, solution to his state of disillusionment as a way of combatting the "void that invades us," which is introduced in the second strophe of 'Barche sulla Marna':

Ma dov'è / la lenta processione di stagioni / che fu un'alba infinita e senza strade, / dov'è la lunga attesa e qual è il nome / del vuoto che ci invade.

Interestingly enough, this void pertains to the same genre of 'Vasca' and 'Crisalide' where there is a phenomenon without a name. The void is seemingly such because the lacunous quality of what, in the present, one carries with oneself from the past is empty, as compared to its original, seminal experience. At best, Montale's memories and illuminations occur intermittently, like the flashes of 'Il balcone,' the illumination "a tagli" of 'Mottetto 15,' or even the peace that illuminates "a spiragli" and everything that rolls on with "rari guizzi" of 'Tempi di Bellosguardo.' Therefore, it is not surprising that after Montale establishes the dream and of what it consists, he immediately uses images of "bagliore" ("glow"):

> *Il sogno è questo: un vasto, interminato giorno che rifonde / tra gli argini, quasi immobile, il suo bagliore / e ad ogni svolta il buon lavoro dell'uomo, / il domani velato che non fa orrore.*

The perfect dream would be an interminable day where splendor – illumination or epiphanic understanding – was not in flashes or streaks, but continually replenishing itself. As in a dream, there is no duration, no separation between the stimulus and the response. There is no after-image, but the pure coexistence of infinite spatial moments all of which are equidistant. In dreams, the brain experiences the world as an unencumbered brain does in the void behind the screen of images. For, in the void, the brain is immediately connected to Deleuze's being-memory. "Bergson," Deleuze reminds us, "introduced a profound element of transformation: the brain was now only an interval [*écart*], a void, nothing but a void, between a stimulation and a response."[13] It is not "only" a void, however, it is especially a void: there is harmony when its virtual quality is not encumbered by the ephemeral material illusion of the body – it transcends the physical limitations of the body. This would be a day not of becoming, but of pure being or presence, "quasi immobile." Despite any cosmic changes – the "acqua in fuga" – there would be a permanent image in the human interval, for the cosmic and the poetic-memorial time would be rather comparable. The morning would be part of the evening as the evening would be part of the morning, where life is not divided by past or future, but seen as one continuous noumenon. These are not the "soste umane" of 'Mottetto 15,' which are a humanly imposed order on an indifferent atemporal cosmos. Here day and night are both part of one process, not cycles that stand in and of themselves. The future, or the unknown "domani velato," is not distressing, for in this halting of time there is less threat: with time not moving forward there is less left behind; less past; less on the goat path behind the speaker of 'Voce giunta con le folaghe.'

Suddenly there is an interruption with 'Barche sulla Marna.' One returns from ideality to reality with the simple word "Qui":

> *Qui...il colore / che resiste è del topo che ha saltato / tra i giunchi o col*

suo spruzzo di metallo / velenoso, lo storno che sparisce / tra i fumi della riva.

The present overtakes both Montale's nostalgia for the past and his fantasies for a greater order. Yet the image of the present is one where the succession of the events in the present is in itself too much to absorb, though no less thrilling to the senses. The brain, limited to the capacity of optic nerves in the body, is subject to the paradox of cinematography, it lives in constant Bergsonian *durée*. A film can indefinitely contain images, but because of the limitations of the eyes, each image has to be perceived not simultaneously but as a linear reproduction – motion orders them. It is an illusion, however, for to exist it must destroy, obliterate each image. In the true void, all images retain their integrity, not as after-images but as if on a perfect cinematic hologram. Montale will realize this in *Farfalla di Dinard*, but for now he constructs atemporal poetry. "Time is therefore conceptualized within the problematic of determining what is storable, what is representable. Memory is representation itself; time its inconceivability."[14] Montale's poems remove time but, paradoxically, without time there would be no memories. One begins to see that memories are not remembrance of a time past but a pure experience of recalling what has been there all along.

Montale uses rather litotic language to emphasize just how fleeting the present can be, let alone a memory of that present. Even in the present, one will be lucky to get even a glimpse of present reality. He describes facetiously how the color of the mouse jumping among the brushes is the one that *resists*, when it is obvious that at best this would be a series of after-images of the darting mouse. And with further imagery reminiscent of the *Ossi*, he adds the presence of the splash of the disappearing starling which seems like "metallo velenoso" ("poisonous metal").[15] Images similar to much of Montale's poetry come bounding into the scene in a simultaneous contradiction of banality and otherness, a mysteriousness which only Montale's scrutiny could give it. This is truly where he is unhappy with regards to the carefree cork ('Barche sulla Marna') moving on the Heraclitan river of time; unlike Esterina or the woman of 'Sul Llogebrat.'

Yet in the fading lines of 'Barche,' the poet seems to be somewhat resigned to reality in the face of his own ideality: "La sera è questa." There is, for once, less concern with the differentiation between cosmic time and human intervals and the memory associated with them. The inference on the part of the reader is that perhaps the poet has temporarily accepted his role, knowing, feeling, that he is right in his assumptions about the empirical world: "Ora ["now"] possiamo / scendere fino a che s'accenda l'Orsa." Now the poet and his company can move forward aware of the illusion of time, of the planets and constellations, rather than fighting cosmic time with a presumption of individual importance in the indifferent universe.

Not only is the statement parenthetical, but perhaps it was added much later. The sentence includes the adjective "domenicali" to describe the boats as pertaining to Sunday. Mentioning Sunday cancels out any sentiment of a "domani velato." The connotation, in fact, of Sunday can be interpreted as the day which one would want to perpetuate because of its association with rest, church, relaxation – Sunday activity. So it is a day in which one is aware of tomorrow and in which one wants to perpetuate the present, so, once again, Montale is destined to live in the past, for all presents flee from the now becoming immediately past: "L'avvenire è già passato da un pezzo,"[16] claims Rombi referring to such poems as 'A Pio Rajna' (*Quaderno di quattro anni*):

Chi scava nel passato può comprendere / che passato e futuro distano appena / di un milionesimo di attimo tra loro.

In the beginning of the poem it was the current of the river that represented movement, the passing of time; cosmic, geologic time fleeing despite the images seemingly dancing on the current. In the last line, the boats themselves are "in corsa" as the image that moves along in his memory to mark the occasion, like Calvino's photographer. The photographer, before becoming obsessed, criticized people for snapping photos. One can live in the present, he comments, but "la scansione dei fotogrammi si insinua tra i vostri gesti non è piú il piacere del gioco a muovervi ma quello di rivedervi nel futuro."[17] Like a photographer, in this regard, Montale is preparing for the future where the fog of memory, which will remain of this moment, will take away from the clarity.

'Nuove stanze' is another example of Montale viewing the present through the filter of memory. In fact it is also a poem in which he arrives at an understanding of the past only in the present:

Il mio dubbio d'un tempo era se forse / tu stessa ignori il giuoco che si svolge / sul quadrato e ora è nembo alle tue porte: / follía di morte non si placa a poco / prezzo, se poco è il lampo del tuo sguardo, / ma domanda altri fuochi, oltre le fitte / cortine che per te fomenta il dio / del caso, quando assiste. // Oggi so ciò che vuoi.

He resolves his "dubbio d'un tempo" ("earlier doubt") and comes to a greater understanding of Clizia. Yet her way, which could ease his existential state if he emulated it, remains mysterious to Montale even though he has recognized it. His epiphany in the line "Oggi so ciò che vuoi" is brought to only a potential conclusion – perhaps like the "Provisional Conclusion" of *La bufera* – in the "chi può" of the terzultimate line. Obviously, the "chi può" would be opposing Nazi-Fascism, for the poem is about the threat of World War II and anti-Semitism, yet it is the same force of opposition in his friend's eyes that would be needed by all to defeat this scourge. It is a similar countenance and attitude of life that Montale would need to combat his "male di vivere."

Clizia has been the same all along, like a platonic form in the abstract which is in all of us at birth awaiting our recollection of it. Now that Montale better perceives this aspect of her, he needs to go back and address what had seemingly not been present in past times. In 'Mottetto 4' she was, in retrospect, spiritually present, though physically absent. Only now does Montale reconstruct what he should have seen all along. It is like a second movement to 'Falsetto,' for Esterina seemed so separate from the race of people on the ground to whom Montale pertained ("la razza che rimane a terra."). Now, in 'Nuove stanze,' there is the possibility that in some odd way Montale himself could pertain to her race; her kind. He could be a sempiternal, platonic abstract; part of a noumenal world for which the empirical life is but one long preparation to meet one's entelechy.

Two images encourage the reader to consider this. The first image is an unseen window:

La morgana che in cielo liberava / torri e ponti è sparita / al primo soffio; s'apre la finestra / non vista e il fumo s'agita.

The second image looks beyond the thick curtains: "oltre le fitte / cortine che per te fomenta il dio / del caso, quando assiste." The window is unseen, yet open – a "varco," if you will – and very much a part of the climate in the *rooms*. In terms of the break in the net or the gap in the stone wall or the "varco" – all images from Montale's earlier poetry – the window could represent a way out, which may have been there for him previously, but which he had missed. The heavy curtains could be the "schermo d'immagini," the phenomenal world of cinematic illusion projected over the noumenal, as a holographic world.

The "schermo" could be a screen on which to project, a screen of all the material around Montale or the receptor of images connected to the optic nerve, but it could also be keeping something out or in – a barrier. At this point, for Montale the heavy curtains are a barrier; for Clizia they are a circumstance that changes little with regard to her spirit. She still manages to look beyond them in two ways: though she is in the room she is keenly aware of what is on the other side of that wall in the literal sense and, in general, she is capable of seeming more than that which Montale and others are capable of intuiting in the realm of the metaphysical. The curtains confound Montale and the others. Understanding it now is perhaps the "Nuove" ("new") part of the title 'Nuove stanze.' While 'Stanze' finishes with "La dannazione / è forse questa vaneggiante amara / oscurità che scende su chi resta," 'Nuove stanze' ends with:

> Ma resiste / e vince il premio della solitaria / veglia chi può con te allo specchio ustorio / che accieca le pedine opporre i tuoi / occhi d'acciaio.

With a 'new' something, one implies (*a priori*) the presence of the old and, likewise, we see poetry not only concerned with memory, and driven by memory, but poetry that is memory. The obsession with recollection culminates in the expectation of revisiting that which Montale remembers. The expectation is the "attesa" which has been so thematic in the *Occasioni* and which manifests itself in 'Notizie dall'Amiata.'

In order to conclude the discussion of the *Occasioni*, and to make the transition to the *Bufera* collection more meaningful, it is necessary to address the final poem, 'Notizie dall'Amiata.' Surely the opening lines of the first of the three parts preface what is to come in *La bufera*: "Il fuoco d'artifizio del maltempo / sarà murmure d'arnie a tarda sera." The storm setting, especially with metaphors of fireworks, creates a stepping stone to the more apocalyptic poem, 'La bufera,' which opens up a dialogue about the storm of war about to be unleashed. The "male di vivere" will no longer be the poet's alone, but of everyone, and will Clizia, as a salvific angel, bring some sort of succor? One will no longer reside in the empirical world while holistic salvation lies in the noumenos.

More importantly for the thematics of the *Occasioni*, the opening line of 'Notizie dall'Amiata' employs a future tense, thus creating a sense of "attesa" in the reader and in the poet that someone, or something, will reduce the violence of the metaphorical and the real storm. In fact, in speaking of 'Notizie,' Isella points out how, "Il primo tempo è colmo dell'epifania dell'Assente."[18] Bonora further focuses on how the lines are addressed "all'assente che è invano chiamata a condividere l'esperienza del poeta."[19] This suggests a world as holograph, of which each brain is but a reflection. In this world, the experience of one is potentially the experience of all. Indeed the poem calls Clizia to join the poet in the interior of the humble room:

> La stanza ha travature / tarlate ed un sentore di meloni / penetra dall'assito. Le fumate / morbide che risalgono una valle / d'elfi e di

funghi fino al cono diafano / della cima m'intorbidano i vetri, / e ti scrivo di qui, da questo tavolo / remoto, dalla cellula di miele / di una sfera lanciata nello spazio.

And the suffering of the poet in solitude awaiting a sign of Clizia is further heightened by the use of the word "cellula," which, says Isella, "È però anche la celleta di una monastica attesa solitaria."[20] Perhaps the salvation of Clizia will assist him: the future tense of "essere" ("sarà") of the first lines suggests that a calm will come, which will seem a "murmure di arnie a tarda sera," and the setting will be the stage for Clizia's visitation, as implied by the future tense of "rompere" used further down in the first part: "le vene / di salnitro e di muffa sono il quadro / dove tra poco romperai." And yet the possibility of epiphany is relegated to the banal and melancholy expression in the present tense, which closes the first part: "Fuori piove." This seems rather anticlimactic to the reader who has attentively read the previous three verses where it seemed an epiphany was nigh: "La vita / che t'affàbula è ancora troppo breve / se ti contiene! Schiude la tua icona / il fondo luminoso." In fact, Montale pens the lines (which hark back to 'Mottetto 20': "La vita che sembrava / vasta è piú breve del tuo fazzoletto") with a tone of paradox and irony. Isella paraphrases the verses thus: "La vita del tuo affabulatore (troppo lunga nella sua noia abituale) è persino troppo breve, se, apparendo tu, le accada di colmarsi del tuo pensiero."[21] On the one hand, the poet's life seems long and drawn out when he suffers its monotony awaiting Clizia, but it must be too brief if it can contain Clizia's complexity in a simple, expressible form. Yet the fact that Clizia has an icon already attributed to her ("Schiude la tua icona / il fondo luminoso"), which is recognizable to Montale and capable of illuminating, means that it is based on the compacted, personal meanings accumulated by the poet over time and reduced into a sort of "punto" which can become "dilatato." This is a reflection of Montale's memory, pregnant with charged meaning, ready to find Clizia in even the slightest hint of popping chestnuts or in the veins of saltpeter and mold on the walls:

Il focolare / dove i marroni esplodono, le vene / di salnitro e di muffa sono il quadro / dove tra poco romperai.

Yet, perhaps she is present in the overlap of simultaneous spatial images. The second part of 'Notizie' is greatly concerned with themes of time and of the dead (particularly germane to themes of the dead in 'I morti' and in 'Voce giunta'). The return of the dead will play a great role in the whole of the *Bufera* collection, as well:

> *Come la prima parte delle 'Notizie' si chiude con la triste constatazione della mancata risposta dell'assente all'appello del poeta, la seconda, in cui gli oggetti nominati ancor più si caricano di sensi e soprasensi, si conclude con il ripiegarsi della coscienza in un'accorata meditazione sulla vanità dell'attesa, sul nulla, sulla morte: "Oh il gocciolìo che scende a rilento / dalle casipole buie, il tempo fatto acqua, / il lungo colloquio coi poveri morti, la cenere, il vento, / il vento che tarda, la morte, la morte che vive!"*[22]

Certainly, it is implied that the wind, a naturally occurring phenomenon, will auger a possible dialogue with the dead, much the way the coots will bring Clizia's disembodied voice from afar in 'Voce giunta.' However, more important and problematic is the "nothing" of 'Notizie,' overtly addressed by Bonora in the quote above, and which Montale insinuates with the use of "la cenere" ("ashes") – the residue of something that has been, but which is no longer.

Absence and death, both recorded in memory are equivalents of nothingness for they are not material; not part of the phenomenal cinema of illusion. So to experience the epiphany, Montale may have to experience it with time standing still as implied in the line, "l'occhio del campanile è fermo sulle due ore." It could be that the physical clock has stopped at about 2 o'clock, but is is more charged with metaphor than that. Savoca (in *Quaderno per Le occasioni*) offers a fantastic explanation:

> *È come se non si fosse un solo tempo, ma quello di due ore: quali queste siano non è detto, ma è possibile un'ipotesi: l'uomo vive in una dimensione temporale in cui il presente è sempre in relazione all'ora del passato o del futuro, e quindi egli, non vivendo pienamente nel presente, è scisso in due.*[23]

Montale, living within the expectation created by his memory, is ultimately awaiting an absence-presence. This absence-presence exists beyond time in his memory, not in the flow of time's regular continuum, so it is possible that in Montale's mind the topos of the dead and memories resides in the "vuoto inabitato / che occupammo e che attende fin ch'è tempo / di colmarsi di noi, di ritrovarci..." ('Voce giunta'). The explanation provided by Savoca regarding the bell tower stopped on the "due ore" becomes increasingly astute if we look at it in the context of 'Voce giunta,' but also if one keeps in mind what Montale himself said about this void: "Le vide inhabité qui se fait en nous juste avant que nous soyons ou que nous disions oui à la vie: le vide qui se fait dans la pendule une seconde avant que ne sonne l'heure".[24] He offers a cinematic world where there is a void between each frame; each Eleatic spatial movement. The break in the stone wall is a metaphor for the break in the empiric world, which reveals the true reality.

The poet, "scisso in due," as Savoca stated above, imagines a void that is somehow outside of time's continuum, and there, if for a brief moment, Clizia can be with him in a sort of epiphany. The poet cannot live his life in time and simultaneously experience Clizia's presence in the void. But to experience this, the time (as represented in the belltower of 'Notizie') must stop, even for just a moment, so that there is a slight gap in it. In this gap, Montale, a living poet, can experience the absent and the dead right before the clock strikes its hour outside of the durée and without the mediation between stimulation and response.

As such, the previous reference to Clizia's icon ("Schiude la tua icona / il fondo luminoso") takes on a greater meaning. If she is seen as having an icon, then she may be perceived by the poet to be sacred or godlike. Therefore, she would be absent the way a divine figure would be: "Assente come una divinità."[25] So, unless Montale leaves this world, how can he participate in Clizia's illumination? "Il fondo dell'icona è la breve vita inutile che affàbula, deve perciò rompersi questo sfondo, perché l'assente possa entrare nella vita vera che sta vivendo il poeta."[26] But this miracle does not bridge the two times, as one detects not only in the resigned tone of the last line of the first part ("Fuori piove"), but also in the optative subjunctives used in the second part of 'Notizie':

E tu seguissi le fragili architetture / annerite dal tempo e dal carbone, / i cortili quadrati che hanno nel mezzo / il pozzo profondissimo; tu seguissi / il volo infagottato degli uccelli / notturni e in fondo al borro l'allucciolío / della Galassia, la fascia d'ogni tormento.

The poet augurs on the presence as if to suggest that her icon, in fact, did not succeed in revealing an epiphany. Time moves forward ("il tempo fatto acqua") and his "attesa" is futile because it only brings him to consider the vanity of life and death, hence the "colloquio coi poveri morti" of the end of the second part of 'Notizie.'

Montale struggles with time in the third part of 'Notizie': "Questa rissa cristiana che non ha / se non parole d'ombra e di lamento / che ti porta di me?" He no longer knows whether he should put his faith in himself, in miracles, or even in a language that, ultimately, is an extension of his feeble attempts to bring presence into the absence with his poetry. Yet, just when Montale has resigned himself, he experiences a moment of calm pause, filled with hope:

Si disfà / un cumulo di strame: e tardi usciti / a unire la mia veglia al tuo profondo / sonno che li riceve, i porcospini / s'abbeverano a un filo di pietà.

Even in this landscape, bereft by the stormy weather, he re-examines his very words, his "parole d'ombra." The very "gocciolío" of the second part of 'Notizie' becomes more promising to Montale as he resigns himself to quiet contemplation. When the "porcospini" drink from the very same water, produced as runoff from the storm, their action offers Montale the very sign he had been trying to evoke from the beginning, a confluence point in the myriad spatial planes of a holographic world. The sign was around him the whole time, but he did not know it at first, as is often the case with Montale, especially in 'Mottetto 4': Il logorío / di prima mi salvò solo per questo: // che t'ignoravo e non dovevo: ai colpi / d'oggi lo so.

These odd creatures appear as suddenly as the jackals of 'Mottetto 6.' They are simultaneously with Montale and with Clizia. They have bridged the two temporal dimensions by being experienced by Clizia in her dream and by Montale in the natural flow of life. But are Clizia and Montale united? Is this unity not what Montale sought and hoped for in the beginning of the poem? This "filo di pietà" carries Montale through the storm of the eponymous collection following the *Occasioni*. In essence, a holographic world allows for two people to simultaneously hold the string of 'La casa dei doganieri.' It can indeed extend into two, or more, moments. Montale has a faith in the presence of absent ones and a faith in his own poetry as a way of transcending tumultuous times and as a way of filling the void around him as he approaches the secret of the true reality. In this there is a subtle contentment, much like the sweet image of young hedgehogs sipping water in the moment after the storm, a water which connects spatial moments rather than disconnecting them, like the Heraclitean river.

Notes

1. Italo Calvino. "Forse un mattino andando," in *Letture montaliane in occasione dell'80 compleanno del poeta*. (Genova: Bozzi, 1977): 44.
2. Walter J. Ong, "Evolution, Myth and Poetic Vision," *Comparative Literature Studies* 3.1 (1966): 5.
3. Alvaro Valentini, *Lettura di Montale: Le occasion* (Roma: Bulzoni, 1975) 151.
4. Sergio Antonielli, *Letteratura del disagio* (Milano: Edizioni di Comunità, 1984) 200.
5. Galassi 205.
6. Gilles Deleuze. *Cinema II: The Time-Image*. Trans. Hugh Tomlinson and Robert Galeta. (Minneapolis: U of Minnesota Press, 1989): 211.

7. Ibid. n.514.
8. See Lorenzo Greco, ed., *Montale commenta Montale* (Parma: Pratiche, 1980) 37.
9. F. J. Jones. "La linea esistenziale dell'arte montaliana," in *Quaderno del Cenobio* 30 (1963): 23.
10. Cesare Segre, *I segni e la critica* (Torino: Einaudi, 1969) 136.
11. The polemic is Montale's; it was discussed originally in an informal article by Montale in the daily *Corriere della sera* in 1950. This article was later reprinted in Eugenio Montale, "Due sciacalli al guinzaglio," *Il secondo mestiere: arte, musica, società*. Ed. Giorgio Zampa (Milano: Mondadori, 1996) 1489.
12. Gilberto Lonardi, *Il vecchio e il giovane e altri studi su Montale* (Bologna: Zanichelli, 1980) 88.
13. Deleuze 221.
14. Mary Anne Doane. *The Emergence of Cinematic Time.* (Cambridge: Harvard U Press, 2002): 45.
15. Translation mine.
16. Maggi Rombi, *Montale: parole, sensi e immagini* (Roma: Bulzoni, 1978) 73.
17. Italo Calvino, "L'avventura di un fotografo," *Gli amori difficili* (Milano: Mondadori, 1994) 53–54.
18. Dante Isella, ed., *Eugenio Montale, Le occasioni.* (Torino: Einaudi, 1996): 222.
19. Ettore Bonora, *Interpretazione di Montale: Le occasioni* (Torino: Tirrenia, 1979) 39.
20. Isella 226.
21. Ibid. 227.
22. Bonora 46.
23. Giuseppe Savoca, *Quaderno per Le occasioni* (Catania: Bonaccorso, 1973) 129-30.
24. Eugenio Montale, *Poésies, III: La tourmente et autres poèmes, La bufera e altro (1940–1957)*. Bilingual ed. Tr. Patrice Angelini with the collaboration of Louise Herline, Gennie Luccioni, and Arnaud Robin (Paris: Gallimard, 1966) 174.
25. Alvaro Valentini. *Lettura di Montale: Le occasioni.* (Roma: Bulzoni, 1975): 225.
26. Ettore Bonora, *La poesia di Montale*. Vol. 1 (Torino: Tirrenia, 1965) 140.

CHAPTER 5

La bufera: Guarding the Ark of Memory from the Storm

La bufera is the third stage of Montale's poetry, and the role of memory as content and as catalyst is still quite strong. In the eponymous poem of the collection, form and content are typical of that which was seen already in the 'Mottetti' and what will come later in works like 'L'anguilla.' The form of *La bufera* is typical of the vertical tension of which I spoke in previous chapters. The one unending sentence comprised of four stanzas strings together a series of images – on a "schermo," – which appears to draw the reader toward a climax which never occurs:

> *La bufera che sgronda sulle foglie / dure della magnolia i lunghi tuoni / marzolini e la grandine, // (i suoni di cristallo nel tuo nido / notturno ti sorprendono, dell'oro / che s'è spento sui mogani, sul taglio / dei libri rilegati, brucia ancora / una grana di zucchero nel guscio / delle tue palpebre) // il lampo che candisce / alberi e muri e li sorprende in quella eternità d'istante – marmo manna / e distruzione – ch'entro te scolpita / porti per tua condanna e che ti lega / piú che l'amore a me, strana sorella, – // e poi lo schianto rude, i sistri, il fremere / dei tamburelli sulla fossa fuia, / lo scalpicciare del fandango, e sopra / qualche gesto che annaspa… / Come quando / ti rivolgesti e con la mano, sgombra / la fronte dalla nube dei capelli, // mi salutasti – per entrar nel buio.*

Montale ties together images of destruction and unrestrained nature in this third collection and, at the same time, all of it seems to be part of the poet's subjective correlatives which justify the final stanza: "As when you turned" seems incongruous to the previous images until one realizes that, once again, this moment was being filtered through memory and the accumulation of images was preparing the reader to be mentally respondent to Montale's state while experiencing his recollection. Interestingly enough, this poetic moment filtered by memory is reminiscent in content to 'Mottetto 4' ('Lontano, ero con te'), but even more specifically the two poems share a common language. In 'Mottetto 4' the father said 'good-bye' to the poet, "entrò nell'ombra", and in *La bufera* Clizia said 'good-bye' to the poet "per entrar nel buio." "Shade" and "darkness" are rather synonymous, not of dying or of leaving, but of becoming absent and entering into the "punto dilatato." The fact that Clizia's deceased father only entered into "shade" while the living, but far away, Clizia entered into "darkness," means that absence is ultimately synonymous with death. Both states reside somewhere behind the screen of images of the void.

The vertical tension keeps the reader framed within the instant, so more likely the reader will be in the same rough time frame mentally to have the recollection and consequently make the correlation. The effect is like that of a fulcrum point of a lever where the last lines – though few – have a strong enough content or impact to counterbalance the many lines above them.

However, an interesting process unfolds in the poem that I must address in terms of absence-presence and the "schermo d'immagini." The last stanza is a manifestation of Montale's realization of how the external "schermo" is a correlative to a memory he had of Clizia in a specific moment of the past. Yet, ironically, as he is describing the effects of the storm – real or allegorical – which will serve as the subjective correlative of the last stanza, he is including Clizia herself. She is a participant of the very unraveling of events that will be used as a comparison to a memory of her. He speaks to her – "entro te scolpita / porti per tua condanna...strana, sorella" – in a present tense, when she is clearly absent, to only then speak to her of the past in the present. This furthers the presence in the void of absence to a two-fold quality. Yet one absence is mostly spatial (in the present), for Clizia is far away, and the other absence is temporal, for it is an event which they spatially shared in a past. In Montale's intuition (a pre-holographic sentiment), they are equidistant, eternal images.

The intermittent flashes and "barlumi" of his previous poetry are more distinctly and dramatically incorporated here: "Il lampo che candisce / alberi e muri e li sorprende in quella / eternità d'istante." The "lampo" which lights up the "eternità d'istante" is carved, sculpted within her, much like in 'Il balcone' where, even in tenebrous places, she carried light. Then the last line – "per entrar nel buio" – is two-fold, as well. He recalls her saying 'good-bye' then "enter into darkness" and this highlights how her leaving and becoming present only as an absence is equivalent to leaving light and entering darkness. Yet this is also a darkness of leaving the known, the safety of prewar Europe to the unknown, unsure disaster and destruction of World War II. Consider 'Incantesimo' (*La bufera*):

Intorno il mondo stinge; incandescente, / nella lava che porta in Galilea / il tuo amore profano, attendi l'ora / di quel velo che t'ha un giorno / fidanzata al tuo Dio.

Through Montale's memory, the reader knows that this is not entirely true, for right now in Clizia's apparent absence, there is still a sign of light and vitality:

I suoni di cristallo nel tuo nido / notturno ti sorprendono, dell'oro / che s'è spento sui mogani, sul taglio / dei libri rilegati, brucia ancora / una grana di zucchero nel guscio / delle tue palpebre.

Whether that grain is still truly burning is irrelevant, for if it burns still in his memory, it burns for Montale. Conversely, his access to this moment is not through memory. Rather it is access to an ideal world devoid of illusion where illumination is eternal and all beings are part of a being-memory.

Perhaps this taking notice of how much more is out there in the empiric reality is a form of struggle conducted in Montale's head. Perhaps living in his memory, finding some sort of presence in Clizia's absence, is too much for Montale. There is more on earth and, even in the seemingly quotidian aspects of life, there is a strange mysteriousness, and 'Su una lettera non scritta' is example of this: "Oh ch'io non oda / nulla di te, ch'io fugga dal bagliore / dei tuoi cigli. Ben altro è sulla terra." Following Plato's myth of the cave, Montale is accustomed to living in illusion. He can only glimpse the noumenos, but even then he attributes it to a temporary illusion, or deviation from the norm. Greco comments on this shift in Montale:

Lo scarto dai 'Mottetti' è netto. In 'La speranza di pure rivederti' la realtà valeva solo come schermo d'immagini, qui ['Su una lettera non scritta'] nonostante l'assenza della donna, il poeta non rimane indifferente di fronte allo spettacolo della vita.[1]

The external world was previously his medium for composing with his existential alphabet. Now, with confidence that the true reality is behind the screen, he can examine the "spettacolo della vita" as a metaphor for understanding the noumenos. Yet what happens when he looks out onto the "schermo d'immagini" is revealing. 'Su una lettera' is one of the earliest of the *Bufera* poems and as such serves as a guage of interpreting how *La bufera* differs thematically from the two previous collections.

Sparir non so né riaffacciarmi; tarda / la fucina vermiglia / della notte, la sera si fa lunga, / la preghiera è supplizio e non ancora / tra le rocce che sorgono t'è giunta / la bottiglia dal mare. L'onda, vuota, / si rompe sulla punta, a Finisterre.

Montale says he does not know how to disappear ('Sparir non so') and one thinks of "svanire / è dunque la ventura delle venture" ('Portami il girasole'). Neither can he lean out nor show himself again ('né riaffacciarmi'), as one sees in 'Il balcone.' He is utterly indecisive; he wants to cut himself off from the prison of his memory, from his past, and yet he does not "write" the letter so that he is not hoping or looking towards the future for some consolation. Perhaps this lack of hope is based on his isolation in terms of expressing himself:

> *L'immagine di quella bottiglia affidata ai flutti spiega la natura del discorso poetico di Montale, è una forma di autocoscienza del poeta, ma non in sede puramente estetica, bensí umana, esistenziale; esprime il disperato desiderio e la impossibilità di comunicare.*[2]

It is much like in 'Ezekiel saw the wheel...' where Montale suppresses the future by trying to suppress the past, as if he wanted to live undisturbed in the presence of one memory, outside of time.[3] He is in the present for once, and almost interminably, so that even prayer is irrelevant and, therefore, a "supplizio" ("torment"). Hope brings him to a future, and the distance separating *now* from the future focuses on how, in a parallel way, memory is the distance between *now* and the past. If the first line of the second stanza is indicative of any states of mind regarding the first two collections with respect to the third, the last line of 'Su una lettera' is similar: "L'onda, vuota, / si rompe sulla punta, a Finisterre." If he is not indifferent to the *spettacolo* of life here, then he is seeing the landscape as he did in the *Ossi*; like a cruel father. If the sea is not one that brings memories and takes them away, it is just a sea that reminds him how insignificant he is, much like a letter in a bottle floating adrift. Of course, this assumes that he chooses to accept the screen of images as reality.

In 'Serenata indiana,' Montale fuses the landscape of his memory with the external landscape. When Montale had been previously indifferent to the life around him, the external landscape was an expressive tool; his "schermo d'immagini." In 'Su una lettera non scritta,' the poet looks away from the past and memory to find the spectacle living around him; not necessarily to be utilized as an expressive tool of language. Yet in 'Serenata indiana,' by his own volition or not, the metaphysical connections are too great, and his instincts were better than he might have imagined.

The first stanza speaks of the undoing of the evening:

> *È pur nostro il disfarsi delle sere. / E per noi è la stria che dal mare /*

sale al parco e ferisce gli aloè.

Perhaps this is the all or nothing to which Clizia pertained in 'Mottetto 10' ("nulla finisce, o tutto, se tu fólgore / lasci la nube") and to which all humans belong. As in the *Occasioni*, Montale quickly imagines her presence there with him, but it is once again a question of metaphysical doubling (as in 'La casa dei doganieri'). In the second strophe of 'Serenata indiana,' Montale speaks to Clizia as if she were present: "Puoi condurmi per mano, se tu fingi / di crederti con me, se ho la follia / di seguirti lontano." He speaks to her presence in the void, but he suggests that she pretend to believe herself with him.

Previously, to simply remember was enough. It was enough to evoke Clizia into the present, on the screen of images around him that could be the potential expressive material for the manifestation – proof – of her existence. Memory is not enough, however. In 'Serenata indiana' Montale realizes that her presence is an eternal constant, independent of his memory: "ciò che stringi, / ciò che dici, m'appare in tuo potere." It is not enough to look out onto the external life, for without the perfect juxtaposition of images, or a sign sent from Clizia, he cannot project her presence in her absence:

Fosse tua vita che mi tiene / sulle soglie – e potrei prestarti un volto, / vaneggiarti figura. Ma non è, // non è così.

There is not – objectively – any proper juxtaposition on the screen to manifest her presence. It is not possible. Then, practically within the same poetic breath, Montale has a sudden, subtle epiphany, which is contrary to anything he had before:

Il polipo che insinua / tentacoli di inchiostro tra gli scogli / può servirsi di te. Tu gli appartieni // e non lo sai. Sei lui, ti credi te.

In this way, Montale had all along been using (as implied by the verb "servirsi") images on the screen, like an octopus, as signs of Clizia's presence. Now he cosmically associates Clizia with the other objects. If this is the case, then Clizia has always been with Montale, regardless of the intersecting points between occasion and memory. This is how she can be an all or nothing, for in the seeming voids or "interstellar spaces" of Borges' 'Adrogué' (an invisible metaphysical plane), there is never just a simple emptiness. 'Nuove stanze' had been a great example of this with the possible soteric quality in the character of the "chi può," who could have the same spiritual fortitude as Clizia. Yet, here, in the fusion of his memory of her with a more objective view of the landscape around him, Montale has risen up to a different metaphysical level. In the overall entelechy of the universe, everything and nothing is important. All and nothing are constantly present: the universe is a hologram – a perfect recollection or perpetual presence.

Montale, however, examines the connection between the screen and pure presence in 'Gli orecchini.' There, he confronts these concerns in one of his more eerie poetic compositions:

> *Non serba ombra di voli il nerofumo / della spera. (E del tuo non è piú traccia). / È passata la spugna che i barlumi / indifesi dal cerchio d'oro scaccia. / Le tue pietre, i coralli, il forte imperio / che ti rapisce vi cercavo; fuggo / l'iddia che non s'incarna, i desiderî / porto fin che al tuo lampo non si struggono. / Ronzano èlitre fuori, ronza il folle / mortorio e sa che due vite non contano. / Nella cornice tornano le molli / meduse della sera. La tua impronta / verrà di giú: dove ai tuoi lobi squallide / mani, travolte, fermano i coralli.*

The first two lines of 'Gli orecchini' create an image that will surface in 'Voce giunta': that there is little difference between death and absence of a person, especially since all is an illusory cinematic projection on top of the void: "Non serba ombra di voli il nerofumo / della spera." The mirror holds no ghost or shadow of her flight – the angelic presence that she is. Much the way the dead father and Clizia appear to Montale in a relatively similar state – either could be simply absent or dead, based on their immaterial state – the lack of a sign of Clizia's flight reveals no more or less. She could be dead or just far away. Savoca's comments, in an article which I find pertinent to our discussion, that: "E forse si potrebbe obiettare che il discrimine tra vita e morte in Montale è sfumato e labile, e quindi non si darebbe differenza sostanziale tra il fantasma di una morta e quello dell'amata assente."[4]

The mirror, or "schermo," does not show any light. The image crafted is of dark gloominess, for a mirror no more reflects light in light's absence than a mind recalls when memories are flickering and dimming. His memory is fading. Even as he understands the secret behind the screen, he is no less bound to the optic limitations of his body's nerve endings and impulses. "È passata la spugna che i barlumi / indifesi dal cerchio d'oro scaccia." 'Barlumi' (light flickers), associated with the Clizia character as early as 'Il balcone' ("la vita che dà barlumi"), are chased from any contact with the mirror; the same light that came from Clizia, so she is dying in his memory. (If absence and death are roughly equal in memory, then a dying in memory is equivalent to a sort of real death). Yet the images are simultaneously real and metaphoric. He looked for her in the objects – talismans – associated with her: the precious stones, her coral earrings. He imagines them having a volume that transcends and connects various spatial planes of experience, but he finds neither the real thing nor a sign as an image on the screen in which to put provisional faith as a possible manifestation of her presence.

The poet flees her ("fuggo") on two levels. To be salvific she may have to be an angel, or a goddess ("l'iddia"), but at the same time if the goddess will not take a material form ("non s'incarna"), then how can he put faith in her? On one level he can not relate to her salvific qualities, but, being salvific, she is not incarnate and in not finding her there he pulls away. Until he receives a sign he can do nothing but remain in earthbound, in the illusory real: "Fuggo / l'iddia che non s'incarna, i desideri / porto fin che al tuo lampo non si distruggono." Previously, it had been the meeting of his memory's template with an external object on the screen of images that coincided to evoke her manifestation in the void. He begins to search for other attributes around him. In the meantime the sounds of planes ("Ronzano élitre fuori") and the general mad undoing of humanity ("ronza il folle / mortorio") is what this war offers. To this dark cruelty he attributes the lack of Clizia's presence both physically and in his memory. Ultimately, if inanity of war can claim lives indiscriminately, then what do his life and that of Clizia amount to?: "e sa che due vite non contano." Humanity is relative and momentary and any moment can bring all or nothing; take away all or nothing. It is as disparaging as the image in 'Marezzo' (*Ossi*): "la memoria ti appare dilavata. / Sei passata e pur senti / la tua vita consumata."

Suddenly, there are shadows on the mirror. In the dark evening, faint fluid motion is detected in the frame, the analogy for the limited visual field incapable of seeing the void before an image appears (cf. 'Forse un mattino andando'): "Nella cornice tornano le molli / meduse della sera." They do not necessarily represent Clizia's return, for Montale specifically says in the next line: "La tua impronta / verrà di giú." *Yours*, as opposed to other signs, will come from below; from that dark place of the void; or perhaps from below because Montale fears her claimed by the underworld, like Orpheus' Eurydice. The "squallide mani" could be referring to her hands, as Montale remembers them, faded by time in his dimming memory. They could be her hands as he imagines her dead; a composite of his remembering her earrings and of what the scene would look like were she to replace them in her current state. Perhaps they are the hands of one of her compatriots in that place ("dove" ("where"), refering possibly to "giú" ("down") burried underground and revisiting her as a shadow; an "ombra" (taken either as "shadow" or as "ghost"). The darkness of war and inhumanity is his perceived reality; the ideality is still Clizia and the hope of the truth behind the screen.

The poem 'La frangia dei capelli' is consistent with the trend of the *Bufera*, which wrestles with memory and the external landscape:

> *La frangia dei capelli che ti vela / la fronte puerile, tu distrarla / con la mano non devi. Anch'essa parla / di te, sulla mia strada è tutto il cielo, / la sola luce con le giade ch'ài / accerchiate sul polso, nel tumulto / del sonno la cortina che gl'indulti / tuoi distendono, l'ala onde tu vai, / trasmigratrice Artemide ed illesa, / tra le guerre dei nati-morti; e s'ora / d'aeree lanugini s'infiora / quel fondo, a marezzarlo sei tu, scesa / d'un balzo, e irrequieta la tua fronte / si confonde con l'alba, la nasconde.*

Part of the problem is similar to that of 'Gli orecchini': When Clizia is in her incorporeal, angelic form, he looks for an external sign or manifestation of her. Could it be him forcing his own memory onto the external screen or is it truly an epiphanic moment of her presence? He looks for a latent trace of her as if on Freud's 'Mystic Writing-Pad.' Is Clizia affecting the landscape, or do the occurrences in the landscape present themselves at serendipitous times misleading Montale from realizing their coincidental nature? Hence the puzzling, contradictory tone of the last lines:

> *A marezzarlo sei tu, scesa / d'un balzo, e irrequieta la fronte / si confonde con l'alba, la nasconde.*

Montale begins by insisting that Clizia should not disturb the perfect bangs that hang on her forehead like some sort of charm warding off bad tidings. Yet Clizia is not physically there, so he is speaking to her in his memory. He is in a parallel chronology where the bangs can exist as pure being rather than as the constant becoming of the rest of the cosmos. He employs an optative similar to that of 'Non recidere, forbice, quel volto.' That is, Montale only has so much by which to remember her and yet that seemingly insignificant fact is all for him – an all-or-nothing. Ironically, he uses the word "Anche" ("also") to say, "Anch'essa ["la frangia"] parla di te," as if it were one of many things on the "schermo d'immagini" that might speak of her. But salvation may not even be possible here and now, and it may have to be remanded to a place beyond this world. The closest connection Montale has with this *beyond* is his memory which seems to come from its "punto dilatato" and vanish to it in an instant. It is this that starts to bring him even closer to 'Voce giunta,' and 'Il giglio rosso' plays a pivotal role in this.

'Il giglio rosso' could easily be included in the 'Mottetti,' for the thematics as well as for the structure. It reflects a style which Montale has used before:

Il giglio rosso, se un dí / mise radici nel tuo cuor di vent'anni... il giglio rosso già sacrificato / sulle lontane prode / ai vischi che la sciarpa ti tempestano / d'un gelo incorruttibile e le mani, – / fiore di fosso che ti s'aprirà / sugli argini solenni ove il brusío / del tempo piú non affatica ...: a scuotere / l'arpa celeste, a far la morte amica.

Grignani speaks of the poem's process of stylization in reference to 'Punta del Mesco': "Nel testo delle *Occasioni* la forma dapprima è quella del ricordo (prima strofa con i tempi all'imperfetto e al perfetto), poi quella tipicamente montaliana della visione «vedo il sentiero»..."[5] 'Il giglio rosso' captures perfectly the motivation from the past revisited through memory and then the exterior landscape projected with an airy, resultant hallucination.

Metaphorically speaking, the red lily is simply an association with the crest of Florence. It is rooted in Clizia's heart, for she was greatly enamoured of the city. The fact that it has been "sacrificato" and replaced by cold mistletoe speaks of Clizia's being in a country where any reference to Christ or Christ(mas) is associated with the cold North and mistletoe, which adorned hearth and home in that period. The cold-warm dichotomy is exposed in the first strophe as the warmth of a new sun:

(Brillava la pescaia tra gli stacci / dei renaioli, a tuffo s'inforravano / lucide talpe nelle canne, torri, / gonfaloni vincevano la pioggia, / e il trapianto felice al nuovo sole, / te incoscia si compí)

It is also seen in the tempestuous, incorruptible ice in the second. But the strength in the poem comes after the so-called death, or sacrifice, of the past icon of Clizia: the red lily. Tempered by memory, his mind imagines the fate of the Clizia-red lily character. In the fusion of memory with the present, this character is sublimated to a past experience as an iconography, to an hypostasis where its earthbound reality gives way to the ideality of Montale's hopes and memories. When the lily blooms next for Clizia, it will be impenetrable to the erosion of time which exacts itself on memory: "fiore di fosso che ti s'aprirà / sugli argini solenni ove il brusío / del tempo piú non affatica..." From real to iconographic to apotheosis, the image of Clizia will be outside of time and not susceptible to human intervals: in cosmic time Clizia is pure being, not becoming. She is stronger, albeit her symbol weakened, because she remains outside of time.

The poetic development of 'Il giglio rosso' is the schematic version of the "punto dilatato." In theory, there is a flash in the poet's memory of the lily: 'Il giglio rosso' followed immediately by a comma. Then, there is a moment of speculation which reminds the reader of the consciousness between a then and a now: "Se un dí / mise radici nel tuo cuor di vent'anni." This is followed by a parenthetical statement ("Brillava la pescaia...te inconscia si compí"), which is a poetic aside, as if we have been privy to something that occupied the immediate flash in the "punto" and perceived by the poet. So what was immediately recognizable to Montale in his memory occupied an instant flash, but the six-verse parenthetical aside is the incision of the fundus that his mind perceived, and all that is named ("pescaia", "renaioli," etc.) has a distinct designation in the harmonic totality of the flash. The ditch of things, the "fossa fuia" of *La bufera* and the "fossa / che circonda lo scatto del ricordo" of 'Voce giunta,' is full of all these things so that they spring forward when the point in the mind charged with their memory releases in a "scatto." Memory is Montale's attempt at reading them in linear succession rather than at once. Memory is the series of cinematic after-images as he reviews the film of those images.

In fact, it does not seem accidental that the flower at hand becomes a "fiore di fosso." It is certainly accurate in the sense that it has come to him as a memory-image from the depths of a ditch; hence a ditch flower. Yet no sooner had it come to him from the "fosso" is it relegated to a memorial death. It has been supplanted by another image more easily associated with Clizia: the mistletoe. One sees the correlation between dream and memory when one recalls that in 'Nel sonno' the image could return to him, "overflow from ditches" ("traboccar dai fossi"). But it is doubled: it came (as a memory) from the ditch and, as a dead memory, goes to the ditch; because, as in 'Voce giunta,' in the afterlife the poet's characters will no longer live as phenomenon, but as noumenon. The lines "fior di fosso che ti s'aprirà / sugli argini solenni ove il brusío / del tempo piú non affatica" recall very clearly the "vuoto inabitato [perhaps an empty "fosso"] / che occupammo e che attende fin ch'è tempo / di colmarsi di noi, di ritrovarci..." The "scatto" sends the mind to the point of memory in a synaptic impulse. The point then instantaneously becomes a "punto dilatato," which is rather synonymous with a "fosso" or a "fossa." In fact, in 'Voce giunta' the dilation of the ditch opens around the moment of the flash – where "scatto" and "punto" are one: "e il respiro mi si rompe / nel punto dilatato, nella fossa / che circonda lo scatto del ricordo."

The idea of a "fossa/fosso" seems to permeate the work of Montale. It is always a revisitiation of his childhood. Whether in *Farfalla di Dinard* or in

'L'anguilla' or in 'I limoni,' and even in 'Flussi', 'Nel sonno', 'Voce giunta' or 'Nel vuoto', it conveys memories of infantile bliss searching barefoot for eels. It has a domestic edenic quality: familiar, warm and positive. Perhaps it is even why in 'Il giglio rosso' it is a ditch flower that will open up to "you" in the after life. It is a ditch flower by virtue of it occupying the ditch of memory. It is a consolation in the sense that it confirms the past and ensures that there will be a future in the afterlife, rather than nothingness, according to Federici: "Il recupero del passato è, in fondo, la coscienza della sua lontananza, ma al tempo stesso la verità del suo accadimento."[6]

The meaning has not died with the symbol, and even the symbol will be rejoined with its reference in the afterlife:

Fiore di fosso che ti s'aprirà / sugli argini solenni ove il brusío / del tempo piú non affatica...: a scuotere / l'arpa celeste, a far la morte amica.

The ditch, from its limitless void, produces memories and to it Montale's characters will return; all of the bounty in the ditch, that never truly left the ditch, will "make death a friend." In the afterlife, there is the potential to have perfect recollection to each moment of terrestrial life – a pure presence which contains all moments.

The fan of the eponymous poem, 'Il ventaglio,' is a physical manifestation in the present absence of its owner who is, herself, in the ditch of memory. 'Il ventaglio' begins with the line "*Ut pictura...*" implying that as with painting so goes poetry. Montale omits "poesis" because what follows the Latin beginning is the poetry (*poesis*) itself, and the poetry itself is demonstrating how as with painting so goes poetry: it renders mobility immobile. It fixes outside of time that which would dissipate in time as one experiences it in the fleeing present of the empirical world; a world where memory is not a true recollection but a by-product of experience, a consolation. It is a presence-absence, as its very presence arises from the necessity to document what appears phenomenologically ephemeral:

Ut pictura... Le labbra che confondono, / gli sguardi, i giorni ormai caduti / provo a figgerli là come in un tondo / di cannochiale arrovesciato, muti / e immoti, ma piú vivi. Era una giostra / d'uomini e ordegni in fuga tra quel fumo / ch'Euro batteva, e già l'alba l'inostra / con un sussulto e rompe quele brume. / Luce la madreperla, la calanca / vertiginosa inghiotte ancora vittime, / ma le tue piume sulle guance sbiancano / e il giorno è forse salvo. O colpi fitti, / quando ti schiudi, o crudi lampi, o scrosci / sull'orde! (Muore chi ti riconosce?).

Much of the greatest appreciation comes from what is intimated in absence. For this reason I refer to Marchese's indirect discussion of the topic at hand by mentioning an argument germane overall to this chapteer:

> *A posteriori, la donna è più reale nell'assenza che nella presenza: «Può darsi / che sia vera soltanto la lontananza, / vero l'oblio, vera la foglia secca / più del fresco germoglio, / tanto e altro può darsi o dirsi. // Comprendo la tua caparbia volontà di essere sempre assente / perché solo così si manifesta la tua magia...» ('Ex voto,' in Satura). Così anche l'ultima poesia di 'Dopo una fuga' (Satura) ripone come condizione del recupero memoriale la lontananza dell'interlocutrice, con la rimozione di un miracolo che non ha resistito al tempo.*[7]

In this sense, 'Il ventaglio' is the perfect poetic vehicle for Montale's thematics. How better would Clizia's absence be evidenced than by the presence of an object she had left behind? The poem becomes a physical artifact of an abstract or of an absence. The fan, as a poem, is a re-evocation of memory on two levels: the memory of war (associated with the contemporary threat of WW II) and the poetic memory where poetic phrases previously used take on greater meanings.

The tone of 'Il ventaglio' takes us back to 'Mottetto 4,' 'Lontano, ero con te quando tuo padre,' with its images of war. Montale assures us Greco (in the latter's interview) that the poem deals with "Immagini di guerra viste o sognate in sintesi (il cannocchiale)."[8] More specifically, Macrí refers to its association with World War I in Caporetto.[9] Certainly one cannot help but imagine Caporetto alongside Cumerlotti and Anghébeni from the famous 'Mottetto 4.' In both cases, the suffering from a past war is perfectly woven and assimilated into the suffering of today (if there is even a today as a pure present in Montale), as if they were but one platonic suffering attributed to separate stimuli on the screen of images.

Another interesting motif brought into 'Il ventaglio' was previously seen in the 'Mottetti.' This is the image of a smouldering volcano painted on a souvenir seashell in 'Ma cosí sia.' Though it is a frozen moment, isolated, it has a memorial connotation. The sunset is reflected on the shell, bridging exterior and interior worlds much as the bee swarms of the exterior are in opposition to the interior of the room in which Montale finds himself. The lava seems to be a static photo-like image. However, though the metaphorical implication in 'Il ventaglio' is the painting in miniature of memorial images on the fan, there is a more living, less static feel: "provo a figgerli là come in un tondo / di cannocchiale arrovesciato, muti / e immoti, ma piú vivi." Somehow, because the painting is more a memorial projection ultimately carried out in the words of the poem, it is more alive ("viva") and dynamic; it is but one moment in its quiddity. It is not all of the moments of the volcano but that one moment in and of itself, like one division of the infinite Zenonian arrow: "At any given moment, the arrow [here, the volcano] occupies a space equal to its volume and simply is where it is."[10] The words fix the images, but the images themselves are more alive than the static shell of 'Ma cosí sia.' The scene is set such that through a denouement of "colpi fitti" and "crudi lampi" the Clizia character may just reveal herself: "O colpi fitti, / quando ti schiudi, o crudi lampi, o scrosci / sull'orde!"

Yet, Montale renders meaning to his own lines in Greco's book: "Chi ti ha conosciuto non può realmente morire; ossia nemmeno la morte ha senso per chi ti ha conosciuto."[11] If she is revealed on the screen of images, then salvation is illusory. If she comes to Montale on the void – illuminated briefly as an epiphany – then salvation is imminent. This seems less like a consoling virtue of memory than a reference to true salvation or afterlife, which would be unusual for Montale. Whoever has met Clizia and recognized in her certain character traits may also have them. Anyone who can recognize an absent Clizia (far off or dead) has the ability to sublimate death and absence and appropriate their eternal qualities to a level of hope and survival in the face of the war. Montale, for the first time in his poetry, may be making a firm affirmation of faith. Though in 'Nuove stanze' he intimated at the qualities of her firm faith, he did not claim to have it. Rather in the hypothetical he mentions who might win or resist: "ma resiste / e vince chi può con te allo specchio ustorio / che accieca le pedine opporre i tuoi / occhi di acciaio."

The last aspect of 'Il ventaglio' is in the "cannocchiale arrovesciato." It is a reversed telescope sight to which he compares the locus of the focus of his memories:

Ut pictura ... le labbra che confondono, / gli sguardi, i segni, i giorni ormai caduti / provo a figgerli là come in un tondo / di cannocchiale arrovesciato, muti / e immoti, ma piú vivi.

Images of Clizia, his life, the war, all pass by and he struggles to preserve them in his memory. His narrative alter ego will discover in *Farfalla di Dinard* that all of these moments are preserved on a film. They do not fade – he will see in retrospect. Rather the poet's soul, limited by his body's physical capabilities, cannot order them simultaneously. Therefore, one takes the place of the other for him, leaving him to experience a fading after-image. If one looks into a telescope from the correct, magnifying end, things infinitely enlarge; on the contrary from the opposite end, things tend to infinitely regress to an eventual – theoretical – vanishing point. The image is the same, but from different reference points. An image, once seen, in order to be stored in memory must be compressed and reduced into an infinitely small point in memory. In this regard, this infinitely regressing screen of images in the inverted telescope brings Montale to a point that can be reduced like that of the point which the ditch of memory encircles. This is the precedent of the "punto dilatato" of 'Voce giunta con le folaghe:'

> *Il vento del giorno / confonde l'ombra viva e l'altra ancora / riluttante in un mezzo che respinge / le mie mani, e il respiro mi si rompe / nel punto dilatato, nella fossa / che circonda lo scatto del ricordo.*

Thus, amid the dense blows and the sharp lightning flashes of war, if Clizia reveals herself suddenly to Montale in memory like a *scatto*, the remembered cannot die, and perhaps, on the metaphorical level, neither can the one remembering. One might argue that the flashes of light from the war will illuminate latent images onto the screen of images.

In 'Personae separatae' two people are separated by distance and by time. Yet the separation is doubled. In order to converse or communicate – because of the separation – they must find each other on the plane of memory. But because all moments have been imprinted already, for the characters to experience the same moment, they merely edit the images, focus light onto a cinematic film, revealing the holographic image that was previously invisible, and they are literally in that moment. Montale's hope consists of waiting for this miracle moment during which he will envision what had been around him, but which he had not previously perceived:

> *Come la scaglia d'oro che si spicca / dal fondo oscuro e liquefatta cola / nel corridoio dei carrubi ormai / ischeletriti, cosí pure noi / persone separate per lo sguardo / d'un altro? È poca cosa la parola, / poca cosa o spazio in questi crudi / noviluni annebbiati: ciò che manca, / e che ci torce il cuore e qui m'attarda / tra gli alberi, ad attenderti, è un perduto / senso.*

As I have mentioned, regarding 'Il balcone,' Montale lacks the ability to illuminate himself like Clizia. He remains stuck reading the after-images in a linear manner, which makes him the viewer of the film and not its editor. Yet, he feels that he could move beyond this impediment, if he had his primordial, platonic senses. This "perduto senso" is the sense of memory; or, an ability to view the world holographically so that memory is perfect in that all is immanently present. Perhaps in this way there is no truly good memory, for in order to belong to a memory a thing must no longer pertain to the present. Memory consoles his present, but perhaps it would be better if certain people did not have to be relegated there, despite the poet's will. The poet, nonetheless, is a separated person both in being far from Clizia, but also in his two selves. He is Montale the poet, set in the human intervals of calendric time, and he is Montale the memorial dreamer who steps out of human time into a continuum of cosmic eternity when he steps into the extra-spatial, extra-temporal world of memory. However, the poet lacks conviction – beyond his suspicions – that this world is the true reality behind the void of 'Forse un mattino andando.'

One sees yet another memory-ditch correlation in the "riano" of 'Personae separatae':

La tua forma / passò di qui, si riposò sul riano / tra le nasse atterrate, poi si sciolse / come un sospiro.

"Riano" is a Ligurian term similar to the Genovese "rian" ("torrent") or "rianello" ("stream"). This is clearly another memory-childhood link, like the "fossa" of 'Voce giunta' or the "botri" of 'L'anguilla' and of the "fossi" in 'I limoni.' The inclusion of 'L'anguilla' in this grouping is doubly important for Galassi, who translates the "nasse" as "eel-nets."[12] These last lines are heavily charged with implications of memory. Her form passed "di qui" ("this way"), he remembered her as a non-form, a memory, and she rested on the "riano" (perhaps along the bank or edge of it) with the grounded nets, and then, from the same nothingness from which she came to Montale as a memory, she returned there like a dissipating breath, or ghost. The verb "si riposò" refers to a locus within the confines of memory, for, resting on the ditch means resting where his childhood ditch is, along with the nets, and that is in memory – ditch ("riano") as a symbol of childhood and ditch as a container of memories. For Montale, memory dissolves or fades constantly, as much in 'Non recidere, forbice' as here in the line "poi si sciolse / come un sospiro." With this, one cannot help recalling 'Vasca' or 'Cigola la carrucola.'

'Vasca' pertains to the glimmers of vision or understanding of which Montale's discourse on memory is an extension:

Ma ecco, c'è altro che striscia / a fior della spera rifatta liscia: di erompere non ha virtú, / vuol vivere e non sa come; / se lo guardi si stacca, torna in giú: / è nato e morto e non ha avuto un nome.

Later on, the "in giú" will rarefy itself in meaning in Montale to mean the underworld of memory, a pit, or a ditch of memory. Yet, even in 'Cigola la carrucola,' the image of the face in the well is already a fantastic precursor for 'Personae separatae.' Memory is seen as an ephemeral thing sitting on an everchanging surface: "Trema un ricordo nel ricolmo secchio, / nel puro cerchio un'immagine ride." At its best, a memory must be caught as a glimmer and not a set image; a glimmer on amorphous water. Yet, because Montale participates in memory-images in his terrestrial, empirical present, they are flashes of photograms, frames of a cinema projected onto a screen – or, in this case a meniscus of water. The images, however real they may appear, are not truly there. They are not reflected; rather they "affiorano" (emerge) from nothingness. In the words of Calvino, "non si riflettono ma affiorano di giú."[13] The next images really solidify an early connection between 'Cigola la carrucola' and works like 'Personae separatae.' His face and evanescent lips will not come together – will remain separate – because the memory cannot hold. The pulley creaking in the well somehow caused the 'scatto' of memory and for a glimmer the past pertained to a "her." But then it quickly blended with other fleeting memories to confound an image with that of another – perhaps a shriek from the pulley wheel was enough to distract the remembrance. The face to which the evanescent lips belonged disappears into the depths of the well of memory, and suddenly "una distanza ci divide" ("a distance separates us"). The poet is both separate from the other and from himself, being caught in the same present in which the poem started, in the cornice of the pulley wheel creaking. As in the poem 'Cigola la carrucola,' in 'Personae separatae' he goes back to his earlier self after the flash of memory. The difference between Montale's and Clizia's world is one of illumination and perspective. She is light; he is darkness. She experiences a noumenal world of direct illumination, while he continues in his phenomenal world, living in the intermittent illumination between each frame of a cinematic projection. In this light, it would be difficult to decipher the trope of the screen of images. If the screen is within Montale, then is he not one plane of an integral, but infinitely planed, hologram? Is the screen a curtain, which prevents him from seeing the world as it is? If the former case is true, then Montale is an unwitting accomplice to his own metaphysical confusion. Rodowick communicates a similar notion, which he notices in Deleuze's philosophy:

There is no illuminated matter, but rather, a phosphorescence diffused in every direction that becomes actual «only by reflecting off certain surfaces which serve simultaneously as the screen for other luminous zones».[14] This is why Deleuze states that the brain is a screen and nothing more.[15]

Montale cannot see the full picture, for he is part of it: his human brain presumes, and expects, to see a whole truth, without realizing that each brain has a role as mini-medium for reflecting the resultant whole. The universe is not this or that image, but the entirety. The final words, however, have a more definitive take on the separation of the poet and Clizia. Their separation is not so much of distance but one of a metaphysical difference in how they perceive materially:

> *e ivi non era / l'orror che fiotta, in te la luce ancora / trovava luce, oggi non piú che al giorno primo già annotta.*

Light, wherever it was, was always in Clizia and perceived by her; for Montale, even in the early daytime after sunrise, it is "already night." Montale is once again flustered by a world caught in a cinema, which convinces him of being bound to time. Later, in *Farfalla di Dinard*, Montale detects that he exists not in time but despite time. Though he intuits a noumenal world in the void, Montale is still trapped in the empirical world. This phenomenal world does not possess continuity but the illusion of it: "Il mondo empirico invece è il consueto succedersi d'immagini sullo schermo, inganno ottico come il cinema, dove la velocità dei fotogrammi ti convince della continuità e della permanenza."[16] The real permanence and quantum simultaneity are in the hologram; that is, the void. Perception, whether of real objects or of formless memories, is called into question: matter exists just as it is perceived; and since it is perceived as an image, the mind would make of it, in itself, an image.

'L'arca' is important to the topic of memory because it speaks of the possibility of the locus of memory and of its preservation in that locus. It is a poem composed of four sentences (within a single stanza) of which three begin with the anaphora "la tempesta:"

> *La tempesta di primavera ha sconvolto / l'ombrello del salice, / al turbine d'aprile / s'è impigliato dell'orto il vello d'oro / che nasconde i miei morti, / i miei cani fidati, le mie vecchie / serve – quanti da allora / (quando il salce era biondo e io ne stroncavo / le anella con la fionda) son calati, / vivi, nel trabocchetto. La tempesta / certo li riunirà sotto quel tetto / di prima, ma lontano, piú lontano / di questa terra folgorata dove / bollono calce e sangue nell'impronta / del piede umano. Fuma il ramaiolo / in cucina, un suo tondo di riflessi / accentra i volti ossuti, i musi aguzzi / e li protegge in fondo la magnolia / se un soffio ve la getta. La tempesta / primaverile scuote d'un latrato / di fedeltà la mia arca, o perduti.*

Out of these three, two include a modifier denoting a springtime storm; the other, it could be inferred, is also a spring storm. Springtime is a rejuvenation period; a rejuvinating time. The pun hinges on the spring storms and the storm of the war – as in 'La primavera hitleriana,' which speaks of the spring of 1938 (in retrospect), which would auger bad tidings for Italy, as even the title of the entire *La bufera* collection implies. Somehow, through all its destruction, the storm also remains positive for memory. In this regard it is far removed from the "primavera inerte, senza memoria" of 'Dora Markus (I):' "Poi seguimmo il canale fino alla darsena / della città, lucida di fuliggine, / nella bassura dove s'affondava / una primavera inerte, senza memoria." If inert spring is without memory, then perhaps one can deduce that a tempestuous spring would be full of catalysts for memories.

Indeed the poem 'L'arca' is full of memorial motifs and fantastic images: "l'orto", "i miei cani fidati", "le mie vecchie / serve", "la fionda", "il ramaiolo / in cucina", "la magnolia" and certainly "un latrato / di fedeltà." They are all images from previous works and from his childhood, and all of them – in a bittersweet way – will be reunited by the great leveller of death in the tempestuous war. They will, as memories or as the dead, be joined "sotto quel tetto / di prima" ("under the same roof as before"), the 'before' being from his childhood. The scourge of death from the war on Italian soil will send everything to a place where absence and death, past and present, are irrelevant: for Christians, into the afterlife; for Montale, into his well of memories. This notion appears in the *farfalla* 'Sul limite,' where all is experienced in the compactness of simultaneity that one finds in this very poem which defies time. With the line "piú lontano / di questa folgorata terra" the idea of afterlife and salvation are questioned and Forti elucidates one aspect of this:

> *E non intende precisare, per ora, se sia un luogo di purgatoriale macerazione, o, se piú facilmente, sia il luogo interno della sola possibile salvazione montaliana, la memoria, la cui laica e solitaria "religio" si instaura in questo libro [La bufera] e, specie piú avanti, farà altri passi in 'A mia madre' e in 'Voce giunta con le folaghe.'*[17]

Here, the well is represented by a pot in the kitchen, at the bottom of which, as in the "fossa" or the "riano" or the "botro," or even the well of 'Vasca,' resides memory:

> *Fuma il ramaiolo / in cucina, un suo tondo di riflessi / accentra i volti ossuti, / i musi aguzzi / e li protegge in fondo la magnolia / se un soffio ve la getta.*

It is the simple tree that keeps the memories.[18] The tree protects them as the acacia in 'Mottetto 18' could not. As it was chopped, the implication is that the shears cut and the memory, which Montale feared would empty and fade, clearly cannot fight entropy, but entropy only occurs as a function of dispersion over time:

> *Un freddo cala ... Duro il colpo svetta. / E l'acacia ferita da sé scrolla / il guscio di cicala / nella prima belletta di novembre. ('Mottetto 18')*

The tree harbors the memories from 'L'arca.' Yet, it is not a real tree, like the willow: "La tempesta di primavera ha sconvolto / l'ombrello del salice." The magnolia is a tree of memory – maybe truer than reality for Montale, as it fits his ideality of the world – that resides in the depths of Montale's wells and ditches on the plane beyond the empiric screen of images to gather and take care of the memories. Perhaps the magnolia's very resistance to the storm, unlike the willow, is that it is not directly affected by the storm in the present. The storm is but a phenomenal projection enabled by Montale's brain as a screen. Light and cinematic projections, only exist as they are perceived – otherwise, they travel through the air imageless until they reach a screen onto which they take a form.

The magnolia remains an apt metaphor for the collector and holder of memories, for a true tree is a convoluted perch for *volatili* and this draws a connection between light, airy thoughts and the angel-like Clizia as a bird in flight, the greatest example being in 'Mottetto 12.' In 'Nel parco' and in 'L'ombra della magnolia,' Montale talks of the physical tree – the arc of memory itself – "shrinking" and "thinning out," respectively:

> *Nell'ombra della magnolia / che sempre piú si restringe ('Nel parco');*

and

> *L'ombra della magnolia giapponese / si sfoltisce or che i bocci paonazzi / sono caduti. ('L'ombra della magnolia').*

It is the same for the memories that will survive even war's destruction. In fact, the very destruction of war strengthens memories or stimulates them:

> *La stessa "tempesta," nominata per la terza volta nel finale, ribadisce l'ambivalenza tutta positiva di una metafisica priva di codificati ricorsi teologici, di una realtà fissata di là dal tempo sulla pur complessa base del solo umano ricordo, e perciò fragile, condizionata, e quindi*

raggiungibile e scompigliabile da parte della occasionale tempesta ch'è all'origine della poesia.[19]

The occurrence of the two verbs "gettare" and "scuotere" leads the reader to ultimately believe the ark and the magnolia tree to be one and the same:

Fuma il ramaiolo / in cucina, un suo tondo di riflessi / accentra i volti ossuti, i musi aguzzi / e li protegge in fondo la magnolia / se un soffio ve la getta. La tempesta / primaverile scuote d'un latrato / di fedeltà la mia arca, o perduti.

The magnolia protects the sweet memories of faces in his childhood kitchen as the buffeting of the ark is one of a "faithful baying." The baying, or howling, is, again, not just a reminiscence of his childhood pets, but the quintessence of remembrance in the dog figure. In a mock interview made into a short story, 'L'angoscia' (*Farfalla di Dinard*), Montale gives the reader a key to understanding the role of the dog figure with childhood and memory. Here the interviewee (Montale) speaks of how he had previously preferred cats to dogs: "Ma la mia conversione è recente, è dovuta al fatto che i cani (piú che i gatti) restano nel ricordo, chiedono di sopravvivere in noi."[20] He assumes that existence is proved by remembrance and that remembrance can be preserved through material objects of the empiric world. He then discusses his role in relation to a pet dog, which reveals to the reader how he feels about the lost ("perduti") of his ark ("arca"): "Io sono dunque la sola persona che ancora conservi il ricordo di quel festoso bastardo di pelo rossiccio. Mi amava e quando fu troppo tardi l'ho amato anch'io."[21] A further example of his entrusted position of one remembering for others is found in *Farfalla di Dinard* in 'La donna barbuta,' writing in the third person about himself: "Il signor M. era certamente l'unica persona al mondo che ne conservasse un barlume di ricordo."[22] Perhaps a mere "barlume" is all that can be offered to Montale.

In 'L'arca' the baying loyalty of a dog is associated with strong memories. As dogs are loyal to humans, so then is Montale's memory – personified as a dog – if it serves him well. And perhaps the loyalty is also Montale's: it is his promise, his way of doing honor to the deceased, as he may be the only one to preserve a "barlume di ricordo." In this light, in 'L'angoscia'[23] Montale's character recounts how the dog loved him and how he loved the dog, when it was too late. Yet there is also another level: the level where human and cosmic intervals cross not in the absolute, but within the perception of a human being, and memory ultimately does fade and empty. Despite any loyal attempts at preservation, the empiric world is a cinema that offers the illusion of temporality and linear motion. Montale only hopes to edit his life, or to preserve the after-images as long as possible. "Da una torre" is a recording of that process.

The anaphora – and one recalls the anaphora of "tempesta" in 'L'arca' – of "ho visto," repeated three times in 'Da una torre,' shows this process:

Ho visto il merlo acquaiolo / spiccarsi dal parafulmine: / al volo orgoglioso, a un gruppetto / di flauto l'ho conosciuto. // Ho visto il festoso e orecchiuto / Piquillo scattar dalla tomba / e a stratti, da un'umida tromba / di scale, raggiungere il tetto. // Ho visto nei vetri a colori / filtrare un paese di scheletri / da fiori di bifore – e un labbro / di sangue farsi piú muto.

The verb "vedere" (to see) in the present perfect implies an original vision on the "schermo d'immagini" and then a recalled vision (or after-image) projected onto the screen of images in the brain as a screen. The first stanza establishes what Montale saw. In a supposed reality, he saw a real "merlo acquaiolo." Where and when, precisely, Montale witnessed this is not as important as the fact that it seems to be a simple memory of what he had seen. He recalls it as if the memory placed him once removed from the original occurrence.

The second stanza cites what Montale remembered from an experience he had envisioned, and this is the movement of a dog named Piquillo. Montale recalls what he had either imagined or remembered. The fact that he may have had a vision (imagined) would have been conditioned, however, by the memory of what had come before it in a fantastic accumulation. That which he has seen and which has been incised upon the screen of the visual receptor portion of his brain is adjoined by hope, desire and fantasy to create further visions. Thus, Montale does not merely recount what he remembers of a reality; he relates the memory of a memory, twice removed from any occurrence. This differs little from the memory of a false, empiric projection on the screen of images.

The third stanza is a much more complicated amalgam of memory, vision and self-reflection. What Montale saw becomes, in the poem, a memory of a vision based on the accumulation of memory. Yet, the latter memory is a subject of his previous poetry revisited. He relives what he had previously seen, in the post-war remains of Italy as a "paese di scheletri." He had looked there for a sign of his female figure and amongst the lugubrious setting, which is the perfect objective correlative for Montale's mental state. What he had once only glimpsed as a "barlume" of memory, in this instance came to him even more muted, and less clear: "piú muto" ("quieter still"), as if to say that his previous experience was also not entirely clear.

In this regard, I submit that the two poems – 'Eastbourne' ('33–'35) and 'Stanze' ('27–'29) – remain the best sources of poetic memory revisited. Through a recycling of terms from preceding poems, Montale already expresses abstract and metaphysical reproductions of a woman – through memory – when she is absent. In *Farfalla di Dinard*, are will encounter this projection as pertaining to the overall phenomenal projection of the screen of images.

The opening lines of 'Stanze' begin to elicit little cells or rooms, perhaps even chambers of the human body itself; little "stanze" that make up Clizia's composition. It appears rather miraculous upon deeper meditation: "The topic is Clizia, her provenance, the miracle she is, her paradoxical presence-in-absence."[24] Yet, according to such poems as 'Flussi' and 'Forse un mattino andando,' the world is already an absence as presence. There could be one point (a little room) in Clizia's body that would be a key to unlocking the mystery of her existence, in a locus where the little rooms ("stanze") compose the theatre of memory for which Clizia is one great metaphor. Maybe only Montale realizes that in the daily course of living, the exchange of blood and oxygen in capillaries, even in one point as it self-perpetuates, is miraculous. Within that realm of miraculous minutiae, Montale wonders whether in her absence there might be a quantum point of confluence, a point in a holographic universe where they overlap:

> *Ricerco invano il punto onde si mosse / il sangue che ti nutre, interminato / respingersi di cerchi oltre lo spazio / breve dei giorni umani. ('Stanze')*

This is also Montale's early poetic use of a point of blood, which can be grouped with 'Buffalo' ("le voci / del sangue") and 'Nel sonno' ("sangue oltre la morte").

These images of blood points increase the need to elucidate why Montale concerns himself with the lip: "un labbro di sangue" ('Da una torre'). In my discussion of the 'Mottetti,', I refer to an aspect of the disembodied voice – which, of course, plays center stage when joined with the coots in the 'Silvae' – as the one attribute of a person which is roughly the same whether present or absent. A song associated with a singer can be roughly reproduced in octave and in note clusters so it would seem as if the original voice were present, represented by the same note flurry that it had sung. Perhaps even a gramophone – close to an exact reproduction – can create an audio memory when replayed. Although in 'Il lacerato spirito' the voices came out distorted in timbre, the more important reference is the phenomenon of the excorporeal: "Le voci ne uscivano stridule, scorporate, alteratissime nel timbro."25 In 'Eastbourne,' Montale provides the blood image paired with a forerunner of the lip motif. A lip could be a symbol for a mouth or syneddoche of the mouth from which a voice exudes, as in the "voce di sangue":

E vieni / tu pure voce prigioniera, sciolta / anima ch'è smarrita, / voce di sangue, persa e restituita alla mia sera. ('Eastbourne')

Perhaps it is this voice that was rather mute in 'Eastbourne' and which he recognizes in the moment recalled of 'Da una torre': the already muted, disembodied voice is quieter still and by now it becomes one of Montale's signs for which he searches on the "schermo d'immagini," a lip of blood. Blood is included because of the piercing bittersweetness of the memory of her, which later on in 'Annetta' (1972) will become a "punta che feriva / quasi a sangue" ("a prick that wounded almost to the point of blood"). From this it is evident why 'Il ritorno' (1940) would reveal the woman friend as the presence-in-absence by her "morso / oscuro di tarantola" ("a dark tarantula bite"). This is the memory-charged language of Montale where each syntagm reveals a whole pre-history of meaning. In this sense, the same way a flash of memory, caused by a scent, a song, a juxtaposition of objects, can be endlessly significant in an instant, so can the very language used by the poet.

The next poem in the series, 'Ballata scritta in una clinica,' accompanies nicely 'Da una torre' in the context of the present topic:

Con te anch'io m'affaccio alla voce / che irrompe nell'alba, all'enorme / presenza dei morti; e poi l'ululo // del cane di legno è il mio, muto.

It reads like another perspective on his looking out of the mullioned windows onto the post-war landscape of Italy in 'Da una torre.' Only here it combines an experience from 'Il balcone' as the actual leaning out to the voice of the dead, to meet it as Clizia (in 'Il balcone') could lean into a light coming from her. The voice of the dead immediately motivates the reader to consider aspects of 'Voce giunta': how could Montale not feel responsible for the duty of remembering the dead? After all, here he conveys that the howling is his, as if the ambiguous, baying loyalty of 'L'arca' were now confirmed, and he is the loyal dog. For if the howl of the dog, i.e., an inanimate carved dog, is his, he is supplying the memorial tribute of past pets he has had in their absence now. The dog was an image of loyalty so strong in Montale that he kept, until his death, a carved wooden bulldog among his effects. Perhaps as Dora and others had talismans, now, in the face of war's destruction, the talisman by which he lives is a wooden Bulldog.[26] Though Montale has sensed a truer reality in the void, he has yet to abandon himself with faith, thereby making the transition to the void. Though Montale conceives of this in immanence, he cannot find convincing, material proof in that same immanence.

Notes

1. Lorenzo Greco, ed. *Montale commenta Montale* (Parma: Pratiche, 1980) 74.
2. Glauco Cambon, *La lotta con Proteo* (Milano: Bompiani, 1963) 124.
3. Cf. Kore-eda's 1998 film, *Afterlife,* the premise of which is the following: a group of recently deceased must spend one week in a purgatorial way station with one task, that of choosing one memory with which to spend eternity. They use the time re-viewing the 'films' of their lives from which to extract the singular, eternal moment. From the time the choice is made, the 'afterlife film crew' of this purgatory dedicate themselves to re-enacting and filming the moment in a style where Fellini and Kafka meet contemporary Japanese filmmaking.
4. Giuseppe Savoca, 'L'ombra viva della Bufera,' *Atti del convegno internazionale della poesia di Eugenio Montale.* VV. AA. (Milano: Librex, 1983) 389.
5. Maria Antonietta Grignani, 'Occasioni diacroniche nella poesia di Montale,' *Atti del convegno internazionale della poesia di Eugenio Montale.* VV. AA. (Milano: Librex, 1983) 325.
6. Corrado Federici, 'Le propaggini del 'male di vivere' nella poesia di Montale,' *Rivista di studi italiani* 4-5.1-2 (1986–87): 124.
7. Angelo Marchese, *L'amico dell'invisibile: la personalità e la poesia di Eugenio Montale* (Torino: Società Editrice Internazionale, 1966) 166.
8. Greco 130-31.
9. Oreste Macrí, *La vita della parola: Studia montaliani* (Firenze: Casa Editrice Le Lettere, 1996) 11.
10. Mary Anne Doane. *The Emergence of Cinematic Time.* (Cambridge: Harvard U Press, 2002): 173.
11. Greco 46.
12. Galassi 289. Though he may be correct in his assessment, there would be no absolutely necessary reason for one to believe they were more eel-nets than mullet-nets.

13. Italo Calvino. 'Forse un mattino andando,' in *Letture montaliane in occasione dell'80 compleanno del poeta.* (Genova: Bozzi, 1977): 43. Calvino is inspired here by insight from D'Arco Silvio Avalle's book (particularly the introduction and the two sections dedicated to the poems 'Il nerofumo della spera' and 'Gli orecchini'): *Tre saggi su Montale*. Torino: Giulio Einaudi Editore, 1970.
14. Here, D. N. Rodowick cites from Walter Benjamin. *Illuminations*. Ed. Hannah Arendt. Trans. Harry Zohn (Glasgow: Fontana/Collins, 1973): 39–40.
15. D. N. Rodowick. *Gilles Deleuze's Time Machine.* (Durham: Duke University Press, 1997): 33.
16. Calvino 44.
17. Marco Forti, *Eugenio Montale: la poesia, la prosa di fantasia e d'invenzione* (Milano: Mursia, 1973) 229.
18. Greco 47.
19. Forti 230.
20. Eugenio Montale, 'L'angoscia,' *Farfalla di Dinard* (Milano: Leonardo, 1994) 196.
21. Ibid.
22. Eugenio Montale, 'La donna barbuta,' *Farfalla di Dinard* (Milano: Leonardo, 1994) 46.
23. Montale, 'L'angoscia,' 195.
24. Joseph Cary, *Three Modern Italian Poets: Saba, Ungaretti, Montale.* 2nd ed. (Chicago: U of Chicago P, 1993) 298.
25. Eugenio Montale, 'Il lacerato spirito.' *Farfalla di Dinard* (Milano: Leonardo, 1994) 60–61.
26. Giuliano Dego, *Il bulldog di legno: intervista di Giuliano Dego a Eugenio Montale* (Roma: Riuniti, 1985) 61.

CHAPTER 6
Flashes: Meta-poetic montage

Most interesting in Montale's poetry is how his entire work flashes from the past to be reworked compactly into the present. In this way, Montale reworks the frames of a film strip to accommodate his projection of reality: "In his view" Jones notes about Montale, "memory consists of a series of empty holes into which the individual can, when suitable prompters appear, refit the events of his life."[1] In his interview with Ruberto, Montale explains that poetry is at times the process of accumulation that only becomes sharp after much waiting.[2] Poetic time differs from – and resides outside of the limits of – calendric time. Like a patient film editor, Montale 'refits the events of his life' so that the poems themselves become the locus of these re-editings and re-workings. If he cannot move beyond the empirical world, he can approach the void in the ideality of poetry. In particular, the poem 'Due nel crepuscolo' exemplifies the process of which Montale claims: "Ho compiuto, cioè, il lavoro che avrei dovuto fare allora, se avessi pensato che l'abbozzo poteva interessarmi dopo molti anni."[3] Montale's world seems to be experienced as an afterthought, living in an ever-fleeting present that can only be properly experienced and categorized in remembrance: if the future is open-ended, then Montale's past is open-ended, as well. In fact, he even remands the experience of writing the poem in its present (then) to its completion in a later present (now) when he retrieves it from the past:

> s'io levo / appena il braccio, mi si fa diverso / l'atto, si spezza su un cristallo, ignota / e impallidita sua memoria, e il gesto / già piú non m'appartiene.

All actions of the present (and the present itself) immediately become part of the past as they occur; the present moves constantly forward, leaving the notion of a pure present a mere illusion. In addition this poem is reminiscent of 'Là fuoresce il Tritone' (*Ossi*): "ogni ora prossima / è antica." Federici speaks of a life which is a "perenne scoperta dei detriti prodotti dalle vicissitudini umane, secondo Montale"[4] and that the "recupero del passato è, in fondo, la coscienza della sua lontananza, ma al tempo stesso la verità del suo accadimento;"⁵ to happen is to have been; to know that one exists is to have been, and in this sense one is perpetually redefined by the past as more of one's life pertains to the past as one lives.

Montale speaks of the separation of himself from himself: "se parlo, ascolto quella voce attonito." His whole self is the product of the many subdivisions of himself. Each self can be shorn off as a separate entity, no less part of the whole but self-contained. Each moment of him is an Eleatic arrow: this is Zeno's arrow recapitulated in a poem. He perceives himself as part of the cinematic world; each infinitely divisible moment of self is but a photogram of film. Each is immobile and only becomes mobile through illusion – that of a third party: "cinema works by obliterating the photogram, annihilating that which is static. It appears to extract a magical continuity from what is acknowledged to be discontinuous."⁶ By conclusion, Montale's cinema would be holographic: each part infinitely contains the whole.

In the holographic universe, there is infinite possibility of subdivision, but all pertains to the whole, ultimately. In fact, 'Voce giunta' offers an example of this sort of overlap occurring where three separate spaces and times come together in one moment-poem. This communion is possible in a hologram where all moments are equidistant, and therefore, equi-present. This equi-presence makes communication possible in 'Voce giunta,' where disembodied voices, both of the dead (Montale's father) and of the living (Clizia, far away) communicate. Though the communication in 'Voce giunta' occurs with the "ombre-voci" (voice-shadows), it is more effective than the lack of it here ("Due nel crepuscolo"):

Non so / se ti conosco; so che mai diviso / fui da te come accade in questo tardo / ritorno.

(It should be clear that the "ritorno" (return) is a real one, as the two were ending their walk in the twilight. However, the poet must have seen some great prophetic irony in this while reworking it 17 years later; and so should the reader see it.) This cinematic-poetic editing defines time and can only exist in the a-temporal poetic locus; or, as Montale phrases it: "Sarà forse una contraddizione, ma l'arte che meglio rispecchia il suo tempo non può vivere se non a patto di liberarsene...Al tempo cronologico non mi sono mai del tutto rassegnato."⁷

As far as the voice's destiny is concerned, it appears to open up another interesting area germane to 'Voce giunta.' In that poem, Montale speaks of the "vuoto inabitato," the place from which we come and to which we will all vanish. This term exists because Montale decided to conjoin representatives of his extant language to something quite invisible and abstract to the human intellect. Montale has settled for that description of a concept, but then the reader is resigned to viewing that void as something that can be filled:

Cosí si svela prima di legarsi / a immagini, a parole, oscuro senso / reminiscente, il vuoto inabitato / che occupammo e che attende fin ch'è tempo / di colmarsi di noi, di ritrovarci...

It can never be 'filled' per se, for it is limitless and eternal, but Montale must continue to follow the logic of his language, and not necessarily the logic of his abstraction, or as Brook phrases it, "Pre-linguistic wordlessness is not emptiness but pure potentiality; it can still be, and become, anything. Once the word binds it, it is forced to be something specific, formed, and accordingly restricted."[8]

"Due nel crepuscolo" offers an extension of this. Instead of the appearance of the uninhabited void, which can be "restricted" within the images created by words, here one sees how words can fail to transcend (and even descend) along with their references. The concepts and abstractions will inevitably transcend the ephemeral words and the material world of humans in which they reside. The words (concrete) sink into the void (potential as emptiness) where they will be held for infinity, even though the poet sees them as victims of entropy:

Se parlo, ascolto quella voce attonito, / scendere alla sua gamma piú remota / o spenta all'aria che non la sostiene.

This poem questions where a sound – a voice – goes once it is no longer heard, almost like asking where a moment has gone now that it is not the present. Does it simply die in the air that will host it as a medium? Perhaps it continues infinitely on a parallel continuum of the present – the open-ended past of Montale – as if it has entered the uninhabited void waiting for him it no longer belongs to the time and space as we know them as humans, in human intervals. It has gone where the "fiore di fosso" of 'Il giglio rosso' will reappear: "sugli argini solenni ove il brusío / del tempo piú non affatica..." Time no longer buzzes in the "vuoto inabitato," for this place would be beyond time in immanence. The void will have to wait for Montale as long as he is living in human time: "attende fin ch'è tempo / di colmarsi di noi." Afterwards, when one has passed beyond the world of time, one is joined in it. In the meantime, Montale struggles against time's unraveling in the language of poetry, "e la fuga del tempo diventa poesia della memoria."[9]

Already from the title of the sub-rubric, 'Flashes e dediche' (*Bufera*), one can imagine the inspiration to be of flashes of memory or camera flashes in picture taking. The poetry of this section assimilates stylistically its content so that it fuses with its form and thus approximates the written word to the physical experience of a flash of memory, or a flash of a camera. Like a single snapshot, in terms of their sheer brevity, these poems are disproportionately pregnant with meaning. Manacorda discusses how this process is "la lucida brevità dell'enumerato poetico che per "Lampi e dediche" si assimila programmaticamente al rapido *flash* che fissa in istantanea illuminazione un termine, un valore, un ricordo."[10] On the pictures (visual images) one attributes a context of date and place in the inscription (or the "dedica"). It is difficult for one not to draw the following conclusion: being that in Italian a synonym of flash could be "scatto" (the flash, or click, of a photographic shutter), and Montale has already spoken of these "scatti" before.[11] Could it be that each poem is a "dedica" for the "scatto?" With the fleeing of each moment, and the expectation that one will need a souvenir of it in the future, one snaps a photograph, entrusting it as the "persistence of a visual image in time."[12] Later, the photo, which is a presence indicating an absence, is conjoined to the present to fill a void in order to aid in recalling the past despite time's irreversibility. This discussion reflects a few verses from 'Il balcone:'

Ora a quel vuoto ho congiunto / ogni mio tardo motivo, / sull'arduo nulla si spunta / l'ansia di attenderti vivo.

With "ho congiunto," Montale has conjoined to the absence the memory of Clizia and the written evidence of this is the poem itself. But each attempt to remember and preserve her only reminds him more of the distance that separates him in the present from that moment in the past. In Federici's words,

il recupero del passato è, in fondo, la coscienza della sua lontananza, ma al tempo stesso la verità del suo accadimento ...E, infine, la memoria è funzione del tempo dato che solo nella memoria prendiamo coscienza del tempo quantitativo – documentando le varie fasi di quel che è stato.[13]

With this in mind, a corresponding argument could be found in 'Verso Siena:'

Ohimè che la memoria sulla vetta / non ha chi la trattenga! // (La fuga dei porcelli sull'Ambretta / notturna al sobbalzare della macchina / che guada, il carillon di San Gusmè / e una luna maggenga, tutta macchie...). // La scatola a sorpresa ha fatto scatto / sul punto in cui il mio Dio gittò la maschera / e fulminò il ribelle.

Memory seems to move towards an empty void in the manner of entropy. On the *Occasioni*, Santini comments that there is a "frazionamento della realtà in istanti brevemente percepita e rapidamente consumata."[14] But, here, the reality is not "consumata": time and physical limits impede the visual field from perceiving these sempiternal traces, which reside in the noumenos. Thus, Santini asserts, "ulteriore somiglianza fra le poetiche di Proust e Montale è la concezione della memoria come mezzo conoscitivo di quella realtà che si cela dietro il mondo fenomenico."[15]

What will hold back this process if not for the occasional epiphanic flash of memory or the flashbulb of a camera? The jack-in-the-box which has made its "scatto" seems to be a photographic instant. Interestingly, this release – be it of a camera or of a memory – occurs on the point ("sul punto") where a god unmasks, or reveals, himself and sends a fulmination into the rebel-poet. The flash, which takes a picture of the woman character, could not occur without the auger of this god's lightning and yet it is not clear if the god that comes down is not Clizia herself (a goddess) who has struck his memory in an instant. The poet makes a contradiction: almost as if by the grace of one action the other occurs, and vice versa, to produce the photo of a memory. Though in this case, the photographic image of the memory is preserved in memory itself: "Sul punto," perhaps the "punto dilatato" of 'Voce giunta.' It is infinitely small and infinitely enlargeable, like a photo-negative. The image is impressed – regardless of whether one can physically see it – on a tiny space awaiting the development process which will actualize it visually. The poet is a rebel in the face of the god, like a Prometheus, going against the rules, trying to introduce the past into some present (dilating the present to one eternal instant), or endowing this present with the notion of preserving it in the expectation of the future. But Montale realizes the immanence of his hypothesis: only poetically – for now – can he edit each Eleatic moment onto the screen, thereby creating his own continuity outside of chronological time. Though 'Verso Siena' becomes a poetic artifact of the experience, and therefore a way to preserve Montale's past, the action is, in the poet's words, futile:

Un'opera chiusa è una porzione di passato che pretende di risalire il tempo, operazione destinata al fallimento perché il tempo non è reversibile. L'opera dell'uomo, e non solo l'opera d'arte, dev'essere tanto aperta di morire nell'attimo stesso della sua nascita.[16]

Yet it is within Montale's poetry that he renders time reversible. In *Farfalla di Dinard*, time is neither reversible nor irreversible, for it is a construct.

A reader may tend to concentrate on the first and third strophes, paying less attention to the middle and regarding it as a secondary detail. Yet the middle is where that point is; literally and figuratively. It is a moment collected by parentheses, but it is the memory the poet wishes to hold back based on his statement in the optative mood of the first two lines. It begins by presenting itself like a banal description only to be closed as the camera flashes. Yet it is what was captured and becomes dilated as the poet steps out of time's continuum and into the parallel continuum of its unfolding. It unfolds within the parenthesis, within his rhetorical "punto dilatato."

In 'Verso Siena' the parentheses represent the fact that whatever falls between them is not occurring in the present continuum of time. The mind flashes to that point which contains the memory. The poet cannot hand the reader an abstract reference point and say "this is the net sum of my memory," so he magnifies it in spatial-linguistic terms and in temporality. What is remembered in the flash of an instant originally occurred over the expanse of space and of the duration of time. The parentheses imply a beginning and an end; a closure, which encapsulates the myriad of temporal and spatial descriptive elements – it dilates infinitely but remains distinct. The memory is initiated and closed then, by the structure of the poem, but as the ellipses suggest, what is in the dilated point could infinitely expand. In order to retain it within a singular memory, it must be cut off, closed by the second parenthesis, lest it begin to approximate – in a metaphysical parallel – the continuity of the present in which Montale finds himself. The present is illusory in Montale, who like Cortázar, finds the word "now" to be a terrific lie.[17] The parentheses also represent the inevitable limitations. The words opened up within them portray what is contained within that point in memory, so it has to have – in theory – a recognizable or relative boundary.

In 'Verso Siena' the *boite-à-surprise* clicks – the camera shudder snaps the photo – and the image is fixed, in a sense, on that point, but the subject within the point is, in actuality, still progressing into the present time continuum. As the subject continues in time, it is leaving instants – after-images – behind it infinitely like the contents of the parentheses in the second stanza. The fixed image is a presence that indicates the absence of the subject in the instant in which it was taken. Now is an illusion, so to choose an instant seems rather ridiculous unless, of course, Montale imagines a Eleatic quality of subdivision where instants only exist spatially, outside of time. The struggle of Montale's memory against holding back the entropy of time is a paradox, much like the process of photographing in order to fix time, as with the photographic version of memory in Calvino's 'Avventura d'un fotografo' in which the speaker addresses the issue of capturing a child on film: "Nulla è piú labile e irricordabile d'un infante da sei mesi, presto cancellato e sostituito da quello di 8 mesi e poi d'un anno... solo restando l'album fotografico come luogo dove tutte queste fugaci perfezioni si salvino."[18] However, in Montale's holographic world, every image 'survives' – not that it could 'die' – as a trace; each co-exists with the other as if on the wax of Freud's 'Mystic Writing-Pad.'

Further, Calvino's photographer represents Zeno's theory taken to the point of absurdity. Yet it is only the mind bound to time that undergoes each moment as a contingency, rather than as a pre-existing superposition of moments already there, awaiting recollection. Filming – the need to film – reflects the very contingency present in the empiric world which does not exist in the void of 'Forse un mattino andando' or 'Sul limite.' A filmable subject is a subject bound to time: or, in Doane's words, "The act of filming transforms the contingent into an event characterized by its very filmability."[19]

The following flash is 'Sulla Greve.' The fact that it begins with the elusive "Ora" ("now") complements my argument. The poem quickly explains that in order for there to be a now, there must be a then, and Montale – the perennial denizen of nostalgic places – cannot but recycle a syntagm from a past poem as if the words themselves offer in the present all the historical charge of meaning from their use in the past. This is reminiscent of Deleuze's interpretation of semiotics: "A sign acquires meaning only through its interpretation in another sign, and so on, ad infinitum."[20] This is what Graziosi refers to as Montale's "metalinguaggio retrospettivo."[21] In this case, the imperfect tense of "ti sporgevi" is a counterpoint to the past use of "ti sporgi" from 'Il balcone.' Montale is aware of the process whereby the past is thrust into the present as an apparent illusion. Memories fade because they are not preserved by a language which can accommodate their ineffability. If Montale had the perfect idiolect, beyond simply his pre-linguistic perception, memories would not fade. In 'Sulla Greve' Montale compares two moments: one of his current perceptions and one of his past. The latter gains greater meaning as it becomes linguistically tied to the former:

Ora non ceno solo con lo sguardo / come quando al mio fischio ti sporgevi / e ti vedevo appena. Un masso, un solco / a imbuto, il volo nero d'una rondine, / un coperchio sul mondo...

Once again, the image of the present succumbs to the past, and as in 'Verso Siena,' the image of infinite regression into memory and its continuum is unavoidable for Montale. The ellipses, as in the second stanza of the previous poem, allude to the point in memory which is ever dilatable along a chronological axis to be a parallel of the infinite continuum of cosmic time. Then Montale returns to the "ora" ("now"):

E m'è pane quel boccio di velluto / che s'apre su un glissato di mandolino, / acqua il fruscio scorrente, il tuo profondo / respiro vino.

It is unclear whether the *she* is physically present at his table (as a fixed presence who never really left that temporal-spatial locus) or if she is filtered through memory; projected into the present absence. The confusion arises from two contention points: the word "quel" ("that"); and the expression "il tuo profondo / respiro" ("your deep breathing"). "Quel boccio" ("that [flower] bud") could be a demonstrative used to differentiate the poet, perhaps identifying with "questo" ("this"), or it could be acting with reference to an antecedent of time: it may refer to then, as in the "quando" ("when") of the second verse. The deep breathing of the lady could be physical breathing or her soul represented as airiness. If she is not present, then this is truly a testament to the sacredness of memory and the merits in struggling to preserve it against the entropy of the universe. Through memory Montale revisits a moment of the past and reflects on how much stronger he is now. Though he could not connect with her then, even in her presence, now he has a communion with her, in her apparent absence. In either case, whether she is truly present or not, the poet has sublimated his appetites, desires and perceptions from a visual experience to a more complete experience so that he can imbibe her essence and perceive her with all the senses of the present, as if the moment were continuing into the present. Like a quantum particle in a holographic world, she is there with him. She is instantly there without needing to traverse an intermediary space. Though this would be possible – even ordinary – in the void, ironically it appears to Montale as a miracle on the screen of the empiric world. This passionate mindset is certainly unique in Montale and quite a far cry from 'Falsetto' and 'Sul Llogebrat.' It can be seen as a consummation through memory: there is not simply the satisfaction of revisiting, of projecting presence in an absence; rather it takes an almost religious feeling as he drinks in her essence as wine in a sort of secular eucharist.

If there is a communion in 'Sulla Greve,' then in 'Di un natale metropolitano' there is empty indifference and lack of a great presence in memory. In fact, even peace is absent; it no longer has a meaning: "non è piú guerra né pace." When war is absent one could say that there is – by default, at least – peace. Their souls neither cross in the memory of the one, nor in the prospect of the other:

poi a un crocicchio / le anime, / le bottiglie che non seppero aprirsi, /

non piú guerra né pace, il tardo frullo / di un piccione incapace di seguirti / sui gradini automatici che ti slittano in giú...

Memory fails as a device with which to interact with the past and everything falls into the netherworld like Eurydice, with Orpheus too weighed down to fight the entropy. It is as if there were nothing to hold back ("che trattenga") the memory. This poem produces a vision based on a memory of a vision in which the flash of memory fails. Based on what he knows of Clizia's past, he imagines where she might be now, what she might be doing. So he envisions her "toilette," in which a mirror – reflected, not direct sight – reveals the leftovers of a meal: "nella cornice, una caraffa vuota, / bicchierini di cenere e di bucce, / le luci di Mayfair." It is only in the mirror that is within the vision of memories that a potential flash of memory appears. It is not a recollection of a true thing but a remembrance of a reflection – at best a meeting of two souls. The informed language of the present perfectly recreated the elements of the shared moment, but they were dim and unsatisfactory in the original occurrence, so a re-visitation is that much more unsatisfactory. The meeting should have been inspiring, but it is weak enough to be included in the banality of meal leftovers and cigarette ashes. Illusory reality – like a cinema – moves too quickly over time and can only be appreciated afterwards. Even that after-image of the present – which is now in the past – can only be perceived by a memory which is losing a battle with entropy. Castellani refers to this as a "comunicazione intermittente con una realtà che può essere evocata ma non posseduta."[22] Conversely, in a poet who presents reality as fleeting and mysterious instants that become de facto pasts, memory's flashes, there is roughly no difference between the two statements "I experienced it" and "I recalled it."

Much of Montale's poetry presents a search for a sign or for a truth; some 'thing' to give him faith in a phenomenal world usually experienced as negation (especially in the *Ossi*) or, at best, vicariously through strong female figures who can accept the temporary nature of the present and live moment to moment, from Esterina in 'Falsetto' to 'Nuove stanze' to 'Sul Llogebrat.' Amidst the fleeting nature of cinematic time, Montale attempts to arrive at the heart of a concrete representation. Through language he seeks to get at the quiddity (haeccity, or 'thisness') of the essential "nuce." This quiddity escapes Montale two levels: on the continuum of time; and, as an existential search for truth and meaning. It is precisely this motif that manifests itself in the conclusion of "La trota nera." The haeccity of life escapes even those "Dottori in Divinità:"

Curvi sull'acqua serale / graduati in Economia, / Dottori in Divinità, / la trota annusa e va via, / il suo balenio di carbonchio / è un ricciolo tuo che si sfa / nel bagno, un sospiro che sale / dagli ipogei del tuo ufficio.

The sense of poetry being both a flash and a dedication comes through as this poem blends past and present in terms of the language employed, and content and form become fused. The single-sentence stanza speaks in a present that is related through the language of the past, as if the past belonged to no time: "In Montale i ricordi si presentano quasi independenti dalla memoria ... il ricordo si sviluppa in un minimo di storia,"[23] and outside of time. This he says of the *Ossi* and poems like 'Vecchi versi' and 'Dora Markus [I]' from the *Occasioni*. But, Rombi indicates, in the *Bufera*, "non è quasi mai piú cosí."[24] Adding in 'Keepsake' (*Occasioni*) to point his argument, Rombi speaks of the memories:

> *I ricordi (totalmente privi di riferimenti che potrebbero essere anche delle percezioni) sono allineati in una laconica successione che non è motivata da ragioni conseguenzialmente temporali, né logiche né spaziali, e neppure sentimenti: viene fatto il vuoto attorno a queste nude presenze cosí come, a nostro parere, viene fatto il vuoto intorno alle singole acquisizioni conoscitive e appercettive oltreché mnemoniche di Montale.*[25]

'Keepsake' offers a sudden, impulsive nature of the "ricordi," independent of active memory, which exist poetically as the resultant sum of Montale's chance ability to juxtapose images that were fished out of his active memory. Yet in this juxtaposition, time – though irreversible – comes together in the "lampo," and the sentiment of an hour, a day, a year, a life can be contained within the "punto dilatato" that unfolds to infinitely large, even cosmic, proportions for just a flash. "Montale rifiuta il concetto del tempo ...Il tempo per Montale è la dimensione crudele dell'esistenza umana, è la 'fiaba che brucerà in un lampo,' sono gli 'anni corti come giorni.'"[26] If moments can flee into entropy, then time must be an illusion.

With regard to this dilation, I must address one of Montale's most concise poems that merges so much together into one breath of poetry, 'La trota nera':

> *Curvi sull'acqua serale / graduati in Economia, Dottori in Divinità, / la trota annusa e va via, / il suo balenio di carbonchio / è un ricciolo tuo che si sfa / nel bagno, un sospiro che sale / dagli ipogei del tuo ufficio.*

The graduates and doctors are reminiscent of those of the poem 'I limoni': *Ascoltami, i poeti laureati, / si muovono soltanto fra le piante / dai nomi poco usati: bossi ligustri o acanti.*

To this the poet adjoins his preference for simple, aromatic lemon trees. While in 'I limoni' Montale parodies poetic pretension, in 'La trota nera' he literally places these poets with the "automi" ("Addii, fischi nel buio") who do not see the other (the true reality from 'Forse un mattino') beyond the life in front of them. (They are unaware of the film crew behind the scenes, which is producing the film we will call life in 'Il regista' (*Farfalla di Dinard*).) More interestingly, there are supposedly no trout in the river in Reading,[27] yet our poet catches a glimpse of one: "la trota annusa e va via." He has been given a moment of reprieve from illusions to uncover the secret of the world through one of its attributes. One can surmise that it is the same epiphanic sign of 'L'estate':

Forse nel guizzo argenteo della trota / controcorrente / torni anche tu al mio piede fanciulla morta / Aretusa.

One could argue that this image is Arletta. (She is neither Clizia, nor is she the contemporaneous woman of "La trota nera.") It matters little, for it is a syncretism of these mythologies where the linguistic strength of one expression used in a past situation can reappear meta-poetically to communicate the experience with a woman. The network of self-reference is so compact that each line opens up a dialogue with previous work in a capillary effect. By syncretizing his experience, the present is expressed by the past and vice-versa: the poetic world is the quantum world of com-possibility only expressible as a hologram, where com-possibility is the infinite possibility of each singular image to co-exist with other, infinitely numerous images.

Without an initiation to such works as "Vasca" and "Cigola la carrucola," the reader would extract less significance from "La trota nera." "Vasca" and "Cigola" are the poetic precursors of the image of people bent over looking into water...for something. In "Cigola" there is a 'well' image where "nel puro cerchio un'immagine ride," but it is only a flash and returns to its depths as if it had never been: "Ah che già stride / la ruota, ti ridona all'altro fondo." Likewise, in "Vasca," Montale speaks of "le molli parvenze;" something below/beyond the surface or an *other*. If there is an "other" in the void, it can only be sighted on the screen and taken for an aberration, or an optical illusion. Montale never calls this 'something' by name, but he refers to it:

vuol vivere e non sa come; / se lo guardi si stacca, torna in giú: / è nato e morto, e non ha avuto un nome.

By this point 'Vasca' and 'Cigola' serve as terms for this phenomenon. With particular regard to 'Vasca,' Clodagh Brook remarks how "language may be necessary for the perception and recognition of things, enabling them to be born as they are articulated."[28]

The idea of water and downward pull towards entropy will be played out in the *Occasioni*, as well: "un lugubre risucchio / d'assorbite esistenze" ('Bassa marea'); but not before it is first used within the context of the sea in the *Ossi* ('Crisalide'):

una risacca di memorie giunge / al vostro cuore e quasi lo sommerge. / Lunge risuona un grido: ecco precipita / il tempo, spare con risucchi rapidi / tra i sassi, ogni ricordo è spento.

Montale's beloved's curl is undone in the water of a bath in 'La truta nera': "il suo balenio di carbonchio / è un ricciolo tuo che si sfa / nel bagno." The fading is reminiscent of 'Stanze': "In te m'appare un'ultima corolla / di cenere leggera che non dura / ma sfioccata precipita." The image itself is part of the locus of forehead-feather-bangs-curls. It was initiated in 'Mottetto 12,' 'Ti libero la fronte,' where the senhal for the Clizian only-begetter is established. Then the plumage-forehead relation became conjoined to the reflecting in the water in 'Elegia di Pico Farnese': "nell'acque / specchi il piumaggio della tua fronte senza errore ... il tuo splendore è aperto." They are more rarefied later still in 'La frangia dei capelli:'

La frangia dei capelli che ti vela / la fronte puerile, tu distrarla / con la mano non devi. Anch'essa parla / di te, sulla mia strada è tutto il cielo, / la sola luce con le giade ch'ài / accerchiate sul polso.

He then appends an aviary image: "l'ala onde tu vai, / trasmigratrice Artemide ed illesa," which becomes merged with the bangs in the lines:

e s'ora / d'aeree lanugini s'infiora / quel fondo, a marezzarlo sei tu, scesa [as in 'Ti libero la fronte'] / d'un balzo, e irrequieta la tua fronte / si confonde con l'alba, la nasconde.

The jade jewelry on her wrists is then turned into a further talisman in the poem 'Il tuo volo.' Here, the hair – the bangs, the curls – is practically indistinct from the feathers of a bird, and even synonymous for them: "pendono / sul tuo ciuffo e ti stellano / gli amuleti." It is, therefore, not surprising that the images of stones or jewels become fused into the carbuncle ("carbonchio") of the trout's flash at the surface of the river. And with the flash – the "balenio" – the very nature of Montale's poetry comes full circle as each instant, in reality or in memory, is only appreciated as a fleeting, undoing curl of hair; a flash or glimmer of understanding. The self-referential nature of the poetry approximates for the reader the very process of Montale's memory. The analogy is that all the implication that comes into Montale's mind in a flash during his experience is tantamount to all of the implications that come into the reader's mind with expressions charged with the past of previous poems. Montale's essential alphabet proffers "sottili catene analogiche e differenziali" that tie "gli ultimi presenti a quelli trascorsi."[29]

In that respect, the simple word "vischio" of 'Di un natale metropolitano' conjures up an immediate linkage to emotions connected to, or associated with, Clizia, although in this poem, a certain G.B.H. is the female interlocutor (and though one never knows exactly for what the initials stood, it seems that she was a young Italian divorcée whom Montale had met in Florence in 1945). The relationship between Clizia and G.B.H. approximates Montale's relationship with immaterial memory and material, or concrete, conduits of representation. At the same time the attributes of the earthbound G.B.H. not only become means for a more sublimated discussion of Clizia, but even she is represented as an image impossible to capture by a corpulent Montale all too affected by gravity:

> *Un vischio, fin dall'infanzia sospeso grappolo / di fede e di pruina sul tuo lavandino / e sullo specchio ovale ch'ora adombrano / i tuoi ricci bergère fra santini e ritratti / di ragazzi infilati un po' alla svelta / nella cornice, una caraffa vuota, / bicchierini di cenere e di bucce, / le luci di Mayfair, poi a un crocicchio / le anime, le bottiglie che non seppero aprirsi.*

He revisits his statement from 'Falsetto' about being of the race of those who are earthbound. He syncretizes Orpheus with Baudelaire's albatross and his own concrete stature in reference to 'Falsetto' to produce the last lines of 'Di un natale metropolitano': "il tardo frullo / di un piccione incapace di seguirti / sui gradini che ti slittano in giú." The poet remains a flightless being, hampered by the illusion of corpulence when in fact the true reality in the void presupposes a disembodied process of entelechy.

The point in the poem in which one becomes aware of the indiscriminate nature of the locus femina materializes in the "crocicchio": "poi a un crocicchio / le anime, le bottiglie che non seppero aprirsi." Two souls arrive at an intersection, and nothing becomes of the serendipity in their meeting. The bottles will not uncork and neither war nor peace has meaning as if a positive image or a negative image would still be something compared to the alternative. The two souls that fail to connect are his and Clizia's as much as his and G.B.H.'s. He cannot experience the absent Clizia except as a memory in the present into whose fleeting past G.B.H. perpetually slips. This recalls the paradox of 'Gli orecchini' made manifest in the statement "fuggo / l'iddia che non s'incarna," where the "goddess" may be soteric but cannot be appreciated unless in a carnate form; yet in carnate form she relinquishes the soteric attribute to be lost within the same earthbound gravity in which the poet finds himself. The earthbound G.B.H. will be lost in the present: "sui gradini automatici che ti slittano in giú." Like the fixed images on celluloid, they slide through time, made material and given movement by the very time that undoes them.

The language of 'Di un natale metropolitano' immediately creates a flash of recognition that points to its etymology established in 'Vasca':

Ma ecco, c'è altro che striscia / a fior della spera rifatta liscia: / di erompere non ha virtú, / vuol vivere e non sa come; / se lo guardi si stacca, torna in giú: / è nato e morto, e non ha avuto un nome.

(In this sense the "spera" of the water has become a literal mirror in the later poetic imagery.) The "tu" of "seguirti" becomes as difficult to isolate here as the "tu" was in the *Ossi*, where it was institutional. It was now the poet's alter ego, now just a necessary interlocutor to complete a conversation *à deux* rather than a lonely monologue.

'Argyll tour' is a "flash" that resembles 'Verso Siena' in its application of the poetic style regarding the topic at hand. The cascade of images creates the vertical tension, seen in such works as the 'Mottetti,' as present images accumulate to document the moment of the flash of memory:

I bimbi sotto il cedro, funghi o muffe / vivi dopo l'acquata, / il puledrino in gabbia / con la scritta "mordace," / nafta a nubi, sospese / sui canali murati, / fumate di gabbiani, odor di sego / e di datteri, il mugghio del barcone, / catene che s'allentano / – ma le tue le ignoravo –, sulla scia / salti di tonni, sonno, lunghe strida / di sorci, oscene risa, anzi che tu / apparissi al tuo schiavo...

Not one verb appears until the ninth line: images just build up to what should be a culmination of a moment, and yet, in typical Montale fashion, the apex occurs as a representation of the past. It appears like a photograph or a frame of film. This one plate seems to contain images, one on top of the other, so that they overlap and yet maintain their integrity. After nine lines of substantiation where only one verb reigns supreme, the poet offers an offset line which establishes a narrative past imperfect. It should not be experienced by the reader as following the lines one through nine; instead it should be seen as running simultaneously to them; an instant interior flash resulting from the instant of external observation. This is a flash of the void: time would normally flow from the cinematic montage of this poem, but in the void this is but one co-existent totality. Montale has sighted the holographic real. Then, suddenly from that flash there is a return to the present list of substantives on which (perhaps) the presence will be projected over the void. Montale leaves off with the ellipses how, as present and past are always separated by more distance, this reëvocation-recollection process is nearly infinite. The fact that, based on the mention of sleep ("sonno"), this image may occur in a dream or in real life is irrelevant, for the presence-in-absence quality of dream or recollection is equivalent. The dream may be the only place where Montale can be completely in the spatial and temporal loci of his absent lady without being in the afterlife, for it is an equivalent of that which lies beyond the phenomenic world.

The verse "ma le tue le ignoravo" recalls the "ti ignoravo e non dovevo" of 'Mottetto 4.' It has the same memorial doubling effect perceived in the abovementioned 'Mottetto' and in 'La casa dei doganieri':

che t'ignoravo e non dovevo: ai colpi / d'oggi lo so, se di laggiú s'inflette / un'ora e mi riporta Cumerlotti / o Anghébeni ('Lontano, ero con te');

and

Tu non ricordi; altro tempo frastorna / la tua memoria; un filo s'addipana. ('La casa dei doganieri')

Having had the experience of the two previous works, the reader will be able to intuit more deeply the significance. Montale revisits the moment as if at that time he had the hindsight of the current moment – the prescience that a revisitation could allow. Only in a recollection could he realize that which he should have known in the moment when he could not have known it.

From the privileged position of the present, Montale re-judges his past in his poetry and assigns values to his beloved that had previously escaped him. In the poem 'Sul Llogebrat,' Montale identifies his beloved as the one who physically impelled forward inimical time away from the moment, assuring that it could only be lived as a memory for him. 'Sul Llogebrat" comments on

Montale's metaphysical state as if it were literally a flash of experience coming to him from the past. The poem exemplifies experience of memory as much as it reveals the content within it. The reader is thrust instantaneously into a moment without antecedent or following. Its timeless brevity is much like a plaquette or epigraph as the collection would suggest: 'Flashes'e dediche:'

> *Dal verde immarcescibile della canfora / due note, un intervallo di terza maggiore. / Il cucco, non la civetta, ti dissi; ma intanto, di scatto, / tu avevi spinto l'acceleratore.*

Huffman – referring most probably to the "pitòsferi" of 'Vecchi versi' and the "pietrisco" of 'Giunge a volte, repente' – argues about the precision of the Montale's naming of things in his environment:

> *Montale's experiences are communicated to him and to us through whatever media incite him to perception of the experience. At times the experience is so amorphous, so reluctant to yield its particular truth, that the poet must recreate the experience as precisely as possible in order to approach the understanding of its meaning ... And so I think that this is why it matters exactly what kind of flower he sees, exactly what the nature and composition of a pile of rubble is, because it is that rubble and that flower that are the media of experience.*[30]

While Montale mires himself in naming, Esterina moves forward. In the world of the present, Montale has always questioned too much, observed too much, and thought too much about his surroundings. Therefore, he remains disjointed from the rhythms of time. Like Esterina, who lived in the ephemeral moment which moved progressively forward, the woman moves without resistance through many moments. This is akin to the images of 'Falsetto' from which the later poems take a great linguistic and biographical meaning:

> *La dubbia dimane non t'impaura. / Leggiadra ti distendi / sullo scoglio lucente di sale / e al sole bruci le membra. / Ricordi la lucertola / ferma sul masso brullo; / te insidia giovinezza, / quella il lacciòlo d'erba del fanciullo. / L'acqua è la forza che ti tempra, / nell'acqua ti ritrovi e ti rinnovi: / noi ti pensiamo come un'alga, un ciottolo, / come un'equorea creatura / che la salsedine non intacca / ma torna al lito piú pura. / Hai ben ragione tu! Non turbare / di ubbie il sorridente presente.*

By quickly depressing the car's accelerator, she urged them on into the same future – leaving that moment which Montale is now forced to revisit as a past. She has caused the rift, the distance between present and past, to become greater: she has accelerated the film projection on the screen. Yet, while she moves at the same pace, he lives it all as an after-image. Montale fools himself in this world of perceptions, while Clizia moves on. The paradox is that without the rift there would be no appreciable memory. Now, in the future of that past moment, there is only a sudden flash of opportunity to see it, so that Montale is equally as out of time in its recollection as he was in the seminal moment. His meanwhile ("intanto") was already completed for the interlocutor of 'Sul Llogebrat.' The "intanto" ("meanwhile") is counterpointed by the woman's "di scatto" ("suddenly"). This is a kinetic version, a physical example, of what will separate the one shade (Clizia) from the other shade (the father) in 'Voce giunta.' He who insists on protracting the present will relive the past in the same stasis; his memory will "grow stale on itself." Therefore, the "memoria che giova" of 'Voce giunta' belongs to the one whose mindset in the present resembles that of the woman in 'Sul Llogebrat:' The cuckoo ("il cucco," also the word for a cuckhold) lives in *presente-peccato*, while the owlet ("la civetta," synonymous for a whimsical flirt in Italian), lives the *presente che giova*.

The poem 'Dal treno' greatly approximates Montale's view of the present and its transience, which makes it born – already a past – already a cinematic after-image. The leaning out of the window of a train fuses the outstanding motifs of 'Il balcone,' and also of the illumination "a tagli" of 'Al primo chiaro, quando':

La vita che dà barlumi / è quella che sola tu scorgi. / A lei ti sporgi da questa / finestra che non s'illumina. ('Il balcone');

Al primo chiaro, quando / subitaneo un rumore / di ferrovia mi parla / di chiusi uomini in corsa / nel traforo del sasso / illuminato a tagli / da cieli ed acque misti. ('Al primo chiaro, quando')

In the case of 'Dal treno:'

Le tortore colore solferino / sono a Sesto Calende per la prima / volta a memoria d'uomo. Cosí annunziano / i giornali. Affacciato al finestrino, / invano le ho cercate.

When one has searched for something, there is an expectation, and for Montale this culminates, once again, as is apt for the collection, in a flash-like epiphany: "Per me solo / balenò, cadde in uno stagno. E il suo / volo di fuoco m'accecò sull'altro." The incisive and decisive past absolute encapsulates, isolates and retrogresses the experience.

Furthermore, the differences in verb tenses also accentuate distinctions in memory itself. There is the memory as "peccato" and good memory; and there is, within these parameters, objective recollection – the mental documentation, record, of a fact in a universal sense. The first three lines unfold within the present: "Le tortore colore solferino / sono a Sesto Calende per la prima / volta a memoria d'uomo." Then there is the memory as a distant occurrence, which, unfortunately, no longer pertains to the present, and which, at best, may only be re-experienced as an image immediately undone: it flashed for Montale. This is an overly personal, unrelenting obsession, which will leave Montale less fulfilled. Like the image in 'Vasca,' even this flash falls into a body of water (here, the "stagno" into which it fell), as if it were "born, then died, never having had a name." In Borges' 'Funes el memorioso,' the eponymous character uses names to stand for numbers as well as holistic processes and situations. Each moment is born, and he gives its totality a name.

Yet at the same time, one can associate this memory as a "memoria-peccato" for Montale: "E il suo / volo di fuoco m'accecò sull'altro." Like Funes, Montale is inevitably sucked into the infinite regression of memory, leaving the present behind; missing other experiences. This is the same reluctance to take part in the progressing moment of 'Sul Llogebrat' where he incessantly languors in the moment which will not hold. The flash of 'Incantesimo' is more of an epiphanic release. The release is culminated in the terms that Montale uses, which have gathered momentum over time. So, the memory in 'Incantesimo' is re-evoked by the concepts and words themselves.

Typical of Montale's mnemonic process is his revisiting of a moment with the knowledge that the poet had lacked in that original moment. Montale may not have been aware that he had not known something in the first place, if he had not met Clizia here, "Diotima:" "Nella fiamma leggera che t'avvolge / e che non seppi prima / d'incontrare Diotima." This immediately alludes to images of 'Mottetto 4,' or even of 'Argyll tour.' Concepts and linguistic units come into the present from a poetic usage of the past, recalled in poetic memory. This is further refined as a pre- 'Voce giunta' image in 'Eastbourne:' "E vieni / tu pure voce prigioniera, sciolta / anima ch'è smarrita."

In this way, 'Quasi una fantasia' pulls the reader into Montale's poetic memory. Montale only uses the word "incantesimo," of the eponymous title, one other time, and that is here in 'Quasi una fantasia': "un giorno d'incantesimo." The magical day, or day of incantation, is a moment in the future when Montale will achieve his desired poetic voice and language:

Penso ad un giorno di'incantesimo / e delle giostre d'ore troppo uguali / mi ripago. Traboccherà la forza / che mi turgeva, incosciente mago, / da grande tempo.

Montale had dreamt of the day when his poetic inspiration and the means with which to express it would be one; the unconscious magician – the poet-magus – would come alive. By naming this poem 'Incantesimo' and declaring how he – in the cicada – sings strongest in the tree of Volpe's garden, he is equating the present with the desires of the past, as in 'Corno inglese,' when he awaited a wind that would play the discordant sistrum, which was his heart. Here the Diotima figure is motivation for his cicada-sistrum to emit its melody. In this way, the essential alphabet of 'Quasi una fantasia' is the very poem before the reader. Over accumulated time, usage, and metapoetic allusion, the words composing 'Incantesimo,' have become his de facto "essenziale alfabeto." The alphabet is essential because it contains the past as it graces the present, much like the Volpe character who can only be expressed in terms of the accumulated value of Clizia within the whole allusion of Diotima. When Montale says that she is like Clizia, he need not go into profound detail; it is already intrinsically understood. This much resembles the reasoning of the *osso* at hand ('Quasi un fantasia'): "Tutto il passato in un punto / dinanzi mi sarà comparso." In this sense, the "punto" can be an expressive sign or word as much as the abstract of the infinitely expandable point in which eternal memory is kept in the poem 'Voce giunta.' Epiphany can only be such after the accumulation of experience; otherwise there is no build-up; no tension leading up to the moment, making it vital and crucial enough to be considered epiphanic. The epiphanic moment is not notable or appreciable in and of itself without a context. There is rather an immediate moment in which each and every moment from the past leading up to the epiphany becomes salient; makes perfect sense in a seemingly spontaneous entelechy where all is justified, because each individually assessable moment, from the progression up to the present of the epiphany, assumes an instantaneous relationship to the present. It is no longer a present, but an expression of the past focused into one point; it is a frame by frame projection on the screen of images which exists in front of the void; moments without time, reduced to visual space. This is the cinematographic projection which Montale had preferred in 'Flussi,' a locus where all is "stampato / sopra immobili tende / da un'ignota lanterna."

Then there is a thrust into the present of the magical moment of 'Incantesimo': "In lei vibra piú forte l'amorosa cicala / sul ciliegio del tuo giardino." The cicada's sistrum vibrates best here, emanating melodies within this solitary garden reminiscent of the enclosures out of which the poet tried to break free in the *Ossi di seppia*. Montale has found a voice, but most naturally it dwells in the cicada's form. After all, the cicada image has been part of the process of accumulated poetic meaning, so now the form and the content of meaning both appear in one point – in the poem, as well as in the insect. Ultimately, however, the physical entropy of the world causes the fading of memory: "Il gesto indi s'annulla, / tace ogni voce, / discende alla sua foce / la vita brulla" ('Debole sistro al vento'). This explains the desultory nature of the introduction in which the poet identifies the cicada with a creative melodic influence aborted in the world's torpor: "Debole sistro al vento / d'una persa cicala, / toccato appena e spento / nel torpore ch'esala" (*idem.*). The cicada becomes especially strong as a metaphor, for Montale had previously, in 'Ciò che di me sapeste,' spoken of himself in terms of husks or shells and even as shadows, perhaps of his former self:

Restò cosí questa scorza / la vera mia sostanza; / il fuoco che non si smorza / per me si chiamò: l'ignoranza. // Se un'ombra scorgete, non è / un'ombra – ma quella io sono. / Potessi spiccarla da me, / offrirvela in dono.

In the desolate aridity of the environment of the *Ossi*, it is the cicada that survives the waves of heat: "Non durano che le solenni cicale / in questi saturnali del caldo" ('Egloga'). The cicada can sing incessantly – almost mockingly to whoever must tolerate the dry summer under the exposure of the sun. Yet its inevitable fate will be that the privilege of resistance is balanced by its brief life; it will soon be just a shell, a dried up exoskeleton. Its shell is a perfect correlative of memory; the remnant of a past which burned too quickly to be appreciated in the present.

Montale wrote 'Incantesimo' before 'L'ombra della magnolia,' though it appears later in the order of his compilation. The order is important, for what finally solidifies in terms of cicada imagery surfaces here, more rarefied and more immediately meaningful. Still intriguing is the culmination of memory and cicada in the locus of the magnolia tree, which has already been examined in its being a protector of the poet's dead, his past. What is implied about it is then relevant as well to the epiphany of rediscovering Montale's poetic voice, and furthermore, the endnotes of the poem highlight how tentative this could be:

L'ombra della magnolia giapponese / si sfoltisce or che i bocci paonazzi / sono caduti, vibra intermittente / in vetta una cicala. Non è piú / il tempo dell'unisono vocale.

The tree protecting the past is thinning, and the cicada sings intermittently. But the lone voice of the cicada further represents how Montale can no longer pertain to the voice unified by the strife of the war; as before, he cannot – will not – pertain to the "automi," nor to those "who do not turn back to notice" ('Forse un mattino andando').

As in 'Nuove stanze,' Montale looks to the Clizia figure for inspiration in the venture of not just living but existing. Living and dying were not separated by a great margin during the war; either could have occurred arbitrarily, and surviving was an unexpected gift, but one was too occupied with the struggle to fret about the fragility, and courage was not a choice but a fact of living:

Spendersi era più facile, morire / al primo batter d'ale, al primo incontro / col nemico, un trastullo. Comincia ora la via più dura.

Now, with no war, Montale must find the voice himself, but the voice, if it is to have meaning, to become a culmination of his long-expected essential alphabet, can only be shared with those who have the omniscience to relate instantaneously to its precursors or meta-philology. Without realizing it, Montale has imagined a holographic world where the totality of co-existence renders meaning, action and reaction, in a quantum moment. The only place where this could occur is in the "oltrecielo," reminiscent of the "oltretempo" ('Voce giunta'), a locus beyond time, beyond the screen of images. Clizia draws him there. She is the sunflower and she is the *angelo-procellaria* who is, in 'L'ombra della magnolia,' the "radicata" ("rooted", "earthbound") and yet a "cesena" (a "fieldfare" bird; a *turdis pilaris*) able to rise to meet the heavens. She has the faith in a god, as suggested by the line "le stimme del tuo Sposo." It is she who is Esterina's ('Falsetto') equivalent and yet somehow more sublime. It is she who is the Diotima (literally, "god-honored") to whom Montale compares Volpe. By following her he will perhaps experience a fulfillment of his poetic voice in a place where meanings transcend experience. Hence, his pseudo-suicidal leap into knowledge that will simultaneously be his demise: "è l'oltrecielo / che ti conduce e in lui mi getto, cèfalo / saltato in secco al novilunio." If living in his memories is living outside of the present, the "oltrecielo-oltretempo" would be a mere extension, or continuance, of this state.

In 'L'ombra della magnolia' the cicada only chirrups intermittently and yet even that is fragile and tentative: "la vuota scorza / di chi cantava sarà presto polvere," an image clearly reminiscent of the cicada shell falling into the first mud of cold November in 'Non recidere, forbice.' In the oxymora of the closed freedom of islands of thought in 'Incantesimo,' the poet truly finds his voice. By living in the abstract past of life – in the vagaries of thoughts and memories – Montale is living in an approximation of the afterlife. Death and absence are roughly the same to Montale as in 'Voce giunta': "Il vento del giorno / confonde l'ombra viva e l'altra ancora riluttante." By living in her garden, the amorous cicada comes alive. The world becomes irrelevant – "intorno il mondo stinge" – as when the poet slips consistently out of the present into his memories (a-temporal planes of the hologram).

Suddenly everything coalesces: if Montale could never cross over to understanding while earthbound, clearly the understanding, the truth for which he is searching, will present itself in the "vuoto inabitato." The thin veil that has always separated him from the quid of life will be lifted. There will be lucidity, the same clarity predicted in 'Quasi una fantasia' when "Tutto il passato in un punto / dinanzi mi sarà comparso." There, in the omniscience of a perfect memory, will the essential alphabet become appreciable (recognizable) in a flash and this is spelled out in 'Voce giunta:'

Cosí si svela prima di legarsi / a immagini, a parole, oscuro senso / reminiscente, il vuoto inabitato / che occupammo e che attende fin ch'è tempo / di colmarsi di noi, di ritrovarci.

The final image of 'Incantesimo' is germane: "attendi l'ora / di scoprire quel velo che t'ha un giorno / fidanzata al tuo Dio." The veil, which connects Montale to the truth as a god or as a concept, is ironically the veil that blocked him from obtaining truth on the phenomenal side of the screen. He had not been able to cross over the "varco" without a leap of faith; and perhaps only after death can one paradoxically have the vision to see what was there all along. Montale approaches a vision of this sort by revisiting the past with the knowledge of the present, and integrating the reassessed past into a valid expression of the present. He discovers the totality of an entelechy; intimating that in the holographic noumenos the thing and its entelechy are immediately experienced. Montale sublimates the infinite life of the cicada in spirit which lives, not intermittently in a tree, but fervently in the metaphysical abstract. There, memory and disembodied voice are on an equal plane. In the void is the crossover point: souls yet to be incarnate and souls of those who have left their carnate "spoglie" ("remains", "a mia madre") and the memory of actual occurrence will be the disembodied voices.

Notes

1. F. J. Jones. *The Modern Italian Lyric.* (Cardiff: University of Wales Press, 1986): 495.

2. Roberto Ruberto, "A Conversation with Eugenio Montale." *Italian Quarterly* 68.1 (1974): 51.
3. Eugenio Montale, *L'opera in versi.* Ed. Rosanna Bettarini and Gianfranco Contini (Milano: Mondadori, 1980) 954.
4. Corrado Federici, "Le propaggini del 'male di vivere' nella poesia di Montale," *Rivista di studi italiani* 4–5.1–2 (1986–87): 123.
5. Ibid. 124.
6. Mary Anne Doane. *The Emergence of Cinematic Time.* Cambridge: (Harvard U Press, 2002): 176.
7. Eugenio Montale. *Nel nostro tempo.* (Milano: Rizzoli, 1973): 57, 7.
8. Clodagh J. Brook. *The Expression of the Inexpressible in Eugenio Montale's Poetry: Metaphor, Negation and Silence.* (Oxford: Clarendon Press, 2002) 149.
9. Franco Croce, *La primavera hitleriana e altri saggi su Montale* (Genova: Marietti, 1997) 10.
10. Giuliano Manacorda, *Montale* (Firenze: Il Castoro, 1967) 73.
11. Giuseppe Savoca, 'L'ombra viva della Bufera,' *Atti del convegno internazionale della poesia di Eugenio Montale.* V.V. AA. (Milano: Librex, 1983) 393.
12. Doane 23.
13. Federici 124, 128.
14. Maria Cristina Santini. *La 'Farfalla di Dinard' e la memoria montaliana.* (La Spezia: Agorà Edizioni, 1989): 19.
15. Ibid. 29.
16. Eugenio Montale, 'L'uomo nel microsolco,' *Il secondo mestiere: arte, musica, società* (Milano: Mondadori, 1996) 281.
17. Julio Cortázar, 'Las babas del diablo,' *Las armas secretas* (Buenos Aires: Editorial Sudamericana, 1966) 81.
18. Italo Calvino, 'L'avventura di un fotografo,' *Gli amori difficili* (Milano: Mondadori, 1994) 50–51.
19. Doane 23.
20. Gilles Deleuze. *Cinema II: The Time-Image.* Trans. Hugh Tomlinson and Robert Galeta. (Minneapolis: U of Minnesota Press, 1989): 39.
21. Elisabetta Graziosi. *Il tempo in Montale: storia di un tema.* (Firenze: La Nuova Italia, 1978): 21.
22. Giuliana Castellani, 'Alle soglie della memoria,' *Contributi per Montale.* Ed. Giovanni Cillo (Lecce: Milella, 1979) 143.
23. Maggi Rombi, *Montale: parole, sensi e immagini* (Roma: Bulzoni, 1978) 36.
24. Ibid.
25. Ibid.
26. Fabio Dorigo, *Itinerari montaliani* (Poggibonsi: Lalli, 1986) 61.
27. Montale, *L'opera in versi*, 958.
28. Brook 34.
29. Santini 28.
30. Claire L. Huffman, "The Poetic Language of Eugenio Montale," *Italian Quarterly* 12.47–48 (1969): 105.

CHAPTER 7
Dreams born in the void

Dreams are a combination of many things; perhaps they are a subconscious ordering and reordering of the elements from the dreamer's essential alphabet. It is an ordering because the alphabet is composed of elements from memory or what Montale has already experienced in the past. It is a reordering because the mind juxtaposes these elements from memory (subconsciously) and new possibilities (new forms; presences to be recalled later) arise based on pre-existing structures. It is not so much a conscious, active effort as in regular signs of a language, deliberately ordered for communication. Rather, it is based on recalled experiences and visions. They occur at the pre-lingual level before they are joined to extant words, or even those yet to be coined and, therefore, they form almost spontaneously and autonomously, making Montale, as he says of 'Iride' (*La bufera*), "more its medium than its author."[1] In this sense, free-associative memory occurs naturally; afterwards, Montale merely edits and touches up once it has been thrown down on paper. It is as if a ghost communicated at a séance through the scrawling hand of an attendee and, thereafter, the séance members interpret what has been written. Even Montale himself may not be able to infer any greater meaning from it. It comes from the essential alphabet, which can only exist in relation to a semantic, memorial locus that can simultaneously and instantaneously preserve the meaning, despite the passing of time. Until now, Montale has long sought to edit the cinematic juxtapositions of images on the phenomenic screen. This occurred mostly in vain because he searched for the perfect juxtaposition of objects for which to find names and means of representation; experiences that exist in the void. The notion of void itself was merely the result of a miracle, an epiphany or flash, between the cinematic frames on a screen. A flash of illumination is needed: as a cinematic strip passes, the illumination arrives with each frame. In between the frames – in the interstices – there is light but no images. The illusion, however, maintains a continuous presence. For each brief instant during which each cinematic frame makes room for the next, the viewer is staring into void. The cinematic spectator is the poet in 'Forse un mattino' where Montale is able, "per una combinazione di fattori oggettivi (aria vetro) e soggettivi (ricettività a un miracolo gnoseologico) a voltarsi tanto in fretta di arrivare, diciamo, dove il suo campo visuale non ha ancora occupato lo spazio: e vede il nulla, il vuoto."[2] Montale is aware that his world (the phenomenal) is but a cinematic projection. Further, in 'Il regista' (*Farfalla di Dinard*), he intuits the presence of the metaphysical film crew creating the very illusion-images on the screen that arouse an existential crisis in him.

Montale intuitively relates to some of the images, but neither he nor the reader may be able to get beyond the separate meanings: the images mean exactly what they mean. It is not the burden of the sign to be interpreted. It is just a fact, a memory, which is the objective imprint of a subjective view. This notion echoes the lines in Quasimodo's 'Ho fiori e di notte': "le parole della vita / che non ho mai inteso."

A good example of this is seen within the language of the ideas expressed in 'Iride:'

> *Quando di colpo San Martino smotta / le sue braci e le attizza in fondo al cupo / fornello dell'Ontario, schiocchi di pigne verdi fra la cenere / o il fumo d'un infuso di papaveri / e il Volto insanguinato sul sudario / che mi divide da te; // questo e poco altro (se poco / è un tuo segno, un ammicco, nella lotta / che me sospinge in un ossario, spalle / al muro, dove zàffiri celesti / e palmizi e cicogne su una zampa non chiudono / l'atroce vista al povero / Nestoriano smarrito); // è quanto di te giunge dal naufragio / delle mie genti, delle tue, or che un fuoco / di gelo porta alla memoria il suolo / ch'è tuo e che non vedesti; e altro rosario / fra le dita non ho, non altra vampa / se non questa, di resina e di bacche, / t'ha investito. (part I)*

Here the reader's consideration falls most specifically on the lines: "questo e poco altro (se poco / è un tuo segno, un ammicco, nella lotta / che me sospinge in un ossario, spalle al muro." Immediately in the "ossario" one envisions a reliquary of the past. This ossuary contains his past and is also simultaneously a reference to the enclosures of the *Ossi di seppia* collection. His back is to the wall in this poem, rather than his looking at the wall for a crack in it or a "varco" of passage through or over it to the beyond. He is looking inward, re-evaluating his past with the comfort of his Clizia figure; she has become the very talisman he had admired in Dora Markus. Instead of a garden enclosing life, it is a garden enclosing dead (past) people, and this image recalls to mind the line in Zanzotto's 'Elegia pasquale:' "dagli orti di marmo" (from the marble gardens, i.e., cemeteries). (The fact that it is a "lotta" ("struggle") that is pushing him into the enclosure is something I will address in Chapter 8 in the more extensive discussion of 'Ezekiel Saw the Wheel.')

The way the warmth of summer returns unexpectedly in the San Martino (or Indian) summer, Montale's beloved comes to him: "questo e poco altro (se poco / è un tuo segno ...)." He passes through the next six verses with the parentheses only to join subject and predicate in the opening line of the third stanza:

è quanto di te giunge dal naufragio / delle mie genti, delle tue, or che un fuoco / di gelo porta alla memoria il suolo / ch'è tuo e che non vedesti.

The idea of a "segno" being a nothing and an everything simultaneously has been iterated in lines such as "Nulla finisce, o tutto, se tu fólgore / lasci la nube" ('Perché tardi?'). This is much like the sentiment of 'Stanze' which, in turn, shares an indirect connection with Quasimodo's 'Ho fiori e di notte.' Montale's existence seems to be a mere miracle of coincidence; a coincidental juxtaposition of molecules in a temporal spatial representation called "we." The holographic world of the void is one moment and all moments. Humans have constructed calendric time to give measured order to their lives, but they only delude themselves by calling time something that it is not: linear. It knows no moments of linearity. Quasimodo more clearly states this notion:

Forse muoio sempre. / Ma ascolto volentieri le parole della vita / che non ho mai inteso, mi fermo / su lunghe ipotesi. Certo non potrò sfuggire; / sarò fedele alla vita e alla morte / nel corpo e nello spirito / in ogni direzione prevista, visibile. / A intervalli qualcosa mi supera / leggera, un tempo paziente, / l'assurda differenza che corre / tra la morte e l'illusione / del battere del cuore. ('Ho fiori e di notte invito i pioppi')

This, of course, brings to mind "la morte non ha altra voce / di quella che spande la vita" from 'Palio' which relates to the argument of meaning being based on memory, because only in memory can one appreciate in an instant all that came to make that instant a reality.

The third stanza of 'Iride' also offers some indices of the process of image and meaning assimilation which rarefy in the flash, in this case in the flash of dreaming's subconscious: "e altro rosario / fra le dita non ho, non altra vampa / se non questa, di resina e di bacche, / t'ha investito." Clizia becomes what she represents, and the memory of her is present in the religious equivalent of Catholicism – the rosary. There is a religious syncretism in Clizia's and Montale's background, and this becomes part of Montale's own mythology that exists independent of time, both in memory and in dreams. Perhaps the "bacche" of the rosary could be an American-Christian reference of holly and mistletoe, as Galassi suggests,[3] and certainly her being in America while Montale is in Italy forces his mind to see her in relation to America's version of the tradition of Christmas celebration.

Montale envisions Clizia as pertaining to an eternal process: "Perché l'opera tua (che della Sua / è una forma)" and "perché l'opera Sua (che nella tua / si trasforma)." It gives greater sense to his Nestorian reference of Clizia in the second stanza. And he gives himself consolation: if all people are versions of Christ, then they have a terrestrial form based in time and space, and they have a spiritual, or memorial, form, which will fill the void that exists before and after time; the void suggested later in 'Voce giunta.' For now, the terrestrial form can only partake in the dual nature of the Nestorian in the form of seemingly ephemeral memory. Voluntarily or involuntarily, Deleuze stipulates, memory "gives us eternity, but in such a manner that we do not have the strength to endure it for more than a moment, nor the means to discover its nature."[4] Just as the cold of autumn is suddenly interrupted by the warm reprieve of the Indian summer, the sun of "San Martino si stempra, nero" (the warmth quickly subsides as if a sun went cold and dark). If the poet thinks of her, she brings him to places they shared ("qui mi riporta"), much like the communication between the two absent-present interlocutors of 'Due nel crepuscolo.' Human intervals of time change, but the infinite cosmic time, to which she now pertains in his memory, will not suffer changes. Cosmic time, like memory has no concept of before or after. It is one integral moment: "Non hai sguardi, né ieri né domani," Montale tells Clizia in 'Iride.' To be terrestrial is to be governed by calendric time and therefore a prisoner of memory; to be angelic is to live as cosmic time exists within memory. Montale unifies time poetically. It is in the "punto dilatato" ('Voce giunta'), infinitely expandable and able to be revisited in a flash. In this light, his insistence approximates the hereafter. With, and through, Clizia he experiences more and more of the search for a truth. But if Clizia functions in a Christ-like form ("Perché l'opera tua (che della Sua / è una forma)"), as a Nestorian, she has terrestrial and spiritual forms. This placates Montale's preoccupations, for once he joins his dead (mentioned in his poetry from 'I morti' to 'Voce giunta,' and elsewhere), he will have what he considers Clizia's privileged state. At the same time, as in 'L'orto' ("prediletta / del mio Dio (del tuo forse)") Montale knows his destiny is different from Clizia's and their different gods.

His memory fades – over the passing of time – because he is mired in the phenomenic world:

> *I miei morti che prego perché preghino / per me, per i miei vivi com'io invoco / per essi non resurrezione ma / il compiersi di quella vita ch'ebbero / inesplicata e inesplicabile, oggi / piú di rado discendono dagli orizzonti aperti / quando una mischia d'acque e cielo schiude / finestre ai raggi della sera, – sempre / piú raro, astore celestiale, un cutter / bianco-alato li posa sulla rena. ('Proda di Versilia')*

As Galassi notes, "il compiersi" is "[t]he same rejection of an afterlife as in 'A mia madre,' which involves the sanctification of earthly existence."[5] What is also interesting is how all and any sort of spiritual experience must be mediated by the natural world or the world of objects, which also accrue greater significance in his subconscious evaluation of the world through memory. He is dependent upon the random appearance of the proper alphabet with which to express his relation between the present and the past. He is passive, and depends upon these chance miracles of language with experience as he waits in 'Proda di Versilia' for the goshawk ("astore") to place his dead (in memory?) on his shores. This is clearly like the free-voice which is prisoner and is dependent upon the coots to bring it in 'Voce giunta con le folaghe.' It is precisely the ties to memory which can prevent the fulfillment in the afterlife. The earthbound live much of their lives in memory and remember the dead through memory, therefore, having memory in the afterlife is a sign of being still tied to the earth. The "memoria-peccato" in 'Voce giunta' shows that the poet's father is too concerned with terrestrial time constraints to make the jump over into the Montalian equivalent of the leap of faith from *Purgatorio*, XXVII, needed to get into *Paradiso*. Perhaps he imagines that a memory, though it defies time in an abstract sense, can still fade. One might arrive at this conclusion in the world of illusion if the screen of images blinds the visual field from the void where memory and occurrence are the same moment. Memory is in the soul itself; it is predestined.

In 'Nella serra' and 'Il parco' (*Bufera*), the reader encounters an external world which is merely a linguistic tool with which to describe the poet's interior state. The void has been filled temporarily, but at the expense of Montale's missing it in time. So, the void is not really filled; it is deferred to the parallel of memory; a place which, like the hereafter, seems to be always filled with imagery, and yet, physically invisible and intangible as a locus: a world as hologram.

In 'Nella serra' the dream and memory are fused. Moments of his childhood are described in the first two stanzas:

> *S'empí d'uno zampettío / di talpe la limonaia, / brillò in un rosario di*

caute / gocce la falce fienaia. // S'accese sui pomi cotogni, / un punto, una cocciniglia, / si udí inalberarsi alla striglia / il poney – e poi vinse il sogno.

The images that Montale offers – like those of Fellini – represent themselves and somehow more than themselves, like the mysterious horse, or Oswaldo, of *La strada*. In a scene reminiscent of the domestic Pascoli, we are given elements such as the "caute gocce" of the scythe where beyond the narrative they would seem to be perfect representatives of the essential alphabet. Needless to say, they have convincingly placed the reader in Montale's past in Liguria. In a childlike way, all that precedes the second hemistich of verse eight succumbs sweetly to sleep: " – e poi vinse il sogno," and here one cannot help but think of 'Proda di Versilia,' where Montale recalls how as a boy he would fall asleep in the little nook adjacent to the kitchen:

A quel rezzo anche se disteso sotto / due brandelli di crespo punteggiati / di zanzare dormivo nella stanza / d'angolo, accanto alla cucina, ancora / nottetempo o nel cuore d'una siesta / di cicale, abbagliante nel mio sonno.

The time frame of the subsequent lines begins simultaneously as the child version of Montale drifts into a dream. ("Sogno" ('Nella serra') can be "sleep," metonymically, or "dream"; conversely "sonno" ('Proda di Versilia') can be "dream," metonymically, or "sleep.") Because dreams and memory function in the continuum parallel to, but outside of, calendric time, they are not human intervals; moments within either can intertwine or insinuate themselves outside of chronological, human intervals. The result is a synthesis worthy of Montale's self-commentary on his 'Iride.' The dream transcends time as does the memory, so it is not unexpected that a dream, begun in childhood, could spill into the present, or the future of that past. The ellipses at the end intimate the infinite continuity or interchangeability found in 'Verso Siena', 'Sulla Greve', 'Di un natale metropolitano' and 'Argyll Tour.'

In the third and fourth strophes of 'Nella serra' there is further interchangeability between those functions which lack true material form:

Rapito e leggero ero intriso / di te, la tua forma era il mio / respiro nascosto, il tuo viso / nel mio si fondeva, e l'oscuro // pensiero di Dio discendeva / sui pochi viventi.

Her form was his hidden breath: "la tua forma era il mio / respiro nascosto."

That is, not only was he so "intriso" with her, but their forms were commensurate in the dream; in the memory. As in the afterlife, intimated in 'Voce giunta,' form is meaningless as matter, for "matter exists as it is perceived."[6]

This matterless form is Montale's form in 'Nel parco,' where in the fourth stanza he refers to himself as "disfatto di me":

E rido con te sulla ruota / deforme dell'ombra, mi allungo / disfatto di me sulle ossute radici che sporgono e pungo // con fili di paglia il tuo viso ...

This, according to Grignani, is a clear reversal of 'Due nel crepuscolo.'[7] Montale exhibits an awareness of the fact that though he can approximate moments that transcend time, he is still earthbound and dependent upon memory as he would be dependent upon the shade of a magnolia which slowly ebbs:

Nell'ombra della magnolia / che sempre più si restringe, / a un soffio di cerbottana / la freccia mi sfiora e si perde. // Pareva una foglia caduta / dal pioppo che a un colpo di vento / si stinge – e fors'era una mano scorrente a lungi tra il verde.

The mention of the "cerbottana" and its dart, "la freccia," refer to the past of his childhood. Yet present and past become indistinguishable, one conditioning the other, when he insists on including the two verbs "sfiora" and "si perde" in the present along with the actual situation under the shade of the magnolia. The second stanza is, then, immediately introduced with an ambiguous imperfect tense ("pareva") where the reader is not certain if it is referring to this actual moment in the present or that moment from the past.

Montale works actual versus past tenses into the cornice of the flash of memory. He intimates an infinite succession of memories that can be catalyzed by one flash:

Un riso che non m'appartiene / trapassa da fronde canute / fino al mio petto, lo scuote / un trillo che punge le vene, // e rido con te sulla ruota / deforme dell'ombra, mi allungo disfatto di me sulle ossute / radici che sporgono e pungo // con fili di paglia il tuo viso ... ('Nel parco')

Both the woman and Montale are together as presence in the void. In 'Due nel crepuscolo,' Montale was disembodied – deconstructed metaphysically from himself. He raises his arm which shatters and shears off, no longer pertaining to him; or, it only pertains to the 'him' of one Zenonian moment in the trajectory of his movements. Each movement is a separate, discrete moment divisible from himself, like the infinite and divisible arrows that comprise the moments of Zeno's arrow. The memorial moments are infinite divisions that pertain to him, but are not him. In 'Sul limite,' Montale's guide in the afterlife explains how the poet will not recognize the moments of what he had previously called his life, when he views the film of it. Relativity and subjectivity are but illusions of the phenomenal world. In the void, Montale is part of a holographic totality out of time, with pure presence, though this pure presence is comprised of infinite planes, or cross-sections, of the hologram.

'L'orto' continues the theme of moments in memory, independent of ordered time, which spill into each other:

Io non so, messaggera / che scendi, prediletta / del mio Dio (del tuo forse), se nel chiuso / dei meli lazzeruoli ove si lagnano / i luí nidaci, estenuanti a sera, / io non so se nell'orto / dove le ghiande piovono e oltre il muro / si sfioccano, aerine, le ghirlande / dei carpini che accennano / lo spumoso confine dei marosi, una vela / tra corone di scogli / sommersi e nerocupi o piú lucenti / della prima stella che trapela – // io non so se il tuo piede / attutito, il cieco incubo onde cresco / alla morte dal giorno che ti vidi, / io non so se il tuo passo che fa pulsar le vene / se s'avvicina in questo intrico, / è quello che mi colse un'altra estate / prima che una folata / radente contro il picco irto del Mesco / infrangesse il mio specchio.

The long, drawn-out use of the "io non so" anaphora brings the tension of the poem within a moment, a singular moment in which, like a flash, a mere calendric instant has passed. Meanwhile, while only a moment has passed, the poetic time that captures the myriad images associated in a split second within the essential alphabet, has dilated from the single flash point, or synapse. The single sentence implies the suddenness of one moment which expands spatially, as if time did not bind its infinite versions. To represent all these images in a picture would be simultaneous; to represent them to a reader requires verses that will physically span more time than the seminal, rapidly moving, moment. Each moment has a name, let us say 'A' for which the Zenonian representation would be A1, A2, A3... ad infinitum, but it would not be a linear representation – it would be a hologram with infinite depth and dimension. In the one instant he revisits the past and is unsure if, in the crucible of memories, the past and the present have not been fused into the eternal instant outside of time. Montale has, after all, received a visit from

Clizia, ("messaggera / che scendi") in the 'moment' from his childhood, including the very clear reference to his early summers in Monterosso:

un'altra estate / prima che una folata / radente contro il picco irto del Mesco / infrangesse il mio specchio.

Because the moments seem to coincide, he is unsure where experience stops and where memory begins; hence the "io non so" anaphora. He cannot see that memory – already in the soul's entelechy – is experience, not phenomenon, though he experiences it that way.

As in 'Mottetto 4,' and other poems, Montale experiences an epiphany *ex post facto*. All the moments are part of an eternal continuity and can therefore be experienced disjointedly and out of order if one is not dependent upon linear chronology. He begins to understand the notions reflected in *Farfalla di Dinard*, whereby a life can be filmed in its entirety before it is 'lived'. So he wonders if the presence which brushes his shoulder was not present before he knew to recognize it as such. This is most clearly seen in the last two examples, 'Nel parco' and 'L'orto.'

The idea of the continuous, infinite time in which events can unfurl irrespective of calendric time is later explained in the fourth strophe of 'L'orto' with the "solco solo" ("single groove"):

Se la forza / che guida il disco di già inciso fosse / un'altra, certo il tuo destino al mio / congiunto mostrerebbe un solco solo.

Infinity is not the preponderance of time, but the lack of it. The idea of a destiny decided and determined before and after time, because it is in no time of human intervals, is implied in 'Sotto la pioggia' (*Occasioni*):

Strideva Adiós muchachos, compañeros / de mi vida, il tuo disco della corte: / e m'è cara la maschera se ancora / di là dal mulinello della sorte / mi rimane il sobbalzo che riporta / al tuo sentiero.

The "sobbalzo," or jump, is a skipping on the single groove of the disc to demonstrate how if all is predetermined, then metaphysically speaking he can jump into any one of the moments before or after his time, as he will see in 'Sul limite.' Like a skipping record, Montale can rejoin a point in the continuous groove of the disc and so join the company of any of his female protagonists. Time and history do not have eluctible direction for Montale.[8] In this sense, if the garden is a sort of reliquary of memories (of the past), it is represented as "questo intrico" in 'L'orto':

io non so se il tuo passo che fa pulsar le vene / se s'avvicina in questo intrico, / è quello che mi colse un'altra estate.

In 'L'orto,' Clizia herself, as a past, is present in the first two strophes, as "predilected messenger" (transl. mine) and as a "muffled step," but present in a time during which Montale had yet to know her. This is possible because the time of memory and the presences that come from it are cosmic. They are not bound by that which binds humans themselves, "tempo d'uomo" and "spazio d'uomo." Suddenly, in the third strophe, all of the past and poetic motifs of the past are interrupted by the image of the present aftermath of war:

L'ora della tortura e dei lamenti / che s'abbatté sul mondo, / l'ora che tu leggevi chiara come in un libro / figgendo il duro sguardo di cristallo / bene in fondo, là dove acri tendine / di fuliggine alzandosi su lampi / di officine celavano alla vista / l'opera di Vulcano, / il dí dell'Ira che più volte il gallo / annunciò algi spergiuri, / non ti divise, anima indivisa, / dal supplizio inumano, non ti fuse / nella caldana, cuore d'ametista.

What is completely Montalean and wholly intriguing is how the present enters the poem but can only be spoken of in terms of the past and past poems. The whole third strophe (above) rings of the poetics of 'Nuove stanze,' replete with verses that re-evaluate the past in relation to the new understanding of the present: in the platonic sense, one has recalled to the point where one has perfect knowledge, or realized one's entelechy.

Montale was unsure in 'Nuove stanze' about the nature of Clizia's religious integrity, thoughit would have been clear all along had Montale seen it for what it was. His doubt is not a reflection of Clizia, but of himself, much like the disturbing series of "io non so" that builds up in 'L'orto' to the climax of the present. In 'L'orto' neither reader nor Montale could see her for what she is – "anima indivisa" – without a comparison to what she had been before. Through memory, Montale sees that she was not shaken from her faith by the "supplizio inumano." Though the misdeeds leading up to the empowerment of the Nazi-Fascists were done clandestinely, as in Vulcan's workshop-lair, Clizia had already known her course and righteously saw through the hidden intentions:

L'ora della tortura e dei lamenti / che s'abbatté sul mondo, / l'ora che tu leggevi chiara come in un libro / figgendo il duro sguardo di cristallo / bene in fondo.

The "prediletta" messenger makes a visitation in the opening of the poem. This moment of the present is superimposed onto the past as if yet one more layer of etching into Freud's 'Mystic Writing-Pad'. The template of the past is his adolescence and suddenly the memory is dissipated so that we are left with a present which only makes sense when viewed through the filter of the past, as if one could view simultaneously all of the etchings of the writing-pad in one visual field – hence, the imperfect tenses along with the past absolutes. Then, in the fourth, and last, strophe, the past and the present are examined within the structure of Montale's paradoxical metaphysics where life, like a poem, contains all time and no time:

O labbri muti, aridi dal lungo / viaggio per il sentiero fatto d'aria / che vi sostenne, o membra che distinguo / a stento dalle mie, o diti che smorzano / la sete dei morenti e i vivi infoncano, / o intento che hai creato fuor della tua misura / le sfere del quadrante e che ti espandi / in tempo d'uomo, in spazio d'uomo, in furie / di dèmoni incarnati, in fronti d'angiole / precipitate a volo ...

Clizia has taken on a spiritual form that transcends time and space as she travels on a path of air: "O labbri muti, aridi dal lungo / viaggio per il sentiero fatto d'aria / che vi sostenne." Her enduring nature is commensurate to her faith, her heart of amethyst. In a line reminiscent of Quasimodo as much as of Eliot, Montale fails to see the very afterlife, or beyond, that his memory intimates. For our poet – despite his intuitions – death is the final stage: "il cieco incubo onde cresco / alla morte dal giorno che ti vidi" (second strophe of 'L'orto'). In the garden which holds his memories dear, he and Clizia can approximate a single destiny, as in the fourth strophe: "o membra che distinguo / a stento dalle mie, o diti che smorzano / la sete dei morenti e i vivi infocano," the last line of which seems to be the forerunner of the dynamics of 'Voce giunta.' Then, the poet closes off his introspection into memory and the prospect of Clizia's metaphysical presence in her apparent absence: "precipitate a volo..." The last four lines express the contradiction within Montale: though he intuits a timeless world of pure, objective presence, he is bound by the illusion of matter on the screen of images:

Se la forza / che guida il disco di già inciso fosse / un'altra, certo il tuo destino al mio / congiunto mostrerebbe un solco solo.

Because he experiences himself as a presence, and Clizia as an absence-presence, he must relinquish one aspect of his life to garner the experience of the other. In time he is alone, left to himself. In memory Clizia's presence fills the absence, but Montale is missing the moment in its becoming. Perhaps this paradox is the impossibility of the single groove of their destinies within the empiric world. In a holographic world, one single groove could proffer infinite connections as the light of the universe illuminates it from infinite Zenonian angles. In this respect, one can see how Proust anticipated much of Einstein's theories and how his *Recherche* shares a commonality with Montale's poetics: "what will the Proustian novel be, taken in its totality, if not an immense landscape whose turning light makes successively multiple aspects appear?"[9] The illumination which Proust's "magic lantern" provides is the "ignota lanterna" of Montale's 'Flussi.'

What makes 'Nella serra' more pertinent is how the dream and memory amalgam is sublimated to the level of overcoming Montale's earlier poetic and human polemics in his childhood dreams. The domestic aspect is the heart of the poem, and it is the very memory of the domestic security that also re-evokes his childhood slumber; the very slumber that won everything over in 'Nella serra':

> *dormivo nella stanza / d'angolo, accanto alla cucina, ancora / nottetempo o nel cuore d'una siesta / di cicale, abbagliante nel mio sonno, / travedevo oltre il muro.*

Dreams, like memory, transcend time and place. In his dream he found the "break in the wall," the "link that did not hold," and got beyond his physical state into the void beyond the screen of images. In earlier works like 'Fine d'infanzia,' reading the "oltre" ("beyond") was futile: "Poco s'andava oltre i crinali prossimi / di quei monti; varcarli pur non osa / la memoria stancata." Now he dares to do just that.

With the accumulation of the essential alphabet throughout the poetry itself, this revisitation of the past takes on greater meaning, especially in the cicadas. Thus far cicadas had been symbolic of much of the metaphysical world. However, in 'Incantesimo' the cicada came to be associated with the face, the name, the voice, for which Montale had been searching all along, specifically since 'Vasca.' In the more mature moment of 'Proda di Versilia,' the blinding quality of the "siesta / di cicale" seems to be positive, whereas in the era contemporary to the *Ossi di seppia*, they would be part of the "remote spectral landscapes."[10] They do recall to the reader the confines of the "muraglia / che ha in cima cocci aguzzi di bottiglia" ("Meriggiare pallido e assorto"). The presence of the wall (along with the "broli", "cortili" and "macerie") in 'Proda di Versilia' reveals metaphoric enclosures as containers replete with memories:

Broli di zinnie tinte ad artificio / (nonne dal duro sòggolo le annaffiano, / chiuse lo sguardo a chi di fuorivia / non cede alle impietose loro mani / il suo male), cortili di sterpaglie / incanutite dove se entra un gatto / color frate gli vietano i rifiuti / voci irose; macerie e piatte altane / su case basse lungo un ondulato / declinare di dune e ombrelle aperte / al sole grigio, sabbia che non nutre / gli alberi sacri alla mia infanzia, il pino / selvatico, il fico e l'eucalipto.

In 'Voce giunta,' by some miracle, a denizen of the external world becomes a conduit, like the goshawk of 'Prodi,' and brings the presence of Clizia to the enclosure of the past; to the garden of marble, the cemetery of his dead. It is an accident of the confluence of human time and cosmic time as in 'Delta:'

Quando il tempo s'ingorga alle sue dighe / la tua vicenda accordi alla sua immensa, / ed affiori, memoria, piú palese / dall'oscura regione ove scendevi.

Here, in 'Proda,' Montale wants for them what he cannot have for himself: "il compiersi di quella vita ch'ebbero / inesplicata e inesplicabile." Death and memory are fused in their sense of past and present absence. For, in the void in which the world-memory resides, there is no death or absence; the wind (an element of nature, indifferent in terms of human space and human time) confuses the shadow (memory) of the living and the shadow (ghost) of the dead: "Il vento del giorno / confonde l'ombra viva e l'altra ancora riluttante" ('Voce giunta').

In fact, shadows have been a motif of presence-absence in Montale, but the Italian homonym "ombra" (both "shadow" and "shade") has been used to describe the expanse of a tree (keeper of memory and of the dead, like an ark) beyond just its physical measure. If in 'Nel parco' Montale finds solace in the ever-shrinking shade of the protective magnolia tree, then 'Proda di Versilia' holds the dual nature of the word "ombra" within the locus of the garden: "sabbia che non nutre / gli alberi sacri alla mia infanzia, il pino / selvatico, il fico e l'eucalipto." Additionally, within the very dream from his childhood he recalls his relatives now as "care ombre" who were cleaning and preparing the eels – one of the most intimate and dear bestiary symbols of his youth that will evolve into a figure (in 'L'anguilla') that will transcend the confines of human time and human space:

Nel cuore d'una siesta / di cicale, abbagliante nel mio sonno, / travedevo oltre il muro, al lavandino, / care ombre massaggiare le murene / per respingerne in coda, e poi reciderle, / le spine.

These are the "anni di scogli," as Montale calls them, in the fourth strophe of 'Proda' – as if years were measurable in these terms. These were the times of the "topi familiari" ('Proda'), from a time that was measurable. But now the poet's dreams, his dead, and his home are all equivalents of that which transcends human intervals. They have now approached the time of the sea in its infinite turning over the rocky shoreline: "tempo che fu misurabile / fino a che non s'aperse questo mare / infinito, di creta e di mondiglia." He has this clarity in 'Voce giunta,' when he realizes that he is the only thing consistently present in his present, and his dead and his memories can only be experienced in his present by rare flashes into this "punto dilatato." His dead and his past can only truly join him in his present when he is no longer part of the present measured by human intervals. They will be joined in the "vuoto inabitato / che occupammo e che attende fin ch'è tempo / di colmarsi di noi, di ritrovarci," or the filmic space of the afterlife of the *Farfalla di Dinard*.

In 'Voce giunta,' Montale clearly spells out a beyond, a sort of "oltretempo," and will not embrace it: he is reluctant, like his father, who is a shade described as "riluttante." In fact, the way in which the two *ombre* came to be is a good indication of the two sides of the metaphysical polemic:

L'ombra fidata e il muto che risorge, / quella che scorporò l'interno fuoco / e colui che lunghi anni d'oltretempo / (anni per me pesante) disincarnano.

Part of the polemic is also in Clizia's line "ho pensato per te, ho ricordato per / tutti," and on this subject, Cambon has much to offer to my point:

[And] here one cannot help thinking of the analogy to the double ritual Dante must perform in the garden of Eden, on top of the holy mountain, to perfect his purification as a preliminary to rising toward the stars: his immersion in Lethe, the river of forgetfulness, and into Enoe, the river of good memory. Self-contained memory is sheer closure, inertia, and entropy; a character of the Montalian [sic] persona meets in a dreamed-of afterworld in the short story 'Sul limite' ('On the Threshold') from Farfalla di Dinard, says to him that the new dead gradually lose their memory to "acquire another one": The short story evidently reverberates on the poem we are discussing, adding to our understanding of it:

I know, the first time one is still clingling to the stories of the time before. It's like what used to happen to me when I was among the living, no, what am I saying?, among the dead of Pre-threshold [Antelimite] from where you are now coming; I would dream and upon waking up I would still remember the dream, and even that memory would fade. The same thing is now happening to you; there is still an earthly fringe to put to sleep in your mind, but it won't take long. Later, when Giovanna shows you the "recording" of what you have called your life, you'll have trouble recognizing it. It seems to be so as far as Zone 1, the station where Jack and Fred often go, Fred, the painter who did that portrait of you at Spoleto, remember? Then they say that this memory is lost and a different one is acquired.[11]

In the phenomenal world, he experienced matter as cinematic after-images. In the afterlife, he will not recognize pure images. The recording of which he speaks is the one that he had viewed of Montale's life; it is a film of life:

When I heard your name, he says, I quickly reviews the filmed recording of your life. I had already seen it other times before, because it was "inciso" and updated all the way up to today, and for that reason I was able to wait for you right on schedule.[12]

In the void, he has the ability to see the original 'print': in the phenomenal world, he had attempted to edit the images as they fled past him. His effective reality was comprised of after-images. But Montale's alter ego from 'Sul limite' reflects the same concerns of the poet's father in 'Voce giunta.' The forces that rendered Clizia a shade were of an internal fire of faith, which transcends human intervals as an intangible part of life (the soul). The forces that disincarnate ("disincarnano") his father are countable, measurable years relative in the poet's heavy, earthbound form. Because the disembodied father still thinks in human intervals of time he will suffer the same lack of a voice, or identity, that he suffered while living. To make the metaphysical polemic even greater, there is the fear factor which prevents the father from crossing over, and this is rooted in the prospect of what he will lose among the living: his identity is determined not by himself, but by those who do or do not remember him: "Ma l'altro sbigottisce e teme che / la larva di memoria in cui si scalda / ai suoi figli si spenga al nuovo balzo." (The "balzo" is the Dantean leap, as a reader of Dante's *Commedia* will recall.) Despite what is "promised" to him, should he make the leap through the fire from Purgatory to Paradise, he lacks the faith, and we are reminded of the leap made in 'L'ombra della magnolia':

> *The one point of Purgatorio that could be usefully juxtaposed to 'L'ombra della magnolia' is the very end of Canto XXXIII with the immediate sequel of Paradiso I, where the purified Dantes takes off into the heavens under Beatrice's guidance. Characteristically, this cannot happen to the Montalian persona; the "mullet" jumps and dies to confirm what cannot be transcended. For it is human condition as such, the truly historical one unfolding between the two extremes of "hell" and a "paradise," that defines the limits of consciousness.*[13]

I have already mentioned the innate symbolic quality of the sea to represent infinity in 'Proda di Versilia.' In 'Voce giunta,' there is further sense that by joining the sea – i.e., leaving the land – one becomes a part of cosmic, non-linear time. In the fourth strophe it is spelled out in the notion of the father's temptations and affinities:

> *Ancora questa rupe / ti tenta? Sí, la bàttima è la stessa / di sempre, il mare che ti univa ai miei / lidi di prima che io avessi l'ali, / non si dissolve.*

The sea is the constant state of eternity; the shore is of the earthbound race (cf. 'Falsetto') that lives the temporal life, and the "bàttima" is the point where life is and has been all at once, as in D'Annunzio's 'Undulna.'[14] It is not the decisive living in the moment of Esterina. Neither is it the whimsical indifference that creates indistinguishable moments, one simply superimposing the other, of 'Sul Llogebrat,' or the childlike surety before being disillusioned of 'Fine dell'infanzia:'

> *Ogni attimo bruciava / negli istanti futuri senza tracce. / Vivere era ventura troppo nuova / ora per ora, e ne batteva il cuore. / Norma non v'era, / solco fisso, confronto, / a sceverare gioia da tristezza.*

The poet-father cannot join the sea of eternity; the same sea that absorbs memory because it exists before and after time – the metaphor of the noumenos in the void. Clizia is in the eternal sea, and the father wants to stay on the "prode," prolonging the last step in human form, for his mind's 'human' thinking binds him to earth. It is a more extrapolated, rarefied version of the implication made in 'Casa sul mare:'

Vorrei dirti che no, che ti s'appressa / l'ora che passerai di là dal tempo; / forse solo chi vuole s'infinita, / e questo tu potrai, chissà, non io / ... Il cammino finisce a queste prode / che rode la marea col moto alterno. / Il tuo cuore vicino che non m'ode / salpa già per l'eterno.

In 'Bassa marea' the poet imagines the fixity of the sea, as well as its infinity, as in 'Antico, sono ubriacato,' where the sea is described as an "essere vasto e diverso / e insieme fisso." It turns and neaps and ebbs, but it does not change: it is a metaphor for a closed system not susceptible to entropy. Even the cuttlefish bones themselves, which seem resistant to the elements, will be absorbed, only at a slower, imperceptible rate: "Oh allora sballotati / come l'osso di seppia dalle ondate / svanire a poco a poco" ('Riviere'). At the shoreline where the sea meets human existence is the last bastion of human preservation, as in 'Bassa marea:'

Viene col soffio della primavera / un lugubre risucchio / d'assorbite esistenze; e nella sua, / negro vilucchio, solo il tuo ricordo / s'attorce e si diffende.

It is perhaps as Federici puts it: "Per Montale, quindi, la memoria è la verifica tangibile che ognuno porta con sé del delicato ma tenace attaccamento alla vita."[15]

The return of the voices from the past depends upon an external factor like a coot or a goshawk – both birds – to bring them to the recaller. The return of the dead is dependent upon the posterity of an individual, the survivor, or as Moffa states it: "il ritorno dei morti è possibile solo se c'è nei vivi la volontà e l'amore di comunicare con loro, per svelare."[16] What Montale's father fears beyond just his progeny's negligence in his regard is the loss of memory as a necessary fact in the afterlife. Memory results as the distance between two moments and infinity is one moment. So, the father imagines infinity as absent of memory per se: "Il ricordare tutto," notes Dorigo, " ci priverebbe della memoria, rendendo illeggibile l'esistenza."[17] And as we know from 'Mottetto 1,' the loss of memory leaves only a "certain hell."

Unfortunately, however, the very memory of the past is a proclamation of its very distanced location in the past and the impossibility of truly, physically retrieving it. Again, to cite Federici:

L'enunciato per eccellenza in proposito va trovato in "Cigola la carrucola," poiché delinea il crudele paradosso che è la memoria – capace di evocare fantasmi dal profondo pozzo del passato solamente per farli svanire prima che possano essere pienamente realizzati e goduti.[18]

Notes

1. Eugenio Montale, *L'opera in versi*. Ed. Rosanna Bettarini and Gianfranco Contini (Milano: Mondadori, 1980) 962.
2. Italo Calvino. 'Forse un mattino andando,' in *Letture montaliane in occasione dell'80 compleanno del poeta*. (Genova: Bozzi, 1977): 42
3. Eugenio Montale, *Collected Poems (1920–1954)*. Tr., with annotation and commentary by Jonathan Galassi (New York: Farrar, 1998) 574.
4. Gilles Deleuze. *Proust and Signs*. Trans. Richard Howard. (New York: Braziller, 1972): 61.
5. Ibid. 580.
6. D. N. Rodowick. *Gilles Deleuze's Time Machine*. (Durham: Duke University Press, 1997): 24.
7. Maria Antonietta Grignani, *Prologhi ed epiloghi sulla poesia di Eugenio Montale* (Ravenna: Longo, 1982) 67.
8. Roberto Ruberto, "A Conversation with Eugenio Montale," *Italian Quarterly* 68.1 (1974): 50
9. Georges Poulet. *Proustian Space*. Trans. Elliott Coleman. (Baltimore: The St. John's U Press, 1977): 82.
10. F. J. Jones. *The Modern Italian Lyric*. (Cardiff: University of Wales Press, 1986): 407.
11. Glauco Cambon, *Eugenio Montale's Poetry: A Dream in Reason's Presence* (Princeton: Princeton UP, 1982) 108–09.
12. Eugenio Montale, 'Sul limite,' *Farfalla di Dinard*. Translation mine (Milano: Leonardo, 1994) 179.
13. Cambon 149–50.
14. Cf. particularly vv. 109–112.
15. Corrado Federici, "Le propaggini del 'male di vivere' nella poesia di Montale," *Rivista di studi italiani* 4-5.1-2 (1986–87): 124.
16. Mario Moffa, *Eugenio Montale: Lettura della Farfalla di Dinard* (Napoli: Società Editrice Napoletana, 1986) 137.
17. Fabio Dorigo, *Itinerari montaliani* (Poggibonsi: Lalli, 1986) 62.
18. Federici 124.

CHAPTER 8

'Ezekiel saw the Wheel': Reconciling the past

The present has been inimical and ambiguous in Montale from the outset, but throughout the first three collections of poetry there is a contradiction between his feelings about memory and the specific content of these memories. In fact, the best example of the contradiction can be seen in 'Ezekiel saw the wheel...' (*La bufera*): it is odd that a poet, so concerned with drawing memories up from the depths of his past and of his mind, would try to repress his recollection – much like the narrator of 'Sul limite' (*Farfalla di Dinard*), as the lines of 'Ezekiel' imply:

Ma la mano ... frugava tenace la traccia / in me seppellita da un cumulo, / da un monte di sabbia che avevo / in cuore ammassato per giungere / a soffocar la tua voce, / a spingerla in giú, dentro il breve / cerchio che tutto trasforma.

Memory now fails, becomes dim, now persists and gnaws at him.[1] Does Montale want to forget? Is he afraid of forgetting? Does he long to hold onto his past through memories despite any bitterness they may cause him? Can Montale only come to terms with his metaphysical "male di vivere" through the revisitation of memory? In short, is memory ultimately for Montale "memoria che giova" or "memoria-peccato?"

From the beginning one has observed in Montale what Virgillito calls that which oscillates "fra l'insopprimibile amore della terra e l'aspirazione alla 'divina inesistenza'"[2] [a term taken from the poem "Domande senza risposta" (*Diario del '72*)]. Of course, this is best typified in the dichotomy of the two voices in 'Voce giunta.' As a contradiction, Montale's 'love of the earth' is clouded by his feeling of metaphysical isolation or insignificance in the empirical world; a physical world that denies him a voice which may rise above his temporal, earthbound state. This impediment is often synonymous with the dearth of ready-made linguistic expressions and correlative objects with which to give form to the ineffable vagaries behind the screen of images. Not being able to concretize his ideality in the absence of this language, Montale's perceived abstractions cannot exist and there is no surety that in the absence of ideality the final stage of the temporal will not be hell: "e l'inferno è certo" ('Mottetto 1'). Brook succinctly epitomizes the Montalean disconnect: "Language may be necessary for the perception and recognition of things, enabling them to be born as they are articulated." If Montale's ideality cannot be "articulated,"[3] then the abstraction in it cannot be "born" in any meaningful sense – or, even more denigrating, in 'Flussi': "La vita è questo scialo / di triti fatti, vano / piú che crudele," after which he reasserts:

> *cosí un giorno / il giro che governa / la nostra vita ci addurrà il passato / lontano … / la rapace fortuna è già lontana / … / e la vita è crudele piú che vana.*

Grignani describes Montale's memory as a possible solution to his "male di vivere," but she also suggests a more passive option: "e la memoria, sia come atto intenzionale di rivincita sulla fallacia della realtà che si vede, che come meccanismo spontaneo di iterazione."[4] Memory and any approach toward ethereal, divine inexistence are both steps toward nothingness; abstract notions that to a physical world seem immaterial. Without some correlation between the world Montale sees behind the screen of images and a language with which to manifest it, he is reduced to a temporal hell where he sees a real, truer reality, while others cannot get beyond the screen: Brook recalls how the "'vuoto' lying behind them [in 'Forse un mattino andando']" is "the profound 'real' reality."[5]

Yet even if Montale's reality is more true, to record these things in his poetry means a return to reality within the conceptual language Montale uses, as in "Tra chiaro e scuro" (*Diario del '72*): "La nostra mente fa corporeo anche il nulla," yet what can be made corporeal at the pre-lingual, mental level is very different from what can be given form and expression in a spoken language. (This is what Camus says of expression: "L'esprit projette dans le concret sa tragédie spirituelle."[6]) Even when he is merely the medium of his dream language in a poem such as 'Iride,' he must record the poem in physical forms that resemble those which the reader's mind will construct. As Montale struggles with ideality and reality he still has a third dimension that contains both in an abstract form: dreams and memory. As in 'Voce giunta,' or in 'Proda di Versilia,' the subconscious memory is brought to light by an external stimulus: "In Montale's view, the past may be brought to life but only accidentally and not through the individual poet who acts as a conscious medium of its recovery."[7] In fact, it could be argued that in 'Ezekiel saw the wheel…,' Montale experiences a struggle as two moments of memory that are superimposed, one interrupting the other. His visual field cannot appreciate the multiple layers of reality, so he sees the moment as interference on one plane, much like a hologram when viewed from a particular angle, viewed as a confusion of lines and waves. Montale has experienced the multiple layers of Freud's 'Mystic Writing-Pad' without the proper optical capacity to fathom the myriad latent images as distinct entities:

> *Ghermito m'hai dall'intrico / dell'edera, mano straniera? / M'ero appoggiato alla vasca / viscida, l'aria era nera, / solo una vena d'onice tremava / nel fondo, quale stelo alla burrasca. / Ma la mano non si distolse, / nel buio si fece più diaccia / e la pioggia che si disciolse / sui miei capelli, sui tuoi / d'allora, troppo tenui, troppo lisci, frugava tenace la traccia / in me seppellita da un cumulo, / da un monte di sabbia che avevo / in cuore ammassato per giungere / a soffocar la tua voce, / a spingerla in giù, dentro il breve / cerchio che tutto trasforma, / raspava, portava all'aperto / con l'orma delle pianelle / sul fango indurito, la scheggia, / la fibra della tua croce / in polpa marcita di vecchie / putrelle schiantate, il sorriso / di teschio che a noi si frappose / quando la Ruota minacciosa apparve / tra riflessi d'aurora, e fatti sangue / i petali del pesco su me scesero / e con essi / il tuo artiglio, come ora.*

The first six lines of 'Ezekiel' have an incredible amount of material to offer the reader in terms of Montalean mythology and the toil of reconciling reality, ideality and memory: the "intrico," the "mano straniera," the "vasca," the "fondo," and the "burrasca."

'Ezekiel' offers two poignant moments: one seems to have already been in the poet's mind – by what means, I cannot say – and the other seems to interrupt it contrary to the poet's desire. When the strange hand snatched him (in the present perfect tense), Montale had already (pluperfect tense) leaned, gazing into the pool, which recalls that of 'Vasca.' There are two possibilities: either the 'strange' hand may have interrupted Montale in the present during his foray into the solace of the memory of the pool – a mnemonic locus to which he had already gone; or, the 'strange' hand is superimposed over the one memory (in the same temporal-memorial plane, as the poet conflates a later experience on an earlier one). The later is an infusion of memory with the prospect of salvation brought on by a Clizian figure. Montale recalls the episode of his youth when he had fallen, a mere toddler, into the fountain and imagines that salvation, now seemingly offered by Clizia in his memorial revision, to be and have been part of one continuum. Though the poem contains themes of downward entropy and pushing of voices into the ditch of memory, the idea of being "ghermito" by an "artiglio" recalls the birdlike qualities of Clizia coming from the upper spheres, the classic examples of which being 'La frangia dei capelli,' 'Mottetto 12' and 'Il tuo volo.' Although this does not disregard the chosen messenger sent from god in 'L'orto' that has had a long journey on a path made of air: "messaggera / che scendi, prediletta / del mio Dio (del tuo forse)."

The image of the bird seems contradictory in its role in this poem. It seems to be an image which comes from above, but which the poet will aim to suppress downwards. Montale enjoys the salvation from drowning in the pool, yet removed from the moment he seeks solace in its memory and is not permitted to do so because of the uninvited intrusion of another past, which would normally be dearer to him. That Montale would want to suffocate the memory does not necessarily make it a negative memory, however. In fact it is simply a symptom of the general memory with which the poet lives daily. He will not 'recognize' the film of his life because it happened in an a chronological way; he had forced a linear chronology onto it in order to make sense of it: the flashes were such in 'life' because they appeared without context. Perhaps this also exemplifies Huffman's statement about the poet being merely a "conscious medium of its recovery."[8]

If memory is an abstract with neither ineluctable direction nor material form, why is there necessarily a downward association made about the direction? Pushing a voice (a memory) downward is sending it to the ditch of memory of 'Voce giunta': "nel punto dilatato, nella fossa / che circonda lo scatto del ricordo." Though contradictory, it sheds light on the understanding of 'Mottetto 2' ('Molti anni'): "E per te scendere in un gorgo / di fedeltà, immortale." The drainlike whirlpool pulling the poet downwards seems a positive locus of eternal faithfulness. But having nearly arrived to the poetic end of *La bufera*, one can see that this may have been a forerunner of the ditch of memory. Where entropy had been a terminal vanishing point in 'Mottetto 1' ("Lo sai: debbo riperderti e non posso"), by now it is a noble void which includes past, present and future in the "vuoto inabitato" of 'Voce giunta.' This point – infinitely shrinking and infinitely expanding – goes as far back as Dante, of whom Montale surely had a good working knowledge:

Cosí vedi le cose contingenti, / Anzi che sieno in sé, mirando il punto / A cui tutti li tempi son presenti. (Paradiso, XVII, 16-18)

Time, is used figuratively for "all times," implies one continuum experienced spatially. This contrasts with 'Debole sistro al vento' (*Ossi*) which Arrowsmith calls "one of the bleakest poems Montale ever wrote."[9] In the *Ossi* Montale fears the entropic failing of the world and of his memory. The void was absolute nothingness then:

> *Debole sistro al vento / d'una persa cicala, / toccato appena e spento / nel torpore ch'esala. // Dirama dal profondo / in noi la vena / segreta: il nostro mondo / si regge appena. // Se tu l'accenni, all'aria / bigia treman corrotte / le vestigia / che il vuoto non ringhiotte. // Il gesto indi s'annulla, / tace ogni voce, / discende alla sua foce / la vita brulla.*

Since the *Ossi*, however, the notion of void changes to play counterpoint to the illusory world. 'Sul limite' is the poet's self-parody, in this regard: nothingness is a beginning, a communion with the world-memory and not the result of entropy. In 'Incontro' (*Ossi*), Arletta disappears (as Zampa identifies her),[10] like a shadow or wraith: "Poi piú nulla. Oh sommersa!: tu dispari / qual sei venuta e nulla so di te." And why should memory not be thought of in terms of negation when even his very existence and individual voice have been experienced as negation or denial within the early, suffocating enclosures of the *Ossi*? If she (whether recalled consciously or involuntarily) is a ghost, she is a projection of his memory and a synechdoche of it, and his memory is then drowned, lost, in the infernal depths of the "altro cammino" ('Incontro'). With the final line, "ch'io / scenda senza viltà," Montale makes clear in 'Incontro' how his loss of Arletta as memory is akin to Orpheus' loss of Eurydice. In this sense, much less negative than 'Incontro,' yet surely chthonic and orphic, is the poem 'Delta' (*Ossi*). It speaks of a suffocated presence ("presenza soffocata") not dissimilar from the "soffocare la tua voce" of 'Ezekiel':

> *La vita che si rompe nei travasi / secreti a te ho legata: / quella che si dibatte in sé e par quasi / non ti sappia, presenza soffocata.*

Yet in 'Delta' it is different. If one is speaking in terms of Arletta in this poem, then she is either dead or absent,[11] which means Montale is seeing her as a memory. If she is a memory then the line "la vita che si rompe nei travasi / segreti a te ho legata" clearly shows that any hope of breaking out ("rompersi") of the enclosure of the "male di vivere" will have to rely on the salvific presences of the world of memory. In the *Farfalla di Dinard*, Montale presents a world as memory. Finally, there is an approximation to the sea and eternity rather than a feeling of insignificance in its *cospetto*:

> *Quando il tempo s'ingorga alle sue dighe / la tua vicenda accordi alla sua immensa, / ed affiori, memoria, piú palese / dall'oscura regione ove*

scendevi. ('Delta')

This is the earliest notion of the rift between human intervals and cosmic time. The infinite sea becomes the metaphor for vast cosmic time where memories and the dead exist as if in one moment which includes past, present and future, a world-as-memory in a hologram. If relating the poet's "varco" from the enclosures of the *Ossi* to memory means calling this locus a depth from which it comes and goes, then perhaps it would be necessary to revisit 'Vasca:'

> *Ma ecco, c'è altro che striscia / a fior della spera rifatta liscia: / di erompere non ha virtú, / vuol vivere e non sa come: / se lo guardi si stacca, torna in giú: / è nato e morto e non ha avuto un nome.*

Here is the garden pool of the enclosure; of his youth;[12] the same pool revisited poetically in 'Ribaltamento' in *Quaderno di quattro anni*:

> *La vasca è un grande cerchio, vi si vedono / ninfee e pesciolini rosa pallido. / Mi sporgo e vi cado dentro ma dà l'allarme / un bimbo della mia età. / Chissà se c'è ancora acqua. Curvo il braccio / e tocco il pavimento della mia stanza.*

In this sacred ark of Montalean mythology, the poet evidences an early intersection of the phenomenal and noumenal world. The chance at identity disappears into the depths, the same depths from which Arletta's memory arrives and to which he ties his hopes of breaking out. In the process of breaking out, the poet also hopes to obtain an identity, a name. These depths – though dark and obscure – become the letterbox (an image from 'Reliquie' in *Farfalla di Dinard*) of memories in 'Delta' and this, of course, evolves into the ditch of memory in 'Voce giunta.' To this evolution Montale will finally put a terminus in 'L'anguilla' where he gives an affirmation of his identity in the eel, the symbol of life and identity that survives in the void behind the harsh images on the screen. The eel finds life,

> *dove solo / morde l'arsura e la desolazione, / la scintilla che dice / tutto comincia quando tutto pare / incarbonirsi.*

And Montale gives life to that which was ineffable before he had been able to manifest it as language. Then, so do the presences of memory find life when the past had seemed forgotten and the poet was left in absence. This eel occupies the same "travasi segreti" of the underworld seen in 'Delta.' Montale refers to it with earlier poetry as the underworld, but it is a precursor to the void. The eel, as an embodiment of childhood memories, occupies the ditch of memory. It even survives when the ditch seems temporarily arid, that is, when the empirical world seems bleak to our poet:

L'anguilla, torcia, frusta, / freccia d'Amore in terra / che solo i nostri botri o i disseccati / ruscelli pirenaici riconducono / a paradisi di fecondazione.

The idea of hope in eternal memory is seen in 'Ribaltamento,' a revisitation of the 'Vasca' locus, when the poet queries whether there is still water in the basin: "Chissà se c'è ancora acqua." In the same poetic breath, he answers his own question: "Curvo il braccio / e tocco il pavimento della mia stanza." In his memory (poetic time) Montale was so much a part of his past that he reaches out to touch the pool; in his human interval of chronology, he realizes that he is still in the present, in his room when the action of touching the pool (ideality) and the action of touching the floor (reality) converge into one moment. The very fact that the lines become blurred shows that though the possibility of aridity was there in the original, past moment truly is dried up and gone; there is still fecundity in his memory. That Montale is able to give the dreamlike moment a literary locus means that language has served him satisfactorily in its verbal representation of an ineffable experience.

In 'Ezekiel' though the poet tries to suppress his memory, it is so overpowering that he cannot, and in fact it induces further moments of memory. This is similar to Borges' notion that there is only one thing which does not exist: forgetting ("Sólo una cosa no hay. El olvido" ('Everness')). As mentioned above, in certain 'Flashes,' and even in other poems, Montale's use of the points of ellipsis is an indicator of a provoked memory: the one flash in the mind causes a chain reaction of infinite regression – or expansion – of memory and poetically accommodates the interior regression of the mind. The ellipses intimate not an end, but continuity. In that possibility, memory can certainly leave the plain of that which is good to derail the poet indefinitely and become a cumbersome *memoria-peccato*; useless memory. Once again, there is the same dilemma of 'Voce giunta,' and also the dilemma debated by the two interlocutors of 'Reliquie' (*Farfalla di Dinard*). The husband of 'Reliquie' refers to the wife's collection of photos, clippings, small iconic statues, and letters as her "reliquario privato,"[13] with, perhaps, a slight mocking tone. It has become a completely subjective symbol to the wife, having no continuity with the rest of the world; enclosed in a past, yet to her it is an eternal present. The wife will retort further down: "Tu parli del mio reliquario come se fosse una mania che non ti riguarda."[14]

Montale parodies himself in 'Sulla spiaggia (also of *Farfalla di Dinard*).' He seems to have no proper recollection of the character Anactoria, yet she remembers him:

> [...] *mi credevo ricco ed ero invece indigente. Qualcuno che avevo dimenticato m'ha colto di sorpresa; sono io che esisto ancora nella mente di Anactoria o di Annalena, io che sopravvivo in lei, non lei in me.* [...] *Io credo insomma a dimenticanze relative e quasi volontarie, a un processo, come chiamarlo?, tayloristico della mente che mettte in pensione quanto non può giovarle, pur conservando il bandolo e il filo di se stessa. Ma qui non ç'é da discutere: Anactoria o Annabella era stata del tutto soppressa dal mio pensiero per quatttro cinque sei anni, ed ora è tornata perché hla voluto tornare, è lei che mi fa grazia di sé, non sono io che mi degno di ridestarla andando dilettantisticamente alla ricerca del tempo perduta. È lei l'amorevole, la degna intrusa che rivangando nel suo passato s'è imbattuta nella mia ombra ed ha voluto ristabilire nel senso migliore della parola una "corrispondenza".*[15]

He is not merely one being, but the net result of many different perspectives or versions of himself, and he lives because of Anactoria's 'memory' which completes him: "It was I who survived in her, not she in me."[16] There is an infinite amount of people who have preserved some aspect of his life by merely remembering a moment or place in whose plane Montale happened to be. He was the background in someone else's experience; he was what might appear to be an automaton in another's moment in which he or she believes to be 'one who turns to look back', hoping to discover a rift in the space-time continuum while others walk by convinced that the empirical world is the true reality. The complete version of Montale would be the net sum of every person who ever had minimal visual contact with him. He is holistic only when he is projected in totality by all of the brain-screens that have ever reflected his image into being. All of the Anactorias of his life hold an end of the thread of which he spoke in 'La casa dei doganieri,' and now he is guilty of not holding the other end.

Then, further down still, the reluctance of the father of 'Voce giunta' to cross over and the interior struggle of 'Ezekiel' are lucidly stated in the wife's description of why she cannot let go – futiley or not: "Faccio semplicemente l'inventario dei nostri ricordi, l'unico filo che ci lega dopo tant'acqua è passata sotto i ponti."[17] And now one truly appreciates the opening lines of 'Barche sulla Marna' (*Occasioni*):

Felicità del sughero abbandonato / alla corrente / che stempra attorno i ponti rovesciati / e il plenilunio pallido nel sole: / barche sul fiume, agili nell'estate / e un murmure stagnante di città.

Here, the cork's very bliss is founded on its lack of consciousness of time's passing as it (time, inferred by its current) "melts around the upside-down bridges."

In 'Ezekiel,' one returns to enclosures in a few ways. The enclosure of the *Ossi*, the garden, is the physical locus of that poetry. The reliquary garden is also a reliquary box of the past, and Montale's mind holds on to the memories from it like the wife in 'Reliquie.' The pool of water ("vasca") inside the enclosure of the garden is the well of infinite depth from which memories come and to which they go. The "breve / cerchio" into which the poet would like to suppress a memory in 'Ezekiel' is the "punto dilatato" of 'Voce giunta.' It is a restricting enclosure and, paradoxically, it is a void, though it is not a void in the sense of being uninhabited. What Montale cannot see is that it is a naturally occurring landscape, that is, it occurs naturally as mortals leave the body as their complete soul. Its natural form is void, not as nothingness, but as the alternative to ther illusory 'something' of the phenomenal world.

Though Montale wrote 'Ezekiel' chronologically before 'Voce giunta,' it seems to be a more direct, emphatic version of the Clizian message of the latter; and to an extent, along with 'Proda di Versilia,' it shares the commonality of Clizia's exhortation to leave the enclosures of the past. It is an invitation to the poet to leave the useless, fading memories of his reliquary. He has put too much value in the material things which are manifested as material images constructed by the mind on the screen of images. "Clizia lures him to open spaces and away from enclosures."[18] Open space is, in a sense, a void, and the void may be a point, or a "sacred spot,"[19] but how can it be experienced in the sense of its entelechy? That is, how can a thing, whose end is only intuitable, ever reach an actual, rather than potential, form? If completeness means that intended form matches realized form, the "punto dilatato," in its being virtual, is in fact actual. Perhaps the irony of never finding the "varco" is within this rationale: for the purposes of poetry being a medium in visible, written form and for discussion amongst those who are earthbound – terrestrial humans – like Montale, one needs to make the abstract somewhat material or channelled into concepts based on pre-existing forms readily assimilated by human intellect. Speaking indirectly of a need for the abstract to take form in an essential alphabet, Montale himself tells the reader in 'Tra chiaro e scuro' (*Diario del '72*), "La nostra mente fa anche corporeo il nulla." There is the tendency of humans to project human standards even on those abstract or immaterial notions to which they do not pertain. It would seem contradictory that a poet like Montale, so consoled by the presences brought to him by memory to fill his daily void, should not embrace the faith of Clizia in 'Voce giunta' and leave the conviction that life begins and ends in the body, as in the more pessimistic "A mia madre."

The content of the poem 'Ezekiel' doubly exemplifies two aspects of an inimical memory; it is doubly "persistent" and doubly "gnawing."[20] All along Montale has had a fear of his memory fading ('Mottetto 18,' for example) and the obsession of preserving it has led him to the conception of the "memoria-peccato" of 'Voce giunta,' where it "builds mold upon itself." Montale's memory is his consolation and yet it is his personal enclosure; it restricts his world. The appearance of the fused Clizia-Arletta interlocutor of 'Ezekiel' is a testament to the contradiction that creates internal polemic within the poet. She appears only because Montale's memory is so persistent and she is inimical in her ability to spontaneously interrupt the course of another memory. She is the opposite of Anactoria, and Montale becomes Clizia for a moment in 'Sulla spiaggia.' In this light, Zambon constructs a salient argument with respect to 'Il ritorno':

Il riemergere del ricordo della donna: «ecco il tuo morso / oscuro di tarantola: son pronto». È un ricordo angosciante e quasi sinistro, annunciato da una «voce di sarabanda», da «Erinni fredde» che «vantano angui / d'inferno» e da una «bufera di strida»: un'aria mozartiana, come ha precisato Montale (il «cofano» è un grammofono o uno strumento), ma anche una sorta di evocazione infernale, dove quegli «angui» (in una prima redazione assimilati a «una raffica / di punte», immagine che rimanda direttamente ai versi di "Annetta" in cui la presenza/assenza della donna nella memoria è definita come «una punta che feriva / quasi a sangue») sono la manifestazione più degradata e minacciosa dell'anguilla.[21]

She could give him a voice. She could lead him to a life of affirmation, of faith, outside of his internal reliquary; the epicenter of his metaphysical "male di vivere" where he becomes a prisoner within himself. Memory could be understood as an end, but the end is taken for the means.

Montale had looked into a pool within his memory – the pool of 'Vasca,' or the one into which he fell as a toddler, searching for a voice, an identity or the truth:

La funzione della "vasca viscida," che sappiamo legata a un incubo

> *infantile di annegamento (descritto in una lirica del 1976, 'Ribaltamento,' Quaderno di quattro anni) corrisponde dunque a quella dell'antico "pozzo" e della equivalente vasca di un'altra poesia degli Ossi (intitolata appunto "Vasca"), sul cui "tremulo vetro" passa dapprima "un riso di belladonna" e poi, dopo un ciottolo ha infranto "le molli parvenze," "altro" che "striscia" e che "vuol vivere" (remota prefigurazione dell'anguilla che "cerca / vita"?), pur non avendo la forza di "erompere." E al "cerchio d'oro" del pozzo rinvia "il breve / cerchio che tutto trasforma," altra variante del fosso o della fossa del ricordo.*[22]

But the truth is that the memory is part of the reality and the moments of perceived reality were the mental constructions and visual illusions he had taken for reality. The 'salvific' one saves him from an existence without an identity much as she snatches him in her bird-like talon from a figurative and a literal drowning in the "vasca." His reaction is to suppress the absence-presence that is memory, much like the reluctant Montalean alter-ego narrator of 'Sul limite' (*Farfalla di Dinard*), but the "mano-artiglio" ("hand-talon," the second half of the term finally offered in the last line of 'Ezekiel') insists and digs deeper, exposing more of the past to the light of Montale's screen, which is a barrier to the noumenos. She saves him from festering within the all-too-private enclosure, or reliquary, that is Montale's memory as cinematic after-images:

> *Ma la mano ... frugava tenace la traccia / in me seppellita da un cumulo, / da un monte di sabbia che avevo / in cuore ammassato per giungere / a soffocar la tua voce / ... / raspava, portava all'aperto / ... / il tuo artiglio, come ora.*

Montale's poetry – as a physical, linguistic artifact – plays a part in the memorial process like the very components of the reliquary box in 'Reliquie' (*Farfalla di Dinard*). His poetry, especially a work like 'Il ventaglio,' becomes a concrete, visible form of his memories and that which is invisible and spiritual, but as such they exist as aspects of the phenomenal world. It becomes the lingual version of what had been previously pre-lingual, or that which could exist in a thought language but not a spoken one, but the very tangible existence of the poem creates a contradiction that is common to works of literature. Camus words this sort of scenario: "L'œuvre d'art naît du renoncement de l'intelligence à raisonner le concret. Elle marque le triomphe du charnel. C'est la pensée lucide qui la provoque, mais dans cet acte même elle se renonce."²³

The interruption by the memorial intruder of the bird-like Clizia, in 'Ezekiel,' is not unlike the Anactoria-Annabella of 'Sulla spiaggia' (*Farfalla di Dinard*), who motivates the poet to ponder where memory goes, and from where it suddenly appears, and how it often needs to be suppressed lest it lose its positive function of "memoria che giova." These wraiths of memories are not always "grate" ("appreciated" or "welcome"). After receiving mail from a person whom his recollection is not keen on having met, the interlocutor of the short story ('Sulla spiaggia') first opens up the idea of recollections appearing as if in flashes: "Un lampo illumina la mia mente, un vero lampo nel buio."²⁴ He then goes on to expand on the concept, expressing a sense of embarrassment, which, as mentioned above, is a parody of himself – this reflects the hypocrisy of his own insistence on the importance of preserving memory:

> *A dire il vero sono avvilitissimo. Penso agli scherzi della memoria, al pozzo di San Patrizio del ricordo. Io mi credo in credito verso di me e verso gli altri supponevo che infinite cose tramontate vivessero ancora in me, trovassero nel mio petto la loro ultima giustificazione [...] Già; e come può un ricordo sparire fino a questo sogno? Ero consapevole di custodire nello scrigno della memoria una folla di fantasmi possibili, virtuali che non evocavo per non ridestare ombre non sempre grate, ma che tuttavia affioravano talvolta alla superficie della coscienza e ne formavano in qualche modo la ricchezza. Reminiscenze così fatte, spore inesplose, castagnette a scoppio ritardato possono senza fatica spiegarsi, giustificarsi. Ma che dire del fatto che pullula* ex abrupto *dalla nostra inerte materia grigia, che pensare del fenomeno di una scomparsa totale che ad un tratto si rivela presenza?*²⁵

In his parodied form, Montale has taken the phenomenal world to a logical conclusion. He has joined the world of objects and the so-called concrete images that appear on the screen. He has become *de facto* part of someone else's essential alphabet. He has become the Esterina-Clizia-Arletta character who lives in the present. He has become the automaton who does not question while Anactoria has taken on his role. One finally imagines what Montale's situation would resemble if the roles were reversed. It is this very external world of the visible that gives Montale's poetry form, and gives the poet, himself, a certain strength in their connection to the images they preserve. Yet, now, he must deny all of these signs in the screen of images to enter a more spiritual context. Paradoxically, in a spiritual context, without the screen of images giving form to the abstract and invisible, how will he manage? Clizia offers the answer all along: he must have faith and make the Dantean "balzo" from a metaphysical purgatory on the earth to a very unfathomable, yet real, realm of the void. Perhaps this place exists beyond even the screen of images as the *other*; beyond even 'L'anguilla,' for this poem may just be an argument for the locus, the convergence of the spiritual within the living body and the spiritual outside of the living body, which become one and the same within memory; one and the same in the world-brain as hologram. After all, the eel is a "freccia d'Amore in terra" ("an arrow of love on earth"), as opposed to its form solely beyond the realm of the terrestrial. The flash – the brief rainbow – of the eel is a twin of the one in the eye of the interlocutor of 'L'anguilla.' Yet it is also something that transcends generations of men, sons of mankind, mired in the same mud: these are both the children playing in the rivuleti looking for eels to catch from Montale's youth, and they are mankind formed from mud or clay:

> *L'anguilla, la sirena / dei mari freddi che lascia il baltico / per giungere ai nostri mari, / ai nostri estuarî, ai fiumi / che risale in profondo, sotto la piena avversa, / di ramo in ramo e poi / di capello in capello, assottigliati, / sempre piú addentro, sempre piú nel cuore / del macigno, filtrando / tra gorielli di melma finché un giorno / una luce scoccata dai castagni / ne accende il guizzo in pozze d'acquamorta, / nei fossi che declinano / dai balzi d'Appennino alla Romagna; / l'anguilla, torcia, frusta, / freccia d'Amore in terra / che solo i nostri botri o i disseccati / ruscelli pirenaici riconducono / a paradisi di fecondazione; / l'anima verde che cerca / vita là dove solo / morde l'arsura e la desolazione, / la scintilla che dice / tutto comincia quando tutto pare / incarbonirsi, bronco seppellito; / l'iride breve, gemella / di quella che incastonano i tuoi cigli / e fai brillare intatta in mezzo ai figli / dell'uomo, immersi nel tuo fango, puoi tu / non crederla sorella?*

The ability of Montale's memory to come back and even become obsessive against his will is problematic for him, but it is not until 'L'anguilla' that one begins to get a feeling, as the reader, that the poet is beginning to understand the message (accept the message) brought to him by the voice in 'Voce giunta.' All beings when all has burned off.

In this sense, his memories – which the poet now embraces like the very eels that inhabit these memories – become the convergence point where he reconciles his two considerations: the terrestrial life and the life of the beyond. In this sense, it could be said that the mud – the medium – in which the eel travels, is a metaphor for memory itself, according to Zambon:

> *La lirica descrive il viaggio compiuto dal guizzante pesce prima che esso appaia nei "nostri botri," prima di essere agguantato dai "ragazzi" nelle "pozzanghere / mezzo seccate" e carbonizzato sulla brace: ciò verso cui tende in realtà 'L'anguilla,' tacendola, è dunque la sua morte, il momento culminante e rituale del sacrificio, descritto nella prosa complementare della Farfalla. Quasi purificato e sacralizzato a ritroso da questo destino mortale, il lungo viaggio nell'acqua e nel fango diventa la metafora della memoria stessa, dall'oscura sopravvivenza e del misterioso ritorno del passato; sono proprio le "stigmate" della sua passione a investire l'anguilla del messaggio profondo di cui è portatrice: "tutto comincia quando tutto pare / incarbonirsi."*[26]

In fact, it is right in the period of time around the late 1940s and early 1950s – when both the *Bufera* and *Farfalla di Dinard* are being composed – that Monterosso and Genova have endured drastic changes leaving them so different from the places of adolescence from which Montale draws so much of his poetry. Bianca Montale, niece of the poet, describes this:

> *La vasca delle ninfe, in cui Eugenio bambino cadde a capofitto rischiando di affogare, è ora poco più di uno squallido buco ... Rimangono nell'eliso della memoria, e forse soltanto nella cappella al cimitero, unica proprietà Montale rimasta, dove riposano i genitori e i fratelli. Era [the subject is Montale] tornato due o tre volte – la prima per un funerale – e si era sentito completamente estraneo a questa Monterosso, come smarrito e sgomento.*[27]

Within these few lines of biographical testimony by Montale's niece, two aspects help the reader explain with greater meaning the impact of the last few poems in the *Bufera* collection: 'Voce giunta' and 'L'anguilla;' one a polemic between good memory and bad memory, and the other the reconciliation of memory's purpose in uniting the terrestrial and the spiritual in a metaphysical sense. (Memory is the closest that a human being living in the empirical world can come to experiencing the real world beyond the illusory projection, unencumbered by human perception.) The cemetery in 'Voce giunta' is not just the locus of his father's remains, but one of the places perhaps most resistant to the changes of time in Monterosso and, therefore, which most preserves his adolescent memories of that place. The "vasca" has continuously served as a water symbol of reflection and a place that harbors memories in its depths. If the "vasca" of his youth is dried up, then no longer do the depths of the water serve as a metaphor for the haven of memories; rather what remains does. If the present is ephemeral and every moment will be remanded to memory, then even the locus, or symbol, of memory is subject to changes and it will itself evolve into a new symbol. The well is now just a "squallido buco," and only dry mud will remain at its bottom, but the eel can persevere in this medium. In the eel, Montale finally resolves the oscillation "fra l'insopprimibile amore della terra e l'aspirazione alla 'divina inesistenza'."[28] The empirical world of images offers Montale a medium with which to construct his poetic images, but what our poet has only been able to intuit so far is that the material images perceived on the screen of images dwells in front of the void where all things can gather in one point (as in 'Quasi una fantasia') in front of his visual field, for in the void the brain's screen is the world-brain's screen. If Clizia is by now – as an absence/presence – an example of divine non-existence and the poet is still "of the earthbound race" (cf. 'Falsetto'), then the eel is the metaphysical resolution that can only exist on the plane of memory which, itself, is the closest that the poet, while still in human form, can get to his divine non-existence.

In this regard, I conclude this chapter with a citation of a poem that speaks of this non-existence. It is, in itself, an auto-homage to the very themes I have elucidated, especially of the revisitation of the past, whether poetic or metaphysical. This poem is 'Domande senza risposta':

> *Mi chiedono se ho scritto / un canzoniere d'amore / e se il mio onlie begetter / è uno solo o è molteplice. / Ahimé, / la mia testa è confusa, molte figure / vi si addizionano, / ne formano una sola che discerno / a malapena nel mio crepuscolo. / Se avessi posseduto / un liuto come d'obbligo / per un trobar meno chiuso / non sarebbe difficile / dare un nome a colei che ha posseduto / la mia testa poetica o altro ancora. / Se il nome / fosse una conseguenza delle cose, / di queste non potrei dirne una sola / perché le cose sono fatti e i fatti / in prospettiva sono appena cenere. / Non ho avuto purtroppo che la parola, / qualche cosa che approssima ma non tocca; / e cosí / non c'è depositaria del mio cuore / che non sia nella bara. Se il suo nome / fosse un nome o piú nomi non conta nulla / per chi è rimasto fuori, ma per poco, / della divina inesistenza. A presto, / adorate mie larve!*

Notes

1. Eugenio Montale, *Collected Poems (1920–1954)*. Tr., with annotation and

commentary, by Jonathan Galassi (New York: Farrar, 1998): 581.
2. Rina Sara Virgillito, *La luce di Montale (per una lettura della poesia montaliana)* (Milano: Edizioni Paoline, 1990) 79.
3. Clodagh J. Brook. *The Expression of the Inexpressible in Eugenio Montale's Poetry: Metaphor, Negation and Silence.* (Oxford: Clarendon Press, 2002) 34.
4. Maria Antonietta Grignani, *Prologhi ed epiloghi sulla poesia di Eugenio Montale* (Ravenna: Longo, 1982) 52.
5. Brook 115.
6. Albert Camus, *Le mythe de Sisyphe* (Bussière: Gallimard, 1967): 171.
7. Claire Huffman, "T. S. Eliot, Eugenio Montale, and the Vagaries of Influence," *Comparative Literature* 27 (1975): 203.
8. Ibidem.
9. Eugenio Montale, *Cuttlefish Bones (1920–1927)*. Tr., with preface and commentary, by William Arrowsmith (additional commentary by Rosanna Warren and Claire Huffman) (New York: Norton, 1993): 229.
10. Giorgio Zampa, ed. '*Introduzione*' to *Eugenio Montale: Tutte le poesie*. (Milano: Mondadori, 1984): xxviii.
11. Eugenio Montale, *L'opera in versi*. Ed. Rosanna Bettarini and Gianfranco Contini (Milano: Mondadori, 1980): 917.
12. Piero Boragina, and Giuseppe Marcenaro, *Una dolcezza inquieta (l'universo poetico di Eugenio Montale)* (Milano: Electa, 1996): 23.
13. Eugenio Montale, 'Reliquie,' *Farfalla di Dinard* (Milano: Leonardo, 1994): 136.
14. Ibid.
15. Ibid, 185–6.
16. Ibid. 185.
17. Ibid. 137.
18. Glauco Cambon, *Eugenio Montale's Poetry: A Dream in Reason's Presence* (Princeton: Princeton UP, 1982): 118.
19. Ibid. 111.
20. Galassi 581.
21. Francesco Zambon, *L'iride nel fango: 'L'anguilla' di Eugenio Montale* (Parma: Pratiche, 1994): 80.
22. Ibid. 79–80.
23. Camus 132.
24. Eugenio Montale, 'Sulla spiaggia,' *Farfalla di Dinard* (Milano: Leonardo, 1994): 184.
25. Ibid. 185.
26. Zambon 42–43.
27. Boragina 23.
28. Virgillito 79.

CHAPTER 9

Perhaps one morning a hologram

In 'Forse un mattino andando' Montale proposes a void behind the world as we know it. Additionally, one discovers in *Farfalla di Dinard* that not only is there a void behind the phenomenal world, but the phenomenal world is a holographic film projection made by the denizens of the 'noumenos,' as seen in 'Il regista' and 'Sul limite' (*Farfalla di Dinard*). Montale has provided notions of synchronicity, especially in such works as the *Mottetti*, but with the knowledge that informs Montale's poetic world in *Farfalla di Dinard*, those synchronicities were one moment during which the projection of two or more layers of holographic reality overlapped. In the *Farfalla di Dinard* Montale clearly states, once and for all, that memories are not stored in the brain. They reside outside of the mind, albeit perceived by the mind in one holistic holographic world reminiscent of Deleuze's 'being-memory'. On holograms, Michael Talbot remarks: "We do not perceive [matter] as being on our retinas. We perceive it as being in the 'world-out-there'."[1]

The case for imagining Montale's world as holographic comes precisely from his notion in 'Forse un mattino andando' that if he could succeed in casting his visual field on the screen before the images manifested themselves there, he would see the blank screen; not nothing as the opposite of something, but void the only pure aspect of the world that is not illusion. In the physics of holograms there is, as Talbot holds, a similar obsession: "Perhaps most astonishing of all is that there is compelling evidence that the only time quanta [groups of electrons] even manifest as particles is when we are looking at them."[2] At other times, they are waves, not particles. In fact, another scholar of holographic related quantum physics, Nick Herbert, uses the metaphor of Midas, the fabled king who could not experience human touch, for everything he touched turned to gold. In Herbert's analogy, "humans can never experience the true texture of quantum reality, because everything we touch turns to matter."[3]

The whole study of holograms was pioneered by Karl Pribram who, like Montale, was fixated on finding the location of memory.[4] Holography seemed to be the best explanation, as well as a metaphor. As with the many unions of visual experience which superimposed on Montale's screen of images, holograms created on photographic film can hold many different images on the same seemingly single-planed surface. "If our brains function holographically," says Talbot, "a similar process may be responsible for the way certain objects evoke specific memories from our past."[5] The study of quantum physics reveals that memory is not 'where': each experience shares a point in space, but in holographic physics all points in space are equal to others. This is non-locality theory, which is analogous to Montale's "punto dilatato" of 'Voce giunta con le folaghe.' The "punto dilatato" is a prescient analogy of the non-locality of memory; or more precisely, the non-locality of noumenal experience behind the illusion we call reality (or Maya). Because a quantum (an electron particle seen as light) "literally has no dimension,"[6] it can be simultaneously anywhere and nowhere. Each is part of an indivisible whole – the whole is interconnected. "Although particles such as electrons appear to be separate from one another, on a deeper level of reality they are actually just different aspects of a deeper cosmic unity."[7] Every part of a hologram contains all of the information possessed by the whole. The whole universe is but a constant enfolding and unfolding. The apparent movement of the phenomenal world is but the projection of a hologram. There is a particular holistic unity in Plato's view of memory that would support the notion of the brain-as-universe, or unified hologram brain that is, indeed, the universe. Frances Yates synthesizes Plato's view quite succinctly:

Plato...believes that there is knowledge not derived from sense impressions, that there are latent in our memories the forms or moulds of Ideas, of the realities which the soul knew before its descent here below... In the Phaedras...he again develops the theme that knowledge of the truth and of the soul consists in remembering, in the recollection of the Ideas once seen by all souls of which all earthly things are confused copies. All knowledge and all learning are an attempt to collect the realities, the collecting into a unity of the many perceptions of the senses through their correspondences with the realities.[8]

At a certain level, by remembering, voluntarily or otherwise, we share a holographic network that unifies us. The "confused copies" are merely the phenomenic world, which we cannot see as anything but the true reality; we 'fall for,' this never realizing that proof of the noumenos itself is offered by the very process that allows us to experience the world Platonically.

The movement perceived in Montale's world is but holo-movement and Montale would have that our experiences of it in our minds are part of the being-universe. If there is a deeper cosmic unity, our brains and the brain-universe are one. If the world of illusion in Montale is a hologram, then the whole of human activity is already recorded on it. "Tutto è già stampato," Montale has been telling his reader all along. But who 'stamped' it? In *Farfalla di Dinard*, Montale hypothesizes a response.

The *Farfalla di Dinard* could be considered a more prosaic rendering of the poetic collections' thematics. Reading the short stories, however, the reader gets a sense of being *dietro le quinte*, or behind the scenes. Montale no longer speaks to his institutional 'tu' or his alter-ego; rather he speaks more directly to the reader. The reworking of past thematics and the directness of the prose combine to offer interpretative clues to the reader, allowing him/her to understand the more hermetic poetry. The reader begins to discover the framework for Montale's logic and his paradigm, though, even when Montale relates explicitly, the nature of the argument still leaves many questions. Montale asks his reader to get beyond the phenomena immortalized in his poetry and to enter a world of ontological causation. If the world is but an illusion, what mechanism, he queries, allows fantastic, if brief, synchronicities to miraculously bridge two moments seemingly isolated by time and space? In *Farfalla di Dinard* Montale picks up where he had left off in 'Voce giunta con le folaghe,' in the last stanza of which, "the poet propounds a seemingly strange belief in memorial predestination as the logical conclusion to his thought."[9] Events seem to move in their own "predestined paths"[10] as if they were strips of film, holographic or otherwise. The collection of prose stories is laden with terminology relating to flashes, photograms, film strips, memory, LP records, and disembodied essences in the cosmos; all revisited aspects of his poetry.

Germane to this is the *farfalla*, 'La casa delle due palme.' As with most of Montale's works, this one catches the reader in medias res. It begins thus:

Il tuo treno stava per giungere. Fra un tunnel e l'altro, in un breve squarcio – un batter d'occhio se il treno era un diretto e un'eternità se si trattava di un omnibus o di un trenino operaio – appariva e spariva la villa, una pagoda giallognola e un po' stinta, vista di sbieco, con due palme davanti, simmetriche ma non proprio equali.[11]

So much is captured: a descriptive imperfect, and an iterative imperfect; a memory of a tram enfolded into the compactness of many superimposed memories of a 'train'. Again, as time infinitely expands, the poet's memory infinitely regresses into its folds. The past, a previous past and a present live simultaneously on the page. There is the train he remembers and then the myriad train forms that are instantly retrieved as if cross-correlated. This instant retrieval of seemingly disjointed moments is a function of his brain as hologram: every part of a hologram contains all of the information contained by the whole. His mind functions the same way as the screen of images.

The story offers a particular train, and an 'every-train'. Additionally, it immediately correlates the train of the 'Mottetti'. The prose work relates a villa, which appeared and disappeared in the tunnel as if in frames of film illuminated by alternating light and darkness in a flicker on the screen. It is an "illuminazione a tagli" found in 'Al primo chiaro, quando':

Al primo chiaro, quando / subitaneo un rumore / di ferrovia mi parla / di chiusi uomini in corsa / nel traforo del sasso / illuminato a tagli.

The closed men are immobile yet mobile. They are in a movement-in-stasis, like the unchanging, yet moving, sea in the *Ossi*. They only appear when illumined. All that the poet sees is not the continuous shape of things; rather he sees the lie in the illusion of continuity of a cinematic movie. He sees the lie that is the phenomenal world of appearances. The world is not even evolving, but already stamped. Each frame, like a Zenonian arrow, is a visual representation of one aspect, one singular moment, of a thing. It is the viewer that gives the hologram the appearance of movement, hence change, as he or she changes angular perspective. Yet each image, part of the whole, also contains the whole, and is therefore predetermined. If it is predetermined, the way we perceive this phenomenal illusion is unique to each of us based on the editing that we conjoin to the experience by living uniquely and approaching the screen from varying angles of incidence. The hologram functions only when illuminated from a light source – usually a laser – to produce images, or presences in absence.

In Montale's story, 'La casa delle due palme,' the train traveler does not recognize the porter, yet he seems familiar: "Tieni – disse Federigo consegnandogli la valigia e interrogandosi tra sé e sé 'Chi è costui?', perché la faccia non gli era nuova; finché un lampo non gli illuminò il cervello ed egli aggiunse un cordiale 'Oh, Gresta, come va?'"[12] From this moment, the narrator begins to digress into Federigo's inner mental workings. Through his protagonist, Montale posits a hypothetical question on memorial predestination after experiencing the miracle of an entire past within a moment, which he had deemed "immaginario":[13] "Federigo credette per un attimo d'impazzire e si rese conto di ciò che avverrebbe se la vita trascorsa si potesse 'risuonare' daccapo, in edizione *ne variateur* e a consumazione, come un disco inciso una volta per sempre."[14] The image of a disc (a record) engraved with all of life smacks of a holographic imprint. Each groove recalls

Jones' "predetermined paths." The sounds, images on the disc are there sempiternally and permanently. Yet for the continuity to be appreciable by the poet, it must be turned so that all the infinitely divisible moments appear to evolve in a flux. Nonetheless, the predetermined quality does not prevent synchronicities and irregularities from occurring. It does not guarantee the linearity of time but the non-linear, atemporal Montalean experience such as that of 'Sotto la pioggia,' where such a 'disk' appears:

> *Strideva Adiós muchachos, compañeros / de mi vida, il tuo disco dalla corte: / e m'è cara la maschera se ancora / di là dal mulinello della sorte / mi rimane il sobbalzo che riporta / al tuo sentiero.*

The "sobbalzo," says Galassi, "is the skip of the record that will allow the poet to escape into his memory of her,"[15] but it is not necessarily allowing him to escape into his memory of her; rather it superimposes that experience right onto the present screen of images. It is the same moment which Montale takes for a memory as it interferes with his putative present.

The inability to decipher memory from experience and past from present is found in 'L'orto' (*La bufera e altro*) where the etched record theme is reintroduced. With the anaphora "io non so se," the poet wonders whether 'her' step, "che fa pulsar le vene / se s'avvicina in questo intrico, / è quello che mi colse un'altra estate." Could this be the hand that once touched his shoulder? He cannot discern his limbs from hers; his fingers from hers; his blood from hers. He concludes hypothetically: "Se la forza / che guida il disco di già inciso fosse / un'altra, certo il tuo destino al mio / congiunto mostrerebbe un solco solo."

Suddenly, Federigo, the protagonist of 'La casa delle due palme,' catches sight of a certain Maria: "E fu come se trent'anni retrocedessero di colpo e lui, Federigo, tornasse ad essere l'uomo di un tempo restando in possesso delle ricchezze accumulate piú tardi."[16] A quick 'jump' and their paths are one and the same; a "solco solo." He is now immersed in "un tempo che non era segnato dalla meridiana."[17] The phenomenal illusion of time is revealed as the protagonist experiences another holographic image of reality from a different groove.

In the *Farfalla*, 'Il lacerate spirito,' Montale offers a meta-commentary on the art of recording. The narrator discusses the advent of wax audio recordings of operatic stars. There was much distrust on the part of the 'divi' who would rather be forgotten by posterity than to be 'counterfeited' so poorly: "Di fronte alla prospettiva di presentarsi alla posterità cosí contraffati pensarono: meglio esser dimenticati che sentiti a questo modo."[18] In this regard, a technology had emerged which would allow its users to imagine a future past; in recording the present to be remembered by a future listener looking to the past, the users have a personal say in memory, controlling the re-experiencing of a moment.

One day, the narrator relates, a certain character was able to capture the prince of 'L'Africa' at the opera by recording him from the stage wings. In recording the performance, he immortalized even "i rumori del retroscena e le ovazioni del pubblico."[19] But even this copy, the reader is told, lacks a certain quality. The recording of a great singer (Meyerbeer) might present to an expert ear something of worth, but to others, it would seem "un brusio interrotto da vociferazioni varie e concluso da un si bemolle duro e calante, sommerso da un'onda di grida e di plausi che sembrano insulti."[20] Without realizing it, Montale's narrator has broached an interesting point. Reality may not be singular, if not illusory; rather it is multiple. What might appear unintended imagery or sounds to a photographer or audio recorder are merely some of the infinite coexistent, cross-correlated projections. A 'perfect' recording of the voice without the whole of the unintended interferences would ignore the true depth of any given experience.[21]

The world for Montale is the 'maya', an illusion projected on the screen of images, but even these images are taken for signs in as much as Montale cross-correlates them with other images, thus gathering instant meaning from them. The narrator of 'Il lacerato spirito' addresses the multiple layer of an experience – from any number of perspectives the moment would be interpreted (or recognized, or remembered) differently. What Montale recognizes is the pure voice he expected on the recording. All of the other unintended noises represent the infinite parts of a moment which, though present in the recorded hologram of life, might go unnoticed. Though unnoticed, they are still part of a holistic moment.

It is precisely this process that is reflected in the *farfalla* 'Sulla spiaggia.' Montale had little, or no, recollection of the Anactoria character and yet she has a recollection of him. As a holographic reality, the common moment was experienced from different perspectives. Because the brain is a hologram, which receives and internalizes that which is part of a whole universe as hologram, the spatial-temporal event which transpired between Anactoria and Montale was, and is, permanently stamped and ready to be perfectly re-experienced, if he who 'recalls' is aligned at a correct angle of reflection in the holographic movie. Montale realizes that the preservation of a memory from his past does not depend solely on himself; it can be preserved regardless of his volition or awareness of it. Anactoria has made clarity of the holographic interference, while Montale has not. He needs a 'flash' – as with a laser projecting a holographic image – to allow him to relive it, as one has seen already in 'Sulla spiaggia': "Un lampo illumina la mia mente, un vero lampo nel buio. Rivedo..."[22] As he suddenly 're-sees' what Anactoria had already clearly seen, the narrator finds it unsettling that someone else could be responsible for guarding his past:

> *A dire il vero sono avvilitissimo. Penso agli scherzo della memoria, al pozzo di San Patrizio del ricordo. Io mi credevo in credito verso di me e verso gli altri supponevo che infinite cose tramontate vivessero ancora in me, trovassero nel mio petto la loro ultima giustificazione: mi credevo ricco ed ero invece indigente. Qualcuno che avevo dimenticato m'ha colto di sorpresa; sono io che esisto ancora nella mente di Anactoria o di Annalena, io che sopravvivo in lei, non lei in me. Già; e come può un ricordo sparire fino a questo segno? Ero consapevole di custodire nello scrigno della memoria una folla di fantasmi possibili, virtuali che non evocavo per non ridestare ombre non sempre grate, ma che tuttavia affioravano talvolta alla superficie della coscienza e ne formavano in qualche modo la ricchezza.*[23]

The adjective "virtuali," the verb "affiorare" and the expression "alla superficie della coscienza" speak of experience as reflection received by a receptor rather than a true material manifestation. If something that Montale had forgotten could be simultaneously remembered by Anactoria, these moments had never truly disappeared. They exist constantly and ever latently until they properly receive illumination in the hologram, which is holistically projected over the void. Thus, the phenomenal reality of the hologram, though more advanced than a photograph, shares similarities, especially those elucidated within Benjamin's philosophy: "For Benjamin, the larger the interval of exposure, the greater the chance that the aura of an environment – the complex temporal relations woven through its represented figures – would seep into the image, etching itself on the photographic 'plate'."[24] The notion of temporality is the illusion in the phenomenal universe where one experiences the world more as a series of photos or frames in a film than as a hologram of totality. For us, as well as for Montale, "It is montage which constitutes the whole, and this gives us the image of time...Time is necessarily an indirect representation, because it flows from the montage which links one movement-image to another."[25] Though photography is more primitive than the hologram, Benjamin's "seeping" offers an holistic view of experience – latent, visualized, or otherwise. The virtual quality of a hologram presupposes the "aura of an environment" and accounts for a multidimensional layering effect on the plate where all is co-existent and temporality is a by-product of a mind still resigned to believing that the images around it are to be digested in an order rather than absorbed simultaneously.

Thus the reality projected over the void (the 'real' reality) of 'Forse un mattino andando' is a holographic film, the creation of which is treated humorously in the two *farfalle* 'Il regista' and 'Sul limite.' Visually, it is a three-dimensional experience, but all of the senses are stimulated in the holographic brain, which is part of the universe-brain. The sense of touch, for example, is easily explained by the phenomenon of the 'phantom limb' whereby amputees will still feel impulse in a removed limb. It is there and not there, but if the electric impulses convince the brain, then it is, in fact, there. In 'Il regista,' Montale imagines that his alter ego has a special awareness of the virutality of the universe, as if he were privy to the joke. His narrative conceives of a camera crew which constantly resides behind the scenes, as it were, filming the virtual life, which the poet has until then believed to be material and real. Indeed, he meets a friend who is part of the film crew responsible for creating not only reality for the next 5000 years, but also the sensation of memory.

The story, 'Il regista,' begins in an aura of a reality, the presence of which is indicated by the form of a man who is "aureolato"[26] in the morning fog. Montale had believed this man (Amerigo) to be dead, so from the start the reader cannot pin down the setting: a memory, a hallucination, a jaunt into the afterlife, a peak behind the phenomenic curtain into the void. Even within this a-temporal moment a memory occurs. Amerigo recalls how Montale had indirectly saved his life. Fulfilling his debt, Amerigo will share something of great import with our narrator: Amerigo and his crew are making a film of the next fifty centuries. He warns the narrator, however, not to divulge this to anyone, "altrimenti ti lascio andare per la tua china e nessuno parlerà piú di te."[27] The implication is that the film crew can create a memory of Montale in others so that they will speak of, remember, him. Speaking and remembering are synonyms just as seeing and living are synonyms in the virtual world: "Stiamo girando il film dei prossimi cinquanta secoli che poi gli interessati vedranno, anzi vivranno, a turno e per il piccolo tratto che li riguarda."[28] The film is memorial predestination materialized. Furthermore, Amerigo reminds Montale of certain distinctions: "Tu, come uomo vivo, appartenevi al film precedente."[29] That is, the film that is presently being 'shown', in which case the reader wonders if this moment is but another illusion on the screen of images, or if it is a privileged view into the void, a miracle moment where the world reveals its secret. Montale realizes just how pre-determined the filmed life is, as Amerigo continues: "Ora...non si tratta di darti una parte nuova, la tua sta per finire e non è stata nemmeno brillantissima. Non per colpa tua, lo so."[30] Thus, all is decided beforehand so that even a first experience for our poet is but a recollection from the film. However, Amerigo assures Montale: "posso ficcarti di straforo nel nuovo film, assegnarti una parte nel ricordo dei nuovi attori."[31] "Nessuno ti leggerà nel nuovo film,"[32] Amerigo tells him, referring to creating a role for him as a writer, "ma tu sarai ricordato come una figura già esistente, come uno vissuto in altri tempi."[33] This is crucial to understanding Montale's phenomenalistic perception of memory and its role.

In the Dinardian film, one can be born already a memory. The filming, then, would be a prolepsis which contains the analepsis. Memory is not part of reality, but it is the reality that terrestrials know. The reality on the screen of images is but a record of events, a world as memory tempered by individual perception. The film-memory is produced from a predetermined set of images which can be manipulated so that time becomes irrelevant. Characters such as Montale belong to a past before he existed and a future which is not a continuation of his present. Since the new film, Amerigo points out, "organizza e ricucina i dati del film precedente, non possiamo far tabula rasa di tutto."[34]

The most curious part of this already outlandish parody of his memorial poetics is the ending. The story ends in the same fog in which it began. As our narrator walks along with Amerigo, he pays no mind to the traffic lights. Consequentially, a line of cars in the traffic nearly overtakes him. The cars abruptly halt to the sound of a police whistle. The traffic officer intends to give Montale a ticket for crossing illegally: "Un poliziotto vestito di un impermeabile nero mi si avvicinò di corsa. – Siete in contravvenzione – gridò – Levatevi di qui e seguitemi sul salvagente."[35] Reacting to this, Montale wonders if Amerigo will receive the same penalty: "Anche lui...in contravvenzione? – dissi guardando Amerigo ch'era saltato sul salvagente con noi."[36] The officer is unaware of Montale's reference: "Lui? Di chi parlate? – disse l'agente tirando fuori un taccuino per 'verbalizzare'. – Siete ubriaco?"[37] The officer has not seen what the narrator has: "Evidentemente non vedeva nulla nella nebbia dov'io vedevo il volto che mi aveva sorriso in Vallarsa piú di trent'anni fa."[38]

Perhaps Montale had literally experienced a miraculous moment of grace whereby he glimpsed the void behind the screen. Perhaps he experienced a 'reorganzied, resewn' version of another moment with Amerigo from the past. Like a film editor, he has experienced the montage of a series of frames, which can be infinitely combined over the screen of images. Montale and the officer are possibly present in a moment not equally experienced by two participants, just as with the moment which Anactoria had perfectly preserved that which escaped Montale. Likewise, it is possible that the officer's position did not align at the correct angle to receive the holographic projection, which Montale perceived. The officer lacks the prodigious moment of grace which seems to accord Montale a privileged vision of the real, noumenal reality behind the phenomenal world. The end of 'Il regista' implies that Montale does not tell the officer his secret. So, he will move on just as he had said he would in 'Forse un mattino andando': "Ed io me n'andrò zitto / tra gli uomini che non si voltano, col mio segreto." And he has kept his secret, as well as the one which Amerigo had advised him not to reveal. Yet, in actuality, he has not revealed it to anyone but his reader. Montale has seen the flaw in the phenomenal world and knows it is just an illusion; it cannot "hold up," as he says in 'Debole sistro al ventro': "Dirama dal profondo / in noi la vena / segreta: il nostro mondo / si regge appena." In fact, as he had predicted in 'Quasi una fantasia,' all of the past had appeared in front of him in one point.

Notes

1. Michael Talbot, *The Holographic Universe*. (New York: Harper Perennial, 1991): 25.
2. Talbot 34.
3. Nick Herbert. "How Large is Starlight? A Brief Look at Quantum Reality," *Revision* 10.1 (Summer 1987): 31–34.
4. Talbot 411.
5. Talbot 22.
6. Talbot 33.
7. Talbot 42.
8. Frances A. Yates. *The Art of Memory*. (Chicago: U of Chicago Press): 36–7.
9. F. J. Jones. "Montale's Dialectic of Memory." *Italian Studies* 28 (1973): 105.
10. Ibidem.
11. Eugenio Montale. 'La casa delle due palme,' in *Farfalla di Dinard*. (Verona: Arnoldo Mondadori Editore, 1960): 49.
12. Montale 50.
13. Ibid. 51.
14. Ibidem.
15. Jonathan Galassi, trans. and ed. *Eugenio Montale: Collected Poems* (1920 – 1954). (New York: Farrar, 1998): 514.
16. Montale 52-3.
17. Ibidem.
18. Montale 80.
19. Ibid. 81.
20. Ibidem.

21. In fact, Talbot would suggest that the true experience is nothing but interference in the hologram until we focus on one aspect of the whole. "A hologram is produced when a single laser light is split into two separate beams. The first beam is bounced off the object to be photographed. Then the second beam is allowed to collide with t reflected light of the first. When this happens they create an interference pattern which is then recorded on a piece of film. To the naked eye the image on the film looks nothing at all like the object photographed. In fact, it even looks a little like the concentric rings that form when a handful of pebbles is tossed into a pond. But as soon as another laser beam (or in some instances just a bright light source) is shined through the film, a three-dimensional image of the original object reappears" (Talbot 14–5).
22. Montale 231.
23. Ibid. 232.
24. D. N. Rodowick. *Gilles Deleuze's Time Machine*. (Durham: Duke University Press, 1997): 8. Cf. Walter Benjamin's "Short History of Photography" (trans. P. Patton) in *Classic Essays on Photography*. Ed. Alan Trachtenberg. New Haven: Leete's Island Books, 1980: 199–216.
25. Gilles Deleuze. *Cinema II: The Time-Image*. Trans. Hugh Tomlinson and Robert Galeta. (Minneapolis: U of Minnesota Press, 1989): 34–5.
26. Montale 210.
27. Ibidem. (The 'china,' or path, is reminiscent of the 'percorso' in 'Voce giunta...' It is the way of those who are still in terrestrial form and who believe the illusion of phenomenic reality.)
28. Ibid. 211.
29. Ibidem.
30. Ibidem.
31. Ibidem.
32. Idem. 212.
33. Ibidem.
34. Ibidem.
35. Ibid. 213.
36. Ibidem.
37. Ibidem.
38. Ibidem.

Printed in the United States
109043LV00001B/63/A